CANDLES IN THE DARK
SIX MODERN MARTYRS

CANDLES IN THE DARK

SIX MODERN MARTYRS

MARY CRAIG

HODDER AND STOUGHTON
LONDON SYDNEY AUCKLAND TORONTO

For my Polish friends

British Library Cataloguing in Publication Data

Craig, Mary
    Candles in the dark.
    1. Christian martyrs – Biography
    I. Title
    272'.092'2   BR 1601.2

    ISBN 0-340-34254-4

Contents

Photographic Acknowledgments

Martin Luther King Jr. *Keystone Press*
Maximilian Kolbe *Popperfoto*
Janani Luwum *Keystone Press*
Oscar Romero *Popperfoto*
Maria Skobtsova *Portrait by N. Verevkina, photo by Greg Hackel*

Acknowledgments

I acknowledge a special debt to:

Canon Donald Allchin of Canterbury Cathedral, Julian Filochowski, John Harriott and Olgierd Stepan.

and also to

Metropolitan Anthony of Sourozh, Miss Monica Byrne, Mrs Lotte Cromwell, Mme Geneviève de Gaulle-Anthonioze, Frances Gumley, Peter Hebblethwaite, Sergei Hackel, Rev. Christopher Hill, Mlle Marie Kastchenko, Bishop Festo Kivengere, Mme Tamara Klépinine, M. Igor Krivoshein, Mlle Rosane Lascroux, Malcolm Muggeridge, Peter Reddaway, Archbishop Robert Runcie, Jon Sobrino S.J., Terry Waite, Dr. Philip Walters and the staff of Keston College Kent, Pauline Webb, Richard West, John Wilkins, Jean Wilson, Mme Tamara Zhaba.

and finally to Enid Oakes who, almost inadvertently, gave me the idea for the book.

If there were no one who said, 'I die, but I shall live', no one who said, 'I and the Father are one', then there would be no hope for those who suffer mute and devoid of hoping. All suffering would then be senseless destructive pain that could not be worked on, all grief would be 'worldly grief' and would lead to death. But we know of people who have lived differently, suffered differently. There is a history of resurrections, which has vicarious significance. A person's resurrection is no personal privilege for himself alone – even if he is called Jesus of Nazareth. It contains within itself hope for all, for everything.

Suffering, Dorothee Soelle

We thank thee for thy mercies of blood, for thy redemption by blood. For the blood of thy martyrs and saints
shall enrich the earth, shall create the holy places . . .
From such ground springs that which forever renews the earth,
though it is forever denied.

Murder in the Cathedral, T. S. Eliot

Contemporary man needs the possibility of holiness more than at any other time. But he needs hagiography less than ever.

Jan Józef Szczepański, 1975

Author's Foreword

Not all the beliefs for which men and women have been prepared to die can be true; some are demonstrably false and some are mutually contradictory. The final judgment about the truth of those beliefs must rest on other grounds than the willingness to forfeit one's life for their sake. Christian martyrs are no exception to the rule: the same criteria must be applied to them as to the others. Did they die stubbornly refusing to abandon a belief-system which had assumed the tyranny of an idol over their lives? Or were they defending universal truths and values without which a human life may not properly be called human? It is only when we scrutinise the lives of the martyrs as a whole that we arrive at an answer to the questions.

And so, in retracing the lives of the five men and one woman who are the central characters of this book, I have set them squarely in the historical and cultural background which shaped them and against which their drama played itself out. They were children of their time, acutely aware of the crucial issues of their time – and driven to take a stand on them. I believe that when they are thus seen in full context they emerge not only as incomparably brave human beings but also as triumphantly right. They are fixed points of reference in an uncertain and threatening world, a witness to what is unchanging and indestructible in man; they are a reconciling force, for in them we see the spiritual heights to which a human being can rise if he learns to overcome terror and pain not only with faith but with the healing power of love. The martyr who witnesses to truth dies forgiving not cursing; loving, not hating.

Ours is a post-Christian world, in which three ideologies

struggle for the minds and hearts of men: nationalism, communism and rampant individualism. All three, when translated into a political system and backed by force, demand total, unquestioning allegiance, and reveal a terrible contempt for human freedom and dignity. In a 'world without God', man's inner core of truth is denied existence. It is to prevent the light of human freedom from being snuffed out, to keep alive that inner heart-beat of truth, that the martyrs of this century – in every country, of every colour and race, and of every shade of belief, religious or secular – have died, and are even at this moment dying. And though by the purely material standards of their persecutors they have lost the struggle in losing their lives, yet, as the Book of Wisdom insists, 'as sparks run through stubble, so will they.' They stand for something that cannot die.

The martyrs in this book were in a sense chosen for me, since they were the ones commemorated at the Martyrs' Chapel in Canterbury Cathedral during Pope John Paul's visit in May 1982. It was the murder of Janani Luwum, Archbishop of Uganda, in February 1977, which prompted the Dean and Chapter of the Cathedral to set aside a chapel in memory of the saints and martyrs of our own times. It was dedicated in July 1978 during the Lambeth Conference of Anglican Bishops held in Canterbury. Twelve men and women (three Orthodox, three Roman Catholic, two Protestant and four Anglican) were selected from the list of many thousands who have died in this 'century of Christian martyrdom'.

During the Pope's historic visit, Archbishop Robert Runcie accompanied him, together with five other Christian leaders, to the Martyrs' Chapel. Each of them spoke aloud the name of a chosen martyr and placed a lighted candle in a seven-branched candlestick. In relighting those seven candles, I hope, as they did, to bring the day of reconciliation a little nearer. Reconciliation not only between Christians but among men and women everywhere.

Mary Craig.
Woolton Hill, Newbury

1.
Dietrich Bonhoeffer
1906–1945

On 27 July, 1945, neighbours of the Bonhoeffer family in the Dahlem suburb of Berlin tuned in to an American radio station and heard a familiar name: Dietrich Bonhoeffer. There was to be a memorial service broadcast from London's Holy Trinity Church that same day, said the announcer. The neighbours walked slowly over to the Bonhoeffer house and gave the news to Dietrich's parents. It was thus that they learned of his death.

Until that moment they had continued to hope that somewhere in the ruins of Hitler's Germany he was still alive. Communications between Berlin and the rest of the country had broken down, but news kept trickling through. Only two weeks after Germany's capitulation, they had learned that their son Klaus and son-in-law Rudi Schleicher had been executed by the Nazis in the last days of the war. And now this – the news that their youngest son Dietrich had been hanged at Flossenburg concentration camp on 9 April, just three weeks before Hitler's suicide and the end of the war. Theirs was an ill-fated family: they had yet to learn that another son-in-law, Hans von Dohnanyi, had died on the same day as Dietrich. But however great their inward grief, they received the news stoically. Susanne, the youngest child, was with them. 'I don't believe we cried,' she said later. 'It was that kind of time when you knew you'd need all your resources just to go on living.'

*   *   *

It was a different world into which Dietrich Bonhoeffer had been born thirty-nine years earlier, on 4 February, 1906. The solid burgher Bonhoeffer family had achieved much distinction in the past, with its generations of judges, men of letters, artists and churchmen. Karl Bonhoeffer, Dietrich's father, must have expected his children to follow in the family tradition. At the time of Dietrich's birth (the sixth of eight children), Karl was Professor of Psychiatry and Neurology, and Director of the University Hospital for Nervous Diseases in Breslau. Shortly afterwards he moved to a similar position in Berlin where his children would benefit from growing up in a cosmopolitan capital city.

Sabine, Dietrich's twin sister, remembers him as an attractive, high-spirited boy, with the blond hair and deep blue eyes of the Teuton. Although he was above average intelligence, he was not, at least by Bonhoeffer standards, unduly precocious. All the Bonhoeffer children were clever.

Dietrich grew up in the shadow of the First World War, in the last months of which his older brother, Walter, was killed. When the war was over, everything changed for Germany. Under pressure from the Americans, Kaiser Wilhelm II abdicated and a Federal Republic was proclaimed at Weimar. Demoralised by defeat and exhaustion, the German people had little enthusiasm for the Republic. They had no experience of democracy, and resented being forced to accept a government they did not want. The only thing to be said in its favour was that it had prevented a take-over by the Communists.

If the establishment of the Republic was a bitter pill for the Germans to swallow, the Treaty of Versailles, which followed in 1919, took their breath away. This punitive treaty blamed the Germans for starting the war (a blame they were unwilling to accept), demanded crushing reparations payments from them, deprived them of long-held territories (such as parts of Poland) and effectively disarmed them; it aroused a sense of bitter injustice which the years would do nothing to dispel.

Economic difficulties dogged the new government right from the start, due in no small measure to the burden of reparations imposed by the Treaty. By 1923 Germany was in crisis: inflation was rampant, the German Reichmark stood at one billion to the pound sterling, food was scarce, money not worth the paper it was printed on, the life-savings of the middle classes were wiped out, and a general hopelessness prevailed. The Germans blamed the democratic government for all their woes.

This was the year when an obscure house-painter called Adolf Hitler staged a political putsch in Munich and rocketed onto the scene with his National Socialist German Workers' Party. Though the putsch came to nothing, Hitler became a national figure, even a national hero.

1923 was also the year when the seventeen-year-old Dietrich Bonhoeffer decided to follow a career in theology, thereby faintly shocking his liberal humanist parents, and outraging his two older brothers, Karl-Friedrich and Klaus. Unmoved by their jibes, Dietrich entered the theological faculty of Tubingen University.

By the following year, Germany seemed to be back on an even keel: thanks partly to economic measures taken by the government and more particularly to foreign loans and to the (American) Dawes Plan which assisted the country to meet its treaty obligations. The years between 1925 and the depression of 1929 were therefore relatively prosperous ones, in which Hitler, waiting in the wings, had to bide his time. While Bonhoeffer was a student, the National Socialists were still something of a joke to the country at large.

In any case, Dietrich was too preoccupied with his work to care much about politics. He was proving to be an outstanding student, already showing great independence of mind, with a most un-German tendency to argue with his tutors. At the end of 1927 he presented his thesis – three hundred pages on the *Nature of the Church*, which made it clear that his view of the Church was somewhat wider than the orthodox one. The Church, claimed this 21-year-old theologian, was all of those who professed Jesus Christ, linked together in brotherhood. It was a union which demanded personal commitment more than a membership card. To this idea of the Church as representing a challenge to man, he gave further expression a few months later in a sermon: 'There is only one hope for our age which is so powerless, so feeble . . . so forlorn – return to the Church, to the place where one man bears up another in love, where one man shares the life of another . . .'

That sermon was preached in Barcelona, where Bonhoeffer had gone in February 1928 to act as curate in a German Lutheran parish made up mainly of businessmen. With a series of hard-hitting sermons, and by immersing himself in the businessmen's problems, he had succeeded in reviving their flagging faith. 'It is not we who go to God,' he told them, echoing the famous Swiss Protestant theologian, Karl Barth, 'it is God who comes to us.' The young curate wasn't at all what the businessmen were used to, nor had he ever met anyone like them before, but their mutual strangeness did not prevent him from becoming immensely popular with them.

When he returned to Germany in 1929, the bad times had returned. The prosperity of the preceding years had been largely illusory, based as it was on borrowings from abroad. The results of the Wall Street crash were disastrous for Germany, as the flow of loans dried up and repayment of the old ones was demanded. Production fell, industries and businesses collapsed, their owners went bankrupt. With increasing unemployment, the people were once again plunged into misery. Although the trouble was worldwide, the Germans yet again chose to blame their own government. Adolf Hitler saw his chance and moved in. From now on the National Socialists' influence would steadily increase. Their membership was 108,000 in 1928; by 1929 it had grown to 178,000. Hitler had already built up an intricate party structure and political machine: he had a whole new state ready prepared for the day when it would be required. He was leaving nothing to chance.

Bonhoeffer scented the danger in the air but tried to ignore it. In order to achieve his ambition to become a university lecturer he had to acquire a further degree ('habilitation') for which he was now ready to present his thesis, *Act and Being*. Here too he developed his theory that the Church was essentially a community in which each man encountered Christ in his fellow men.

When his thesis was accepted he ceased to be a student, though, in spite of his impressive qualifications, he was still too young to be ordained. He would have to wait until he was twenty-five, another eighteen months; and he decided to spend that time in America. Applying for a year's leave of absence, he obtained an exchange studentship at Union Theological Seminary in New York. Three days after he sailed, in the late summer of 1930, the National Socialists won a landslide victory at the polls, and the number of seats held by them in the Reichstag leaped from 12 to 107. From being the ninth and smallest party in Parliament they had gone to being the second largest. Hitler now began to woo the Army and the top industrialists, two sections of society which had never accepted the Weimar Republic and which would doubtless rejoice to see it fall.

* * *

America was a revelation to the young German. At first it perplexed him: he found the state of theology in America incredibly immature, and theological students even more so. (They even made jokes about Luther, his hero.) On the other hand, he discovered on the American theological scene something he had not found in Germany – a real desire to live the Christian gospel, and a readiness to judge the crucial issues of the day in its light.

Characteristically he was prepared to absorb whatever this new experience might have to teach him. After the first few days of culture-shock, he mixed freely with the other students and made friends with them. One of them, Paul Lehmann, who became a life-long friend, describes him as 'blonde, heel-clicking, stiff, with rigorous mental standards, impatient with incompetence'. He had an orderly approach to life and a mania for perfection in even the smallest detail. There was no hypocrisy in him, no obsequiousness. 'Dietrich manifested a contagious freedom, openness and integrity in relating to all sorts and conditions of men, to people as human beings.'

But it was his introduction to the negro life of America which most deeply affected the whole course of his life. Through his negro friend Franklin Fisher he came to know Harlem intimately, and discovered what it really meant to be born a negro in white America. The ghetto was his first encounter with the oppressed peoples on the margins of society, and his most profound sympathies were aroused. It was here that he came to see at first hand the evils of racism, not knowing that soon he would be facing that very evil in his homeland, and even in his own Church, with a different set of victims, the Jews.

Before long he was taking an active part in the Christian life of Harlem. At the Abyssinian Baptist Church where each week he took Sunday school and gave Bible classes for negro women, he discovered that the Church of his dreams really did exist: a community of men and women supporting each other in faith, hope and charity. It was a powerful revelation, a glowing contrast to that officially approved Church which was, he complained, 'more a social event than a confession of faith'.

In Germany, meanwhile, a new and monstrous paganism was gaining ground. National Socialism appeared to offer the demoralised Germans a new national pride and a way out of the economic misery in which seven million people were not only unemployed but hungry. ('To talk of a party,' wrote A. J. P. Taylor in *The Course of German History*, 'is to echo the misunderstanding of those lamentable years. The National Socialists were not a party in any political sense but a movement. They were action without thought, the union of all those who had lost their bearings and asked only a change of circumstances, no matter what.')

The Churches too, particularly the Protestants, were disposed to admire the new movement. The Lutherans disliked the Republic, because within it they were no longer a state Church, as they had been ever since Luther's day. They constantly feared collapse now that state support was removed. So some Lutherans at least were inclined to regard Hitler as a saviour. One group, the Thuringian German Christians went so far as to acclaim him as 'the redeemer in German history . . . the window through which light fell on the history of Christianity'. Another group held that Hitler was the Christ to Luther's John the Baptist, and that the Reformation was about to be truly fulfilled by the new assertion of Germany's spiritual strength and physical power. A third group, the neo-pagan German Christian Movement, rushed to welcome uniformed Nazis to their services – and to provide chaplains for the Storm Troopers.

In April 1932, at Hitler's suggestion, these groups merged as the Faith Movement of German Christians. They preached a religion that was mystically rooted in the 'sacred earth' of Germany and in the pure 'blood' of its Aryan people. In the eyes of these German Protestants, (and many Catholics would have agreed with them), National Socialism was a much-needed counter-weight to godless Bolshevism. They found it heart-warming that so many young Germans were now leading a healthy outdoor life in the Hitler Youth camps, with plenty of bracing exercise and an accent on clean living. They might have been surprised to learn that Hitler had his own plans for the young, saying: 'I want a powerful, masterly, cruel and fearless youth . . . the freedom and dignity of the wild beast must shine from their eyes . . . that is how I will root out a thousand years of human domestication.'

Until this time Dietrich Bonhoeffer had been a conventional, unquestioning patriot. But now, as coming events cast their menacing shadow, he saw dangers in the new rationalisms and militarism of Europe. He became convinced that it was the Church's duty to preach peace, and that it should start by putting its own house in order and healing its own divisions. He was attracted, therefore, to the Ecumenical Movement, then in its infancy, and was appointed secretary of the Youth Delegation to the World Alliance for Promoting International Friendship through the Churches (a forerunner of the WCC). The Alliance was holding a conference in Cambridge in September 1931 and Bonhoeffer was an eager participant. At last he had found a way of protesting against the increasingly introverted nationalistic policies of his own Church.

After Cambridge came his first term as a lecturer at Berlin University. But the savour had gone out of his work even before it began. Although his lectures were well attended, he was oppressed by the prevailing atmosphere, the rabid Nazism of staff and students alike. When at last he was ordained in November he sought release in part-time practical parish work, and readily undertook to instruct a confirmation class of fifty boys from the tough slum area of Wedding. They were said to be unmanageable, but Bonhoeffer had no trouble with them. 'This is real work,' he said, as he prepared to move to Wedding for two months in order to be completely available to the boys and their families. His success with them was astonishing. All fifty were confirmed in March 1932, and he remained in contact with them until his arrest eleven years later.

At the university he shocked his youthful audiences with talk of peace. They would have preferred talk of German rearmament and the coming German mastery of Europe. *Mein Kampf* was having its effect. 'There is a commandment of God,' insisted Bonhoeffer, 'that there shall be no war, because it blinds men to the revelation of God.' There were a few who listened, a few who were drawn to this brilliant young man who had the ability to stand familiar ideas on their head and make his hearers take a long hard look at them. His lecture series on the Church won him many faithful followers. There were some questions in life which were crucial, he told them: What has God done? Where is He? How does He meet us and what does He expect from us? The Church's only reason for existing was to provide a response to those questions. It did not exist for its own sake but 'as part of the explanation of how God became man and saved man'. The Church exists, and God exists, he went on to say, 'and we are the ones being questioned. We are being asked here and now whether we are ready to be used.'

2

Inexorably the juggernaut of National Socialism rolled on. In 1932 violence erupted in pitched street battles between Nazi and Communist. The government was powerless in a situation that was tantamount to civil war. In fact, as one government succeeded another, it seemed as though Germany was no longer governable except by strong-arm methods. The elections of July 1932 showed that many of the disillusioned middle classes had gone over to the Nazis. In the four years since the 1928 elections they had won 13 million new votes.

But they still had only 37 per cent of the vote, which meant that the majority of Germans still rejected them.

Nevertheless the Weimar Republic was clearly in its death throes, and the opposition to Hitler, though numerically great, was weak and divided. Meanwhile, the Conservatives believed that they could use Hitler for their own ends. By the end of 1932 a group of wealthy industrialists approached the aging President Hindenburg and persuaded him to appoint Hitler as Chancellor of a coalition government, the majority of whom were not Nazis, but all of whom wanted to see an end to the hated Democratic Republic.

On 30 January, 1933 Adolf Hitler became Chancellor of Germany and the Third Reich was born. It was an empire which he said would last one thousand years. In the event it would last twelve years and four months, but while it lasted it would bring destruction and terror on a scale the world had never previously known.

Two days after Hitler became Chancellor, Dietrich Bonhoeffer made his first broadcast on Berlin radio. Boldly he spoke of the dangers of charismatic leadership, inviting his listeners to reflect on the meaning of the phenomenon and their own role in creating it. 'To what point is leading and being led healthy and genuine,' he asked, 'and when does it become pathological and extreme? . . . If the Leader allows the led to turn him into an idol, he will degenerate into a mis-Leader.' At this point the broadcast was cut off. Bonhoeffer was not invited to broadcast again.

But Hitler was still one step away from the total power he craved. The Reichstag fire in February was an opportunity which he seized with both hands. Whatever the truth about the fire (did the Communists really start it, or was the whole thing a set-up?) Hitler chose to blame the Communists and to treat the fire as a national crisis. By a series of Emergency Laws he banned the Communists, closed down their newspapers and hounded them all over Germany. Then, using the incident as a dreadful warning, he stoked up fears among the German electorate that if they did not vote National Socialist in the March elections, there would in all probability be a Communist take-over. As truckloads of SS roared through the country, rounding up Communists and Social Democrats alike, the German people went to the polls. On 5 March, 1933 they cast their vote in the last relatively free election they would know until after Hitler was dead. And at this late date the majority still rejected Hitler! He now had 44 per cent of the vote, which was still far short of the two-thirds majority he craved.

Then on 23 March he asked for an Enabling Act which would give him the emergency powers of a dictator. Weakly, with little opposition, Parliament turned over its authority to him, and committed suicide. There would be no more real elections. The Enabling Act alone provided the legal basis for his new Reich, and the way was now clear for a one-party totalitarian state. Within six months he had all he had ever wanted: by then the trades unions and other political parties had been dissolved, free speech and other basic freedoms had been abolished. The way was open for house searches, police terror and the concentration camps; and National Socialism was revealed in its true colours as a system founded on terror and dependent on terror for its survival.

Yet the euphoria persisted, and it seemed as though Hitler could do no wrong. (As General de Gaulle later commented, 'The German people gave Hitler more support and suffered more for him than any other people have ever given any other leader.') For the moment at least the new order, and the new, modest but undeniable prosperity that went with it, were very welcome.

On 1 April a boycott of Jewish shops was announced, and on 7 April the notorious Aryan Laws excluded Jews from the civil service. The long agony of the Jews was under way.

As a good Lutheran, Bonhoeffer believed that the state was within its rights to settle the Jewish question by legitimate means, if it so chose. Yet he could see flaws in the argument where Nazi Germany was concerned and he sensed the beginning of a new and terrible persecution. The Church must reflect seriously on this question, he wrote in a paper on 'The Church and The Jews'. She must ask herself whether racial discrimination could ever be considered legitimate. Did not the Church have an unconditional obligation to any victims of the social order, whether Christian or not? And he made clear his view of where the Church should stand: if a madman were driving a car, he said, it was not enough for a pastor to bind up the wounds of the victims caught beneath its wheels – it might be necessary for the Church to put a spoke in the wheel itself. Bonhoeffer would return to this theme many times, using the metaphor of the mad driver over and over again. But perhaps this was the first time that he had faced the possibility of one day having to 'put a spoke in the wheel' of the Nazi machine. His audience of young Lutheran pastors was horrified at the idea of thus opposing the state, and many of them walked out in protest.

In any case the Church was riddled from head to foot with anti-Semitism. The German Christians wanted a Church that was truly German, and in July 1933 at the Protestant Church elections, they carried the day. They won with the help of the Nazi propaganda machine and with the slogan 'The Swastika on our breasts and the Cross in our hearts'. Bonhoeffer, who had been actively campaigning for a quite different result, had preached a sermon on the Sunday of the election, inviting the congregation to seek the true Church only in the word of God. 'Where people are about to destroy the foundations, the one true foundation comes to light,' he assured them. When the result of the election became known, he suggested to his fellow pastors that they might have a duty to leave a Church that was so patently selling its soul. Most of them derided him as a fanatic, or a deluded radical.

But there were many in the Protestant churches who wanted an independent Church even though they protested their loyalty to the government. A group calling themselves the 'Young Reformers' now approached Bonhoeffer and asked him to draw up a confession of faith which would challenge the German Christians. Bonhoeffer agreed. 'The question is really Christianity or Germanism. The sooner this conflict is brought into the clear light of day the better.' With a colleague he produced a draft Confession of Bethel in August. Unfortunately, by the time it had passed through the hands of a group of overly timorous theologians, it emerged in such an emasculated state that Bonhoeffer refused to sign it.

Worse was to follow. At the first synod after the Church elections, pastors dressed in Nazi uniforms and sang Nazi hymns. Ten German Christian bishops were appointed and Ludwig Müller, Hitler's deputy for ecclesiastical affairs, was made national bishop of the all-German Church. All members of the Church administration who were not sympathetic to the Nazi regime were removed, and it was resolved that the Nuremberg Aryan Laws – and the anti-Jewish terrorism that reinforced them – should henceforth be accepted by the Church.

To Bonhoeffer and those like him it was a synod of shame. What has been called 'the Faith's Party Day' was a bitter day for the Protestant Church. In his acceptance speech, Reich Bishop Müller had referred to Hitler and the Nazis as 'gifts from God'; and a Lutheran pastor had gone so far as to declare: 'Christ has come to us through Adolf Hitler . . . We know today the Saviour has come . . . We have only one task; not to be Christian but German.'

It is easy to shudder at the delinquencies of the German Christians, but to understand them one must take several factors into account. Undoubtedly they were drunk with hero worship for this new Siegfried come among them, but this was not the only element in their behaviour. Firstly they had no tradition of opposition to the state. Until the 1914 War, Lutheranism had always been a state Church, and Lutheran theology gave the state pre-eminence in the temporal sphere, to such an extent that many Lutheran pastors saw themselves as civil servants. The fact was underlined by a declaration made by the Faith Movement in April 1933: 'For a German, the Church is the community of believers who are under an obligation to fight for a Christian Germany . . . Adolf Hitler's state appeals to the Church and the Church must obey the appeal.'

Secondly, although in reality Hitler disliked Christianity, he did not at first parade his dislike, and as a result even the many Christians who mistrusted much of what National Socialism stood for believed that in him they had grounds for hope. Many even believed that Hitler was a personally pious man beset by evil advisers. After all, he had promised 'to allow and safeguard for the Christian Confessions in school and education the influence that is their due'. For the time being, the Jews were the principal target and he needed all the help he could get in his onslaught on them, judging rightly that this help would be forthcoming from within the anti-Semitic ranks of all the Christian churches. The attack on the Christians could wait till the Jews had been dealt with.

How could the German Christians have known that shortly after he became dictator Hitler had told a colleague, Hermann Rauschnig, that he had every intention of stamping out Christianity in Germany? 'One is either a Christian or a German,' he had said, 'one can't be both.' Hitler believed that Christianity would collapse of its own craven cowardice, but that meanwhile the process should be speeded up. 'The pastors will be made to dig their own graves. They will betray their God to us. They will betray anything for the sake of their miserable jobs and incomes!'

Hitler's cynical assessment was probably justified. Apart from the few, like Bonhoeffer, Protestants and Catholics alike were gulled (although there was always a stronger Catholic resistance to the Nazis). Two other factors had a powerful influence. One was the yearning for unity and the hope that a new national Church would unite the hodge-podge of bickering independent Protestant churches. The other was Hitler's undeniable success in the economic sphere, which was doing much to raise the German morale. By a series of audacious measures (much admired in Britain and America) Hitler was banishing unemployment and a new sense of social responsibility and cohesion was replacing the old dead despair. At last the German people had been given an outlet for their deep-rooted need for sacrifice and service.

It was in no small measure this good side of National Socialism which made it so insidiously and seductively dangerous. Recognising this, Bonhoeffer wrote, in his notes for *Ethics*, 'If evil appears in the form of light, benefit, loyalty and renewal; if it conforms with historical necessity and social justice, then this, if it is understood straightforwardly, is a clear additional proof of its abysmal wickedness.' And it was about this time that he told a friend: 'Nowadays, when I pray, deliver us from evil, it is Hitler whom I mean.'

The evil of such an event as the previous September's brown-shirted synod was so nauseating that it could not go unchallenged. A group of the Young Reformers, led by Pastor Martin Niemöller, Dietrich Bonhoeffer and his Jewish friend, Pastor Franz Hildebrandt, who was now banned from the Lutheran ministry, bravely set up a Pastors' Emergency League. They pledged themselves to be true to the word of God, to give aid to the victims of repression and to repudiate the vicious Aryan Laws. The League's protest was circulated with an initial twenty-two signatures – and it came back with two thousand more added. Resistance was taking root. But it was a very fragile plant, and Bonhoeffer felt that even now the full immensity of the danger had not been realised. For himself, he felt an urgent need to 'withdraw into the wilderness', to think things through. He was sure that the time had come for a full confession of faith, but he had not decided how best that confession might be expressed. It was in order to reflect on the possibilities that he accepted a temporary appointment outside Germany – at the Lutheran Church at Sydenham in London.

Reich Bishop Ludwig Müller also knew that the Germans had come to a crossroads, though for him the way forward was not in doubt. As Bonhoeffer left for England the Bishop was proclaiming to his ecstatic followers: 'Old things are coming to an end. New things are beginning. The political battle for the Church is already over. The battle for the soul of the people has just begun.'

3

Bonhoeffer remained in London for eighteen months and made many friends. Chief among these was George Bell, Bishop of Chichester, who was later to play an important part in his life (and who, incidentally, would preach the sermon at Bonhoeffer's memorial service in 1945). The two men had already met and become close friends through the ecumenical movement.

But Bonhoeffer's heart could not be given unreservedly to his work in London. Part of him was still in Berlin, where the Protestant churches were fast becoming a mere arm of the régime. On 13 November, 1933 twenty thousand German Christians had attended a mass meeting in the Berlin Sports Palace. It was a Nuremberg Rally in replica, complete with swastikas, flaming torches, brass bands, Sieg Heils, and Nazi hymns. The Old Testament was denounced for 'its Jewish morality', the censorship of the New Testament was urged and an appeal went up for the removal of 'Rabbi Paul' from the theological scene. A heroic Aryan Jesus, whom one bishop had triumphantly claimed as an archetypal Storm Trooper, was to take the place of the Jewish preacher from Nazareth.

This time the German Christians had gone too far, and a howl of outrage went up from the throat of Protestant Germany. Bonhoeffer and the other temporary exiles in Britain added their voices to the protest. Reich Bishop Müller made haste to disown the German Christians and to seek a compromise with the more moderate Protestants. The moderates rejoiced, believing that victory was theirs. But their rejoicing was premature and unrealistic. Lacking Bonhoeffer's wider vision, they were unable to see that the German Christians had simply ceased to be useful to Hitler, that he was merely trying a new tactic. If he could not have the Church as a useful propaganda weapon, then it must be undermined. Bonhoeffer saw what was happening only too clearly, and knew that when the crunch came Hitler's cynicism about the Churches would be sadly justified: they would commit suicide in a welter of indecision and confusion. 'I believe that all Christendom must pray with us now,' he wrote to a friend in America, 'that "resistance unto death" may become a reality, and that men may be found who are willing to suffer for it.'

The new policy was soon put into effect. Bishop Müller banned all discussion or criticism of Church policies, and threatened sanctions against those who disobeyed the injunctions. Bonhoeffer and his colleagues in Britain were summoned to Berlin and ordered to refrain from ecumenical activities – or else. Bonhoeffer agreed to think the matter over, but when he returned to England he wrote to Müller, refusing to give such an assurance. He was in fact deeply involved in ecumenical activities, and while he was trying to keep the English churches informed about the true state of affairs in Germany, he was always at pains to point out the wider implications. As he wrote to Bishop Bell, 'The question at stake in the German Church is no longer a national issue but the question of the continued existence of Christianity in Europe.'

But at long last the Protestant opposition to Hitler was acquiring a degree of cohesion. In May 1934 the pastors of the Emergency League met in synod at Barmen in Prussia and produced a Confession of Faith. The Barmen manifesto was the first true document of the German Resistance, and at the same time it marked the foundation of a new Confessing Church. Bonhoeffer claimed it now as the only true Protestant Church of Germany and henceforth adopted it as his own.

In June 1934 Hitler instigated a mass purge of all possible rivals. In the Roehm Massacres not only did he arrest and liquidate the Storm Trooper group of his former henchman Ernst Roehm, but murdered anyone and everyone who had opposed him, since the days of the abortive Munich putsch of 1923. There were many prominent Catholics and trade unionists among their number. What happened on the night of 30 June was a blood-bath; it was the clearest possible notice that Hitler was firmly in the saddle, would brook no opposition, and had no intention of turning back.

Yet neither Catholics nor Protestants raised their voice in protest. One Evangelical bishop sent a telegram to Hitler thanking him for 'the rescue operation', and followed it with a circular letter to his flock claiming that the massacre showed 'the unique greatness of the Führer . . . he has been sent to us by God.' Foolishly they deluded themselves that by purging the rough-neck brownshirts, Hitler was making a bid for respectability. They were too naive to recognise that, in thus revealing the fundamentally criminal nature of his regime,

Hitler was throwing them a challenge – to which, he knew, they would be incapable of rising.

'Now the situation grows dangerous,' said Bonhoeffer in England. 'Now we are no longer spectators, observers, judges . . . Now we ourselves are being addressed . . . This has happened to us . . . God is speaking directly to us.'

On 2 August the aged President Hindenburg, last official link with the past, died. He had provided a kind of legality for the regime, but he was no more than a cipher and few mourned him. Hitler did not bother to replace him, but pronounced himself sole head of state: President, Chancellor, Reichs Führer – and Commander in Chief of the Armed Forces, whose members would in future be required to take an oath of allegiance to his person. Had the rest of Europe but realised it, the writing was clearly on the wall: from June 1934 German rearmament, till then relatively covert, was speeded up. Germany was openly preparing for all-out war.

At a meeting of the ecumenical councils in Fanø, Denmark, Bonhoeffer (supported by Bishop Bell) persuaded the delegates to throw their weight on the side of the new Confessing Church (though he did not succeed in getting the German Christian delegation banned) and begged the councils to speak out for peace. 'Peace on earth is not a problem,' he said, 'it is a commandment of Christ . . . Tomorrow the trumpets of war may sound. But today this Council is meeting in assembly and has the power to take weapons from the hands of all those who believe in Christ. What are we waiting for?'

In a quiet moment just after this ringing address, a young Swedish pastor asked him what he would do if Hitler conscripted him to fight. Bonhoeffer, this man recalls, was silent for a long time, before slowly and hesitantly replying: 'Well, my friend, if it ever comes to that, I pray that God will give me the strength to refuse to take up arms.'

Whatever horrors the future might hold, Bonhoeffer knew that he must return to Germany. He would have liked to go to India for a while, to sit at the feet of Gandhi. If Gandhi could force Indian society to change, could not his policies of non violent resistance work in Germany? It was something he was destined never to know; for when the Prussian branch of the newly established 'government' of the Confessing Church invited him to become director of a seminary for young ordinands in Pomerania, he did not hesitate. Returning to Germany he took up residence with twenty-five young men at Zingst on the shores of the Baltic. In his May Day speech for that year (1935) the Führer introduced compulsory military service – on pain of death. Bonhoeffer, the students noted, was visibly distressed. That evening he shocked them to their good Lutheran souls by admitting that he was a pacifist.

4

Discipline
If you set out to seek freedom, then learn above all things to govern your soul and your senses, for fear that your passions and longing may lead you away from the path you should follow. Chaste be your mind and your body, and both in subjection, obediently, steadfastly seeking the aim set before them; only through discipline may a man learn to be free.

First of the Stations On the Road To Freedom
a poem sequence written by
Bonhoeffer in Tegel Prison, 1944

After Zingst the seminary moved to a former private school in the village of Finkenwalde near Stettin. It was a rambling, derelict old house, in much need of repair. Bonhoeffer and his students dug, cleaned, scrubbed and toured the countryside begging for food and unwanted furniture. For these young men (one of whom, only three years younger than himself, was Eberhard Bethge, who would become his greatest friend) Dietrich Bonhoeffer had an ambition. He wanted them to become a real community, with the Sermon on the Mount as their truest guide. Though the Confessing Church's Council of Brothers which had appointed Dietrich were aware of his unorthodox ways, they were shocked to find that here at Finkenwalde he was advocating a new kind of 'monasticism', in which the day began with an hour of prayer, meditation, and singing of psalms. Such practices, they felt, were distinctly un-Protestant. Bonhoeffer had even introduced the practice of mutual confession, arguing that by this means hurts and resentments were brought into the open and not left to fester. 'What are the demands of Christian love?' he asked in his book *Life Together*. 'It is the fellowship of the cross to experience the burden of the other person. If one does not experience it, the fellowship he belongs to is not Christian. If any member refuses to bear that burden, he denies the law of Christ.'

His fellow Protestants were more than ever convinced that Bonhoeffer had gone over to Rome when he sought permission to set up a permanent community of Brothers. He was at pains to convince them that this would not be a monastic order in the usual sense, as the Brothers would not be cloistered or in any way shut off from life, and they would be held together not by vows but by the shared discipline of daily prayer. Despite their misgivings, the Council of Brethren allowed Bonhoeffer to do as he wished, and the House of Brothers which he established drew many of his former students back to Finkenwalde.

Alas, the Confessing Church was not living up to its earlier promise. The pastors had shaken a tiny fist in the face of evil, but they had no taste for heroics. The weakness of the Barmen Confession was that it was a theological, not a political statement, and the new movement had not ventured into political opposition. Already they were fooling themselves that compromise was possible, and the regime battened on their hopes. In the summer of 1935 Hitler set up a new Ministry for Ecclesiastical Affairs headed by Hans Kerrl. The latter organised Church Committees, with a mixed membership of German Christians, Confessing Church and in-betweens. The Confessing pastors longed for security and acceptance; and their Lutheran consciences could not bear being at odds with the state. Closing their eyes to the vile inhumanity of a state which had now, by the Aryan Laws of 1935, deprived Jews of their citizenship and of all human rights, the Confessing pastors consented to swear the oath demanded by Kerrl: 'We affirm the National Socialist de-velopment of our nation on the basis of race, blood and soil.'

In vain did Niemöller and Bonhoeffer plead with them and warn them of the high cost they might have to pay for thus supping with the devil. One by one the regional councils of the Confessing Church reneged on their own declaration at Bar-men and settled for a dubious legal status and an even more dubious hope of a unified Church. To Bonhoeffer the sell-out was incomprehensible. For him the choice simply did not exist. 'Between Church and Unchurch there can be no accom-modation,' he reiterated.

At Finkenwalde, work continued as usual, though the seminarians (who shared Bonhoeffer's views) faced a bleak future compounded of hostility and ridicule. Bonhoeffer urged them to stand firm and have no truck with the Church Committees. As a result some of the young men were arrested. Writing to two of his students who were in prison, Bonhoeffer reflected: 'I believe that we should all prepare ourselves in mind and body for the day when our trial will come . . . If we now become careless and frivolous how can we face our imprisoned brothers, and still more the Son of God, who suffered for our sakes to the point of dying for us? It is a case now of standing firm. That is a trial, but it carries with it a great promise.'

Finkenwalde's days were clearly numbered. A government decree of December 1935 declared all the seminaries of the Confessing Church to be illegal; Bonhoeffer gathered the students together and told them that they were free to leave. None did so, and another two years would go by before the Gestapo moved in and closed the place down.

Early in 1936 Dietrich returned from a holiday with his students to find that his teaching status at Berlin University had been withdrawn. He spent much of his time now writing controversial articles for various periodicals and was in-creasingly condemned as 'a political churchman'. But how could the Church remain on the fence? he asked in a closely-reasoned article for *Evangelische Theologie* in June 1936. Surely it was the Church's sole responsibility to proclaim the word of God, and the nearest approximation to that word had been given in the Barmen Confession. 'Whoever knowingly cuts himself off from the Confessing Church in Germany cuts himself off from salvation,' he wrote, trying to make his readers understand that the struggle of the Confessing Church was man's own struggle for salvation. They chose to misunderstand him, and howls of rage went up over the article. Nevertheless, there was now a growing army of the disillusioned, of those who were sick to the heart of distortions and lies, and who were ready to live up to the Barmen Declaration even if it cost them their lives.

The Prussian Council of Brethren, which alone among the Confessing Church's Councils had refused to join the Church Committees, drafted a memo which rebuked the Führer for his oppression of the Church and for his treatment of Jewish converts to Christianity (the full flood of persecution had not yet been unleashed against the Jews). When this memo went ignored, two young men, one of them a Finkenwalde student, sent a copy to a Swiss newspaper. Its appearance in that paper's columns at the end of July, just before the 1936 Berlin Olympics, caused an international furore. In Germany, where adulation of Hitler was reaching its peak, public fury was so intense that the signatories hastily disavowed the document. Hitler waited for his revenge until after the Games were over and the foreign visitors had gone home. Then he swooped. Dr. Weissler, who had first authorised publication of the memo (and was then disowned by the Confessing Church) was thrown into Sachsenhausen concentration camp, where he was beaten to death. The two young men responsible for sending the document to Switzerland also disappeared into a concentration camp. At Finkenwalde prayers were said for them. From this time onwards one or more of their number would always be in prison.

If the Confessing pastors had imagined that by joining the Church Committees they were promoting Church unity, they were cruelly undeceived in 1937 when their national chairman, Wilhelm Zoellner, came under attack. Hans Kerrl, the Minister for Ecclesiastical Affairs, complained that Zoellner continued to speak of Christ as the Son of God. The only true form of Christianity, protested Kerrl, was National Socialism, the one true fulfilment of God's will for the world.

Speciousness could go no further. It must have been a dreadful moment for the discredited and discouraged pastors. Zoellner felt compelled to resign, the Committees dissolved into the dust, and the government gave up uttering honeyed words about co-operation and compromise. The velvet glove was taken off and the iron hand exposed, although, as Hitler well knew, he had little to fear from the demoralised churches. New orders went forth: church collections were to be handed to the government, sermons were to be censored, and any who continued as Confessing pastors were to be deprived of legal status. Five Confessing Church leaders were arrested and sent for trial, and the Gestapo seized eight members of the Council of Brothers in Berlin. In July Martin Niemöller was arrested and the Church's national headquarters was closed down and sealed. Then at the end of September, by order of Himmler, the head of the Nazi SS, the seminary at Finkenwalde was closed.

The students scattered into different parishes as assistant pastors, and secretly continued their studies with Bonhoeffer. It was at this crucial juncture that he completed the book he had long been writing on the Sermon on the Mount. The central question of *The Cost of Discipleship* – What does it mean to be a disciple of Christ in today's world? – received an uncompromising answer: that discipleship demands a total response. Lip service or mere membership of a Church could not be enough. 'The victory over hatred which the Cross represents is the life-long task of the Christian, and to achieve it, it is not enough to pay lip service to Christ or to declare oneself a member of his Church . . . Such love as this can only be the fruit of grace, that grace which must be sought for and which costs us everything . . . Such grace . . . is costly because it costs a man his life; and it is grace because it gives a man the only true life.'

5

Action
Daring to do what is right, not what your fancy may tell
you, valiantly grasping occasions, not cravenly doubting –
freedom comes only through deeds, not through thoughts
taking wing, faint not nor fear, but go out to the storm and
the action, trusting in God whose commandment you
faithfully follow; freedom, exultant, will welcome your
spirit with joy.

Second of the *Stations on the Road to Freedom*

Even now the weakly conforming Protestant pastors had not
plumbed the depths of shame. They suffered the ultimate
degradation on 20 April, 1938, when, to celebrate both
Hitler's birthday and his successful Anschluss in Austria, the
official Church government ordered them to vow a personal
oath of allegiance to the Führer. Their cup of bitterness must
now have brimmed over. In the course of that summer, most
of the Lutheran pastors took the oath. Bonhoeffer who, as a
practising member of the Confessing Church, did not legally
exist as a pastor, was not asked to take it and so was not faced
with the necessity of refusal.

It was not that he was reckless or foolhardy or that he
craved martyrdom. On the contrary, some of his acquaintances thought he was not reckless enough. Pastor Hellmut
Traub, who first met him at Finkenwalde, reminded him of his
earlier brave words about 'putting a spoke in the wheel' of an
unjust regime. Bonhoeffer nodded in agreement. 'Yes,' he
said, 'but there is no point in doing so thoughtlessly, like an
adolescent.' On another occasion (often held against him) he
was sitting in a café garden with his friend Eberhardt Bethge
when a news bulletin preceded by the usual blast of trumpets
came over the radio. All the customers leaped to their feet to
give the Heil Hitler salute, and burst into the Horst Wessel
song. Bonhoeffer rose with them, gave the salute and joined
lustily in the singing, hissing at the astonished Bethge to do
likewise. 'A mere salute is not worth dying for,' he explained.

A pragmatist, therefore, with both feet on the ground, and

a healthy desire to stay out of trouble: yet he *was* prepared to die if it became necessary. The trouble was that once again he was unsure of what course to follow. So far he had, like Gandhi, turned his back on violent solutions. But would it be possible to go on doing so, in a land ruled over by terrorism? When his brother-in-law Hans von Dohnanyi (later to be executed on the same day as himself for conspiring to kill Hitler) asked him one day how literally one should take Jesus's admonition that those who live by the sword shall perish by it, he replied that the words probably meant exactly what they said. And he added – significantly for himself and Dohnanyi – that the times perhaps demanded men who would be prepared to take that guilt upon themselves. 'Civil courage,' he was to write later, 'can grow only out of the free responsibility of free men.'

In the late summer of 1938 the 'final solution' to the Jewish problem was brought a step nearer by a new law which demanded the stamping of all Jewish passports with the letter I (Israel) or S (Sarah). Many of the Jews realised that the loopholes for escape were being closed. In haste, before the new law could take effect, Dietrich's twin sister Sabine and her Jewish husband Gerhardt Leibholz decided to leave for Switzerland. They were just in time. Hitler was drunk with success now and there was no stopping him. (In September he moved into the Sudetenland and he had his eye on the rest of Czechoslovakia.) On 9 November, after the murder of a German official in Paris by a Polish Jew, synagogues all over Germany went up in flames, as the infamous Kristallnacht – night of broken glass – got under way. Gangs of hooligans smashed the windows of Jewish shops, looting or destroying their contents. The mass deportation of Jews was soon to follow.

There was no protest from the Confessing Church, and the Gestapo reported that resistance from that quarter seemed to be at an end. Bonhoeffer heard the news in Pomerania. 'The synagogues burn today,' he commented bitterly, 'and tomorrow it will be the churches.' Every instinct was pushing him now to make a stand. By March 1939, despite the bloodless take-over of Prague and the spineless behaviour of Britain and France, war seemed inevitable. He would assuredly be drafted. And how could Dietrich Bonhoeffer fight for a Germany which was sunk in such unparalleled evil? On the other hand, how could he not? For his refusal would serve only to increase the danger for the remnants of the Confessing Church which he served.

As he had done once before, he retreated to 'the wilderness', this time to America, and his American friends believed and hoped that he had come to stay, to sit out the coming war with them and be ready to return to Germany to take part in its post-war reconstruction. It is very possible that Bonhoeffer had some such notion himself; but if so, it was not for long. The mere act of leaving Germany seems to have concentrated his mind wonderfully, and hardly had he arrived in America than he was confiding to his diary that he would have to go back. He could not abandon his country to her fate, nor could he turn his back on 'the cost of discipleship'. He had no illusions, but he knew he could not stand on the sidelines as a spectator while Germany was destroyed. Writing to Reinhold Niebuhr, he explained his painful decision: 'I must live through this difficult period of our national history with the Christian people of Germany. I shall forfeit the right to share in the reconstruction of Christian life in Germany after the war, if I do not share the trials of this time with my own people.'

As a conscientious objector he could expect no mercy. With devastating honesty he confided to his American friends that he could not wish for a German victory because that would be to wish for a continuing enslavement of free men and the final destruction of Christianity. 'But,' he wrote in his diary, 'I know what I have chosen. My inner uncertainty about the future is ended. The journey is finished.'

*   *   *

So Dietrich Bonhoeffer returned for the last time to Germany, a Germany where the persecution of the Jews was now at its manic height. And as the shadow of war grew longer and finally enveloped the nations, the very convictions that had always made him a man of peace led him into the violent resistance to evil. It was not only the Church which had to be rescued from this evil, but mankind itself. He prepared now to work for the destruction of Hitler and his regime – and to accept the full guilt of what he proposed to do. Otto Dudzus, a former colleague, had this to say when the war was over: 'By nature and upbringing Dietrich said Yes rather than No. He was a man who would rather have helped build a whole, sound order of things than remove a perverted, distorted order. The smallest offence against order shocked him. For the sake of that order which had been destroyed on a grand scale, he became a revolutionary.'

For the sake of this higher order he was prepared to sacrifice even his own sense of righteousness. Responsible action demanded that he should do so. In one of the short essays which form part of *After Ten Years* (given to members of his family as a Christmas present in 1943), he explained his decision: 'Here and there people flee from public altercation into the sanctuary of private virtuousness. But anyone who does this must shut his mouth and his eyes to the injustice around him. Only at the cost of self deception can he protect himself from the contamination arising from responsible action.' Once again he used the metaphor of the runaway car. As a pastor, he said, he could do more than bind the wounds of the victims or bury the dead; he must throw himself in front of the car and bring it to a halt.

It is essential to understand that Bonhoeffer did not offer excuses for himself. Against those who even today accuse him of treason he would offer no defence. He was, he would agree, guilty as charged. 'Step by step,' writes his English biographer, Mary Bosanquet, 'he was to be involved in a conspiracy which would require the abandonment of much that Christian life demands, expert lying built up into layer upon layer of closely woven deception, and ultimately the willingness to murder. Bonhoeffer never for a moment regarded these evils as anything but what they were – evil. He accepted them as necessary.'

He was about to make his own personal 'confessio' and, as he later told his friend, Bishop Bell, 'our action must be of such a kind that the world will understand it as an act of repentance.'

6

September 1939: German troops marched into Poland and the Second World War began. In April 1940 the Germans occupied Norway and Denmark; in May a blitzkrieg brought about the fall of the Netherlands within four days, of Belgium within three weeks, and of France (unbelievably) within seven. The whole of continental Europe was now either allied to Hitler or prostrate under his jackboot. Britain alone hung on grimly, but few people imagined that she could hang on for long.

When he returned to Germany just before the outbreak of war, Bonhoeffer had gone to Sigurdshof in the forests of Pomerania, where he was doing a little teaching and striving to avoid the attentions of the Gestapo and the call-up. One day in July 1940, during a youth conference somewhere near Königsberg, he was talking to a group of students outside a church when a detachment of Gestapo arrived and ordered them to disperse. The incident, though inconclusive, disturbed Bonhoeffer. Not without cause, as it turned out. Shortly after this, he was notified by the State Security department that because of his known 'subversive activity' he was henceforth forbidden to speak in public. He was ordered, moreover, to report at regular intervals to the Gestapo.

To relieve him of such unwelcome and regular attention from the Gestapo, his brother-in-law Hans von Dohnanyi arranged for Dietrich to be taken on by the German counter-espionage department (Abwehr) as an unofficial but unpaid spy on the staff of its Munich office. It was in fact at the heart of the Abwehr that real resistance to Hitler was crystallising. Hans von Dohnanyi was involved, and the head of counter-espionage Admiral Canaris, together with his second in command, Hans Oster. Twice already, before war actually started, they had planned to arrest Hitler and arraign him before a People's Court. But for one reason or another both plots had failed and their existence had not come to light.

Given leave of absence from the Confessing Church, Bonhoeffer left Pomerania for Munich. Much of the winter of 1940–41 he spent as a guest of Kloster Ettal, a Benedictine monastery whose monks were engaged in a variety of clandestine rescue operations for Jewish refugees. Bonhoeffer was happy in the monastery and in the unaccustomed peace of his new surroundings recommenced work on his projected magnum opus, *Ethics*. In this work he boldly assessed his own Church's share of guilt for the present situation; 'The Church was silent when it should have cried out,' he wrote . . . 'It is guilty of the deaths of the weakest and most defenceless brothers of Jesus Christ.' By which, of course, he meant the Jews.

All the while, he was awaiting instructions from the Abwehr. His first commission took him in February to Geneva, ostensibly on a fact-finding mission for military intelligence, but in reality to seek out old acquaintances from the ecumenical movement. He was to tell them of the progress of resistance within Germany and to sound out the possibilities of a new German government making an approach to the British government, using the Church as mediator. This new government would wish to discuss a peace settlement and a new international order based on justice.

His mission safely accomplished, Bonhoeffer returned to Berlin. His lectureship had been revoked and now, as he was not a member of the National Office for Literature, he was forbidden to publish. Undeterred, he continued to work on the *Ethics*, searching always for a way in which men could discover and obey the will of God in the moral cesspool of Nazi Germany. The old trusty weapons for fighting evil – reason, conscience, freedom, duty, virtuousness were, he noted, as useless in the present context as the rusty swords described in *Don Quixote*. 'The great masquerade of evil,' he wrote, 'has played havoc with all our ethical concepts.' He had always understood that the question of ethics is seldom clear-cut, that men are rarely faced with a straight choice between good and evil. But now, in the jungle of Hitler's Germany, he had to face the question afresh. What could replace the old rusty swords? Nothing less, he concluded, than a renewal of the mind from within, a refusal to be squeezed into a mould. 'The point of departure for Christian ethics,' he suggested, 'is not the reality of one's self or the reality of the world; nor is it the reality of standards and values. It is the reality of God as He reveals Himself in Jesus Christ.' In the end a man may have to sacrifice his reason, his conscience, and all his preconceived ideas of what is right if he is to keep faith with God.

September found him once again pursuing his inquiries in Geneva. Sitting among friends in the home of Dr. Visser t'Hooft, he admitted sorrowfully: 'I pray for the defeat of my nation. Only in defeat may we atone for the terrible crimes we have committed against Europe and the world.' Visser t'Hooft continues to defend Bonhoeffer against those who see such statements as treasonable: 'Bonhoeffer loved his country,' he insists. 'But because of his love, he could not bear to see it become guilty. It was not enough to bewail this fact, to feel sorry about it. A Christian has to try and catch the mad horse, even though it may seem well-nigh impossible or fruitless. There is no fanaticism in this.'

This time his return from Switzerland coincided with the first major deportation of the Jews from Berlin. Admiral Canaris enlisted his help in smuggling a group of distinguished Jews over the border into Switzerland. The details of the operation (known as Operation Seven) are not known, but it was a difficult and dangerous mission and Bonhoeffer carried it through successfully.

As no reply had been received from London to the Abwehr's advances, in May 1942 Bonhoeffer was sent to try again. This time he went to Sweden, where his old friend Bishop Bell was renewing contacts within the Churches. Bell was astounded when two members of the German resistance, one of them Bonhoeffer, came to see him. He was still more astounded when the latter gave him details of an imminent putsch against Hitler and the plans for a new government pledged to renounce aggression abroad and injustice at home. Bonhoeffer even gave him the names of those involved in the plot: Colonel Beck, former Chief of the General Staff; Colonel General Hammerstein; Goerdeler, ex-Lord Mayor of Leipzig; Jakob Kaiser, a prominent Catholic trade union-ist; Generals Kluge and Bock. The resistance was growing, Bonhoeffer assured his friend; it now included Roman Catho-

lics, Evangelicals, trade unionists and Army top brass. All
these details he wanted Bell to pass on to the British Government. What the conspirators needed to know was whether the
Allied governments would be willing to accept that the new
government in Germany would be essentially different from
the one with which they were at war, and that it would take
time for it to restore sanity to Germany.

Bishop Bell wasted no time. As soon as he returned to
England he put the facts before the Foreign Secretary,
Anthony Eden. The latter was cautiously interested but
suspected that the churchmen might be being used as a front
for Nazi peace overtures. The British had heard too many
stories of plots to overthrow Hitler, which never seemed to
succeed. Moreover, they were no longer in a mood to talk
about peace, having determined to secure the unconditional
surrender of Germany. Bishop Bell repeatedly warned
against the folly of such a policy, but nobody listened. Though
Bell never gave up the fight, he was forced to cable Visser
t'Hooft in Geneva: 'INTEREST UNDOUBTED BUT
DEEPLY REGRET NO REPLY POSSIBLE. BELL.'

It was a crushing blow for the conspirators, but they did not
change their plans. Throughout the winter of 1942–3 the
conspiracy moved towards its final stages. Whatever misgivings Bonhoeffer had had about entering a conspiracy to kill
had long since gone. He had weighed the cost. As he had told
Bishop Bell: 'If we claim to be Christians, there is no room for
expediency. Hitler is Anti-Christ. Therefore we must go on
with our work and eliminate him, whether he be successful or
not.'

On 13 March a plastic bomb, intended to assassinate the
Führer at Central Army HQ in Smolensk, failed to detonate.
One week later another similar attempt unaccountably failed.
Fate seemed to be on Hitler's side.

In both of these attempts on Hitler's life, Dietrich Bonhoeffer and Hans von Dohnanyi were implicated. But although
they were being kept under close surveillance by the Gestapo,
it was for reasons unconnected with those events. In Bonhoeffer's case it was his protracted evasion of the call-up which
brought him under suspicion.

Time was running out. On 5 April, 1943, Bonhoeffer telephoned to the Dohnanyi house, hoping to speak to his sister, Christel. An unknown man answered the call. He at once understood that his sister and her husband had been arrested and that the Gestapo were searching the house. Without delay he went to the house of his sister Ursula Schleicher and asked her to prepare him a large meal. Then he returned to his parents' house, planted some documents that he wished the Gestapo to find and hid other more incriminating ones. Having done all he could, he went back to the Schleichers and sat down to wait. At four p.m. the Gestapo came for him and drove him away in a black Mercedes to Tegel military prison in the suburbs of Berlin.

7

On arrival at Tegel he was immediately locked in a cell in that part of the prison reserved for the worst offenders – although nobody could tell him why he had been arrested. Here he was kept in isolation for twelve days, during which time the guards were forbidden to speak to him and the cell door opened only twice a day – for food to go in and slops to go out.

Then, after twelve days, to his mingled embarrassment and relief, it was discovered that Lieutenant General Paul von Hase, City Commandant of Berlin with responsibility for the prisons, was his mother's cousin. Bonhoeffer was restored to the more normal life of the prison, which was almost tolerable. It was a military, not a Gestapo prison, still less a concentration camp. The warders were professional soldiers too old or too enfeebled for service at the front; they had not, as elsewhere, been specially chosen for their brutality.

The prisoners were allowed out of doors, to exercise, to smoke, and were able to read as much as they wished. In his first letter home, Bonhoeffer, trying to be optimistic, referred to his new life as 'a good spiritual Turkish bath'. But the loss of life's minor necessities irked him and he wrote to Bethge with a long shopping-list: 'slippers, bootlaces, shoe polish, writing paper, envelopes, ink, shaving cream, sewing things, and a suit'. Later on he wanted 'matches, a hair brush, a pipe with tobacco, pouch and cleaners, clothes brush, mirror, towel, face cloth, a warm shirt and long socks'. Quite obviously he still had a lot of adjusting to do. Officially he was allowed to write only one single-page (censored) letter every ten days, and he wrote this alternately to his parents and to Maria von Wedemeyer, the nineteen-year-old girl to whom he had just become engaged. In fact he regularly wrote letters, and a friendly guard would smuggle them out and bring food parcels and letters in for him.

Maria, his sisters and parents were even allowed to make supervised visits to him once a month, and sometimes to stand outside and catch a glimpse of him in the exercise yard. They brought him books and he spent hours reading them avidly, trying to stifle the resentment he felt.

For he did resent the loss of freedom, and he was not always as cheerful as his letters home suggested. His prison notes reveal him as harrowed, uncertain about his powers of resistance, anxious about the future, contemplating suicide. He began to agonise over his motives: was it really for Christ that he had become a conspirator – and he worried about the tissue of lies which he had still to tell in order to protect the lives of his colleagues. It had been decided by Admiral Canaris and Dohnanyi that when he was interrogated Bonhoeffer should act out the role of a simple patriotic pastor who had done his bit for the war effort by working for military intelligence, but who was really too naive to understand the import of what he'd been asked to do. Such was the role that Bonhoeffer now played for dear life before his interrogator, Judge Advocate Manfred Roeder. 'I am the last to deny that in an activity which is for me so complicated, so strange and unaccustomed as counter-espionage, I may have made mistakes,' he conceded disingenuously to the court.

At the same time he continued to correspond secretly with the Resistance by means of codes carried in his books and parcels from home. In this way he learned that further unlucky attempts had been made to assassinate Hitler.

The web of deception and the gnawing self-doubt almost tore him apart in those early months. He was far from accepting his lot. 'There are two ways of dealing psychically with adversities,' he wrote at the end of 1943. 'One way, the easier, is to try to ignore them; and that is about as far as I have got. The other more difficult way is to face them deliberately and to overcome them. I am not yet equal to that, but one must learn to do it.' Certainly he had not yet attained the serenity which might have been hoped from the man who a few months earlier had written: 'I believe that God can and will bring good out of evil, even out of the greatest evil. For that purpose he needs men who make the best use of their suffering. I believe that God will give us all the strength we need to help us to resist in all times of darkness . . . A faith such as this should allay all our fears for the future.'

The other prisoners – and many of the warders – would have been surprised to learn that Bonhoeffer was, in his own estimation, 'a man who goes squirming under these ghastly experiences, in wretchedness that cries to heaven.' To them he appeared extraordinarily calm and self-possessed. (He knew this and it only increased his confusion.) During the frequent air-raids to which Berlin was now subjected, he spoke cheerfully to all those around him and kept up their sagging morale. As he had some slight knowledge of first aid he was usually taken down to the emergency post when the alarm sounded; and the warders kept him talking long after the all-clear signal had been given. His talent for giving comfort was well known, and his reputation spread. Soon he was being asked for help in all kinds of ways. He drafted letters of complaint for the other prisoners, obtained psychiatric advice for their defence lawyers through his father, and, last but not least, he provided money for their various legal needs. When there were sick prisoners to be moved he acted as stretcher-bearer, and for the first Christmas he spent in prison, he composed special Christmas prayers for all the prisoners.

Judge Roeder and his investigators were not able to unearth any proof of conspiracy against the state in Bonhoeffer's case. The only charge that could be brought against him was that he had avoided military service. That was a serious enough charge, but if it came to a trial, Admiral Canaris would be able and willing to give evidence about his secret work. But would there be a trial? He had been assured that there would and that he should brief a defence lawyer. But always there was some reason why the trial had to be postponed, and gradually, as the months passed, his hopes of release faded. One year after his arrest, it was decided not to press charges against him, but nevertheless to keep him in prison.

Strangely, yet perhaps not so strangely, it was now, when he had no alternative but to wait in prison without much hope, that he entered the most creative period of his life. All his life he had been prey to depressions, yet at this moment of hopelessness and failure, the depressions faded away. Freed from the tyranny of constantly deferred hope, he at last reached a state of calm acceptance and inner peace. As he wrote to his friend Eberhard Bethge on 11 April 1944, he regretted nothing, 'for I'm firmly convinced – however strange it may seem – that my life has followed a straight and unbroken course, at any rate in its outward conduct. It has been an uninterrupted enrichment of experience for which I can only be thankful. If my life were to end here and now, in these conditions, that would have a meaning that I think I could understand; on the other hand, everything might be a thorough preparation for a new start and a new task when peace comes.'

Peace in that sense would not come for him; but the new start and the new task lay directly ahead. The letters which he wrote to Bethge from 30 April onwards were to change the face of theology in the second half of the twentieth century, though many of his ideas were to be misunderstood and misrepresented.

The months of prison had brought him close to an answer to what had always been the central question of his life: Who is Christ for us today? Living with his fellow prisoners had made him finally aware that twentieth-century man was no longer 'religious'; and that the old 'religious' language, with its abstract metaphysical definitions and categories, no longer spoke to contemporary man in his need. If the Church was truly the community of those who followed Christ, it must face this huge challenge: How can Christ become Lord of the religionless? How do we speak in a secular way about God?

Religion had traditionally used the concept of God to explain the gaps in human knowledge, or as a court of appeal, a *deus ex machina* who could be invoked to help the faithful solve their insoluble problems or give them strength when they had failed. Or again, 'religion' habitually turned into 'inwardness', an escape from the world of problems into an inner world of private and self-regarding prayer. And so, suggested Bonhoeffer, we had pushed God out on to the fringes of our lives, where we reserved a small, well-defined but limited area for His activities. A sort of God-slot. 'But I should like to speak of God not on the boundaries but at the centre, not in weaknesses but in strength; and therefore not in death and guilt but in man's life and goodness.' The Church, he went on to say, stands 'not at the boundaries where human powers give out, but in the middle of the village.'

The reality of God and of Christ should be far more of a challenge to the individual Christian than his 'religion' has allowed it to be. Christians are here to serve God, not beg Him to serve them. One day the Church will discover a new way to interpret and illuminate its mission, but until that day dawns, Christians can speak to the world only through the self-discipline of their own lives. For the Christian is not, as 'religion' has assured him he is, the one who is specially favoured by God, but the one who belongs wholly to the world, as Christ did.

Bonhoeffer elaborated this theme a few weeks later in a letter addressed to Bethge's infant son, on the occasion of his baptism:

It is not for us to prophesy the day (though the day will come) when men will once more be called so to utter the word of God that the world will be changed and renewed by it. It will be a new language, perhaps quite non-religious, but liberating and redeeming – as was the language of Jesus. It will shock people and yet overcome them by its power; it will be the language of a new righteousness and truth, proclaiming God's peace with men and the coming of His kingdom.

Eagerly reading modern scientific works in prison (in particular Karl Friedrich von Weizsäcker's *World View of Physics*) Bonhoeffer had tardily understood how far human knowledge had gone and how much further outwards, therefore, God had been relegated. Man had overcome his ignorance about the world through his own skills and knowledge – without reference to 'God'. In this sense man and his world had 'come of age'. 'God' was no longer the 'god of the gaps', the stop-gap explanation for whatever eluded man's comprehension. But God is greater than we have allowed Him to be: 'We are to find Him in what we know, not in what we don't know . . . He must be recognised at the centre of life, not when we are at the end of our resources.'

Over the next two months, as his own end drew near, he developed this theme in his letters to Bethge. 'I want to start from the premise that God shouldn't be smuggled into some secret place, but that we should frankly recognise that the world, and people, have come of age; that we shouldn't turn man down in his worldliness, but confront him with God at his strongest point.' And, given a 'religionless' world, this brought him to recognise the ultimate demand of faith: that the Christian must live in the world *etsi deus non daretur* – as though there were no God.

God would have us know that we must live as men who manage our lives without Him. The God who is with us is the God who forsakes us. The God who lets us live in the world without the working hypothesis of God is the God before whom we stand continually. Before God and with God we live without God. God lets Himself be pushed out of the world and onto a cross. He is weak and powerless in the world and that is precisely the way, the only way, in which He is with us and helps us. Matthew 8:17 makes it quite clear that Christ helps us not by virtue of his omnipotence, but by virtue of his weakness and suffering . . . Here is the decisive difference between Christianity and all religions. Man's religiosity makes him look in his distress to the power of God in the world. God is the *deus ex machina*. The Bible directs man to God's powerlessness and suffering. Only the suffering God can help.

Finally, in the soaring letter of 18 July, only two days before the failure of the Generals' conspiracy and the beginning of his own road to Calvary, Dietrich Bonhoeffer set out the role of the Christian within this new understanding of God. Summoned to share in God's sufferings at the hands of a godless world, the Christian must live fully in that world without glossing over its godlessness.

To be a Christian does not mean to be religious in a particular way . . . but to be a man – not a type of man, but the man that Christ creates in us. It is not the religious act that makes the Christian but participation in the sufferings of God in the secular life. That is *metanoia*: not in the first place thinking about one's own needs, problems, sins and fears, but allowing oneself to be caught up in the way of Jesus Christ . . . The 'religious' act is always something partial; faith is something whole, involving the whole of one's life.

Three days later, knowing that the plot had failed and that Hitler still led his charmed life, he faced his own mortal danger calmly and prepared himself for the worst. On that day he wrote:

I am still discovering, right up to this moment, that it is only by living completely in this world that one learns to have faith. One must completely abandon any attempt to make anything of one's self, whether it be a saint, or a converted sinner, or a churchman, . . . a righteous man or an unrighteous one, a sick man or a healthy one. By 'this-worldliness' I mean living unreservedly in life's duties, problems, successes and failures, experiences and perplexities. In so doing we throw ourselves completely into the arms of God, taking seriously not our own sufferings but those of God in the world – watching with Christ in Gethsemane. That, I think, is faith . . . I'm glad to have been able to learn this, and I know I've been able to do so only along the road that I've travelled. So I'm grateful for the past and the present – and content with them.

Just after he finished that letter, news came in that von Stauffenberg and others implicated in the plot to kill Hitler had already been executed. Among them was his mother's cousin General Paul von Hase. The net was closing in.

In the few weeks that remained to him at Tegel, an unshakeable peace seemed to descend on him, that ultimate freedom of the spirit which comes from closeness to God. 'It is certain' he wrote to Bethge on 21 August, 'that we may always live close to God, and in the light of His presence, and that such living is an entirely new life for us; that nothing is then impossible for us, because all things are possible with God; that no earthly power can touch us without His will, and that danger and distress can only drive us closer to Him.'

In the last letter of all, on 23 August, the Bonhoeffer of the early letters, demanding coffee, tobacco and clean linen, torturing himself with doubts and fears, had gone for ever, transformed into a man who has no further claims upon life because he has already faced and embraced his destiny.

You must never doubt that I'm travelling with gratitude and cheerfulness along the road where I'm being led. My past life is brim full of God's goodness, and my sins are covered by the forgiving love of Christ crucified. I'm most thankful for the people I've met, and I only hope that they never have to grieve about me, but that they too will always be certain of, and thankful for God's mercy and forgiveness. Forgive my writing this. Don't let it grieve or upset you for a moment, but let it make you happy.

In that letter Bonhoeffer knew he was saying goodbye. Within a short time, the Gestapo had discovered a secret Abwehr file which clearly incriminated Canaris, Oster, Dohnanyi and Bonhoeffer from as early as 1938.

On Sunday 8 October, Dietrich Bonhoeffer was removed from Tegel and thrown into the underground cells of the dreaded Gestapo prison in the Prinz Albrechtstrasse. Of his family, only Hans von Dohnanyi, who fleetingly shared the same prison, ever saw him again.

Men go to God when they are sore bestead,
Pray to Him for succour, for His peace, for bread,
For mercy for them sick, sinning or dead;
All men do so, Christian and unbelieving.

Men go to God when He is sore bestead,
Find Him poor and scorned, without shelter or bread,
Whelmed under weight of the wicked, the weak, the dead;
Christians stand by God in His hour of grieving.

God goes to every man when sore bestead,
Feeds body and spirit with His bread;
For Christians, pagans alike He hangs dead,
And both alike forgiving.

                                    Tegel Prison, July 1944

                               8

Suffering
A change has come indeed. Your hands, so strong and active, are bound; in helplessness now you see your action is ended; you sigh in relief, your cause committing to stronger hands; so now you may rest contented. Only for one blissful moment could you draw near to touch freedom; then, that it might be perfected in glory, you gave it to God.
              Third of the *Stations on the Road to Freedom*

No more secret messages, no more visits from the family. The friends and colleagues who had once supported and encouraged him were now themselves dead or in prison undergoing torture. Prisoners were arriving each day at Gestapo HQ in

Prinz Albrechtstrasse; from there they were tried by a
People's Court and sentenced to summary execution. The
verdict was never in doubt.

Occasionally, on his way to the showers, Bonhoeffer had
brief exchanges with some of his fellow prisoners. One of
them, Fabian von Schlabrendorff, who was in the next cell,
reports that Bonhoeffer was brutally tortured but remained
good-tempered and cheerful with everyone, even the
warders. 'He never tired of repeating that the only fight we
lose is the one we give up.' In secret conversation with
Schlabrendorff, Bonhoeffer revealed that the Gestapo had
not yet discovered the full extent of his complicity, and they
still had no evidence on which to accuse him of treason.

When the Gestapo prison was badly damaged in an Allied
air raid, it was decided to evacuate some of the more prominent prisoners. Accordingly on 7 February, 1945 (three days
after his thirty-ninth birthday), Bonhoeffer was one of a
group transferred from Berlin to Buchenwald near Weimar.
He remained in Buchenwald for seven weeks, not, fortunately for him, in the main concentration camp, but in the cellar of
a house in the woods outside. Food was in short supply but at
least the prisoners did not starve. There was soup at mid-day,
and a slice of bread and jam in the evening. And Bonhoeffer
had the freedom to continue writing a book which he had
started in Tegel, a book on Christianity which would expand
the ideas contained in the letters to Bethge.

A British officer, Captain Payne Best, arrived at Bucken-
wald shortly after Bonhoeffer and in his own memoirs has left
us this testimony:

> (Bonhoeffer) was different; just quite calm and normal,
> seemingly perfectly at his ease . . . his soul really shone in
> the dark desperation of our prison . . . (he was) all humility
> and sweetness – he always seemed to diffuse an atmos-
> phere of happiness, of joy in every smallest event in life,
> and of deep gratitude for the mere fact that he was alive . . .
> He was one of the very few men I have ever met to whom
> his God was real and close to him.

Writing to Dietrich's twin sister, Sabine, after the war, Payne Best recalled that her brother 'had always been afraid that he would not be strong enough to stand such a test, but now he knew that there was nothing in life of which one need ever be afraid.'

As the Allied armies drew close to Berlin and the end of the Third Reich was only a matter of time, the prisoners could sense their imminent liberation. Already, in Buchenwald, they could hear the American guns across the Werra, and their hopes must surely have been high. It was about this time that Dietrich's fiancée, Maria, discovered that he was no longer in Berlin. Filling a suitcase full of warm clothes she set off south, along the line of the German retreat, and eventually arrived in Bavaria. With difficulty she found her way to the concentration camp at Dachau outside Munich, but he was not there. With an endurance born of love and desperation, she made her way on foot to the death camp of Flossenburg, but they turned her away from there too.

Did she have some kind of premonition? For to Flossenburg Dietrich would come in the end. But not before hope had risen a little further. On the Wednesday after Easter a prison van drew up and took a group of prisoners, of whom he was one, away from Buchenwald in a south-easterly direction. They arrived first in Regensburg, where they were locked up five to a cell; and on Saturday they proceeded to Schönberg in the Bavarian forests. The villagers sent in a potful of potatoes for the prisoners and the atmosphere was relaxed and even hopeful.

But on that very day orders had arrived at Flossenburg for the summary trial and execution of (among others) Canaris, Oster and Dietrich Bonhoeffer. The Admiral's diary, containing a wealth of incriminating detail, had been discovered. Canaris and Oster were taken from Buchenwald immediately; and when it was discovered that Bonhoeffer had been sent off on the transport to Schönberg, orders were given for his immediate return.

On Low Sunday morning, Bonhoeffer had been prevailed upon to conduct a service for his mainly Roman Catholic companions. Taking as his theme the Scripture readings for the day – 'Through his wounds we are healed' (Isa. 53:5) and 'for whatsoever is born of God overcometh the world; and this is the victory which overcometh the world, our faith' (1 John 5:4) – he spoke to them of hope. Payne Best remembers that 'he reached the hearts of us all, finding just the right words to express the spirit of our imprisonment, and the thoughts and resolutions which it had brought.'

The men were reflecting on his words, when the silence was grotesquely shattered by the arrival of the SS, demanding Pastor Bonhoeffer. Calmly Bonhoeffer gave Payne Best a whispered message for his old friend, Bishop Bell. 'Tell him,' he said, 'that for me this is the end, but also the beginning.'

Some time that night the contingent arrived at the death camp of Flossenburg. The conspirators were confronted with each other, and a farcical trial went on through the night.

Next morning at first light the prisoners were ordered to strip. The prison doctor has left us his impressions of those last moments:

> Through the half-open door in one of the huts I saw Pastor Bonhoeffer, before taking off his prison garb, kneeling on the floor, praying fervently to his God. I was most deeply moved by the way this lovable man was praying, so devoutly and so sure that God heard him. At the place of execution he again said a short prayer and then climbed the steps to the gallows, brave and composed. His death ensued after a few seconds. In the almost fifty years I worked as a doctor, I hardly ever saw a man die so submissive to the will of God.

It was 9 April 1945. On 30 April Adolf Hitler committed suicide, and the nightmare of Nazism came to an end.

*   *   *

After the war there were, of course, many who claimed that Dietrich Bonhoeffer had died for his political convictions and not as a Christian martyr. Such an accusation betrayed a fundamental misunderstanding of Bonhoeffer's beliefs. It would not have been possible for him to make such a distinction between the 'sacred' and the 'secular'. Had he not said

1at the Christian was a whole man wholly given to the world,
'man for others' as Jesus had been? Bonhoeffer felt himself
responsible for his own society and for future generations of
Germans. It was to provide an answer for those who doubted
1e authenticity of his witness that the memorial tablet set up
1 Flossenburg church was inscribed with the simple words:

'DIETRICH BONHOEFFER, A WITNESS OF
JESUS CHRIST AMONG HIS BRETHREN'

Death
Come now, thou greatest of feasts on the journey to
freedom eternal; death, cast aside all the burdensome
chains, and demolish the walls of our temporal body, the
walls of our souls that are blinded, so that at last we may see
that which here remains hidden. Freedom, how long have
we sought thee in discipline, action and suffering; dying, we
now may behold thee revealed in the Lord.

Last of the *Stations on the Road to Freedom*
Tegel Prison, July 1944

2.
Martin Luther King Jr.
1929–1968

1

Saints, it used to be inferred, were perfect human beings, without sin. They inhabited a sunlit plateau of sanctity beyond the reach of ordinary people. Nowadays we know better. Saints, if we care to use the word at all, can be seen struggling with their own weaknesses like everyone else. What sets them apart is their vision and their willingness to lose everything, even their lives, for the sake of that vision. Martin Luther King is a very modern 'saint', if he can be called 'saint' at all, in view of his somewhat irregular private life. But of his vision there can be no doubt. No man since Abraham Lincoln has done more to advance the cause of the American negro – but his achievement was greater than that. He showed the world that its tensions can be overcome without violence; that a creative non-violent approach to long-festering problems can heal them. He wanted not just to improve the lot of the negro but to lead him away from hatred; and his ideal society would have included whites as well as blacks, with no barriers of race, religion or class. King gave the world an example of the power of *agape*, the Love that has nothing in it of sentimentality or even sentiment, but which is a willingness to see all men and women as worthy of respect because they are all children of God. Like Gandhi, whose devoted follower he was, he proved to be a seminal figure of our tormented age – and, like Gandhi, he had to die because the truth to which his life bore witness was intolerable and not to be faced.

*   *   *

He was born on 15 January, 1929, the son of a Baptist preacher, Mike King, in Atlanta. He too was christened Michael, but when he was five, 'Daddy' King changed both their names to Martin Luther King, Sr. and Jr. From then on he was known to everyone as M.L. A high-spirited lad, he seems to have been accident-prone but a survivor. Once he fell headlong over a banister, twenty feet to the floor below, and then through an open trapdoor into the cellar – afterwards walking away without a scratch. On another occasion, when he had unintentionally hurt his grandmother, with whom the family lived and whom he called 'Mama', he threw himself out of a window and fell twelve feet. Only when he was told that 'Mama', whom he idolised, was all right, did he get up from the ground, quite unharmed. 'Mama' died when he was twelve, and he again threw himself out of the same window, this time with the genuine intention of killing himself. He was badly bruised, no more.

Church was always central to his life. He had officially joined it at the age of five: at a revival meeting at his father's Ebenezer Baptist Church, his sister Christine went forward to pledge herself to Jesus and behind her tagged M.L., determined not to be left out.

As he grew older, he became more critical. He began to disapprove of 'Daddy' King's fundamentalism, to be embarrassed by his old-fashioned pulpit oratory with its noisy and blatant appeal to the emotions. M.L. was an intelligent boy and such rampant emotionalism left him intellectually unsatisfied.

His greatest friend was a white boy, but when they reached school age they had to go to different schools, and the white parents firmly put an end to the boys' friendship. M.L. was bewildered, and his parents had to explain the racial facts of life to him: he was different because he was black, and in a Dixieland proud of its Confederate, slave-owning past, to be black meant to be inferior. The discovery shocked him, and when his anxious parents told him that he must show Christian love to the white people, he replied in amazement: 'How can I love a race of people who hate me?' To return hatred for hatred seemed to him logical, and the conviction gained strength after a white woman slapped him and called him 'little nigger'. One evening, returning from an elocution contest at school, in which he had won the prize, his triumph turned to ashes when he was made to give up his seat on the bus to a white man. 'You black sonofabitch', shouted the conductor. M.L. restrained himself, but inside he was boiling. A 'good nigger', he had already learned, was one who knew his place and stayed in it. M.L. was not out to be a 'good nigger'.

When he entered Morehouse College for Negroes in Atlanta, at the early age of fifteen, it was with the half-formed desire to become a lawyer in order to help his fellow negroes. To his dismay he realised that his education so far had been inferior, and he had to work very hard to catch up with the others. He soon did so, however, winning A grades in most of his subjects. But the idea of studying law lost its appeal, and it was while he was at Morehouse that he decided to become a preacher. Morehouse, under its president, Dr. Benjamin Mays, who became M.L.'s spiritual mentor, showed him that religion could be intellectually mature. Dr. Mays spoke of such things as responsibility and commitment, and the young M.L. came to see that genuine social protest was an essential element in religion.

'Daddy' King, delighted with his son's decision, allowed him to preach a trial sermon at Ebenezer. It was a resounding success. The young man had a remarkable way with words. With his father's blessing he was ordained that same year, 1947, and became assistant pastor at Ebenezer.

Leaving Morehouse, he went on to study Divinity at Crozer seminary in Pennsylvania, one of a mere half-dozen negroes in a small, mainly white theological college. Here too he gained excellent grades, but somehow the curriculum did not satisfy him. He was looking for a way to reply to injustice, but he could not find one. Capitalism, he was sure, was at the root of the trouble, because it was materialistic and selfish. But Communism too was materialistic and, in denying man's spiritual needs, merely replaced one kind of injustice by another. As for pacifism – were there not situations to which the only possible response was violence? The problem was perplexing, for at the same time he was convinced that war was evil.

Suddenly everything fell into place when he attended a lecture on Gandhi. It was a real revelation. At one and the same moment he found his answer, his hero and his own life's commitment. Gandhi, like Jesus, stood out against injustice, firmly but without violence, bitterness or hatred; his anger, like that of Jesus, was creative not destructive. It was not the British in India whom Gandhi wished to destroy, but the social evil they had allowed to flourish. He wanted to 'redeem them through love so as to avoid a legacy of bitterness'. 'We want to change their minds,' he had rebuked a too-violent colleague, 'why should we kill them because they have the same weaknesses as all of us?'

Instantly, M.L. recognised truth in Gandhi's vision, understood that hatred could beget only hatred. 'An eye for an eye?' Gandhi had sadly reflected. 'That way the whole world becomes blind.' Martin Luther King saw that he was right: 'The chain of hatred must be cut,' he mused. 'Only when it is broken can brotherhood begin.' No longer would he hate the whites; his aim now was to save them from themselves. 'Love one another,' Jesus had commanded, and he had meant – respect one another's humanity, show each other the way to freedom of the spirit, redeem each other. *Agape* was the name the Greeks had given to that kind of disinterested love, distinguishing it from *eros*, the love that depended on emotion.

Agape, of which the supreme expression was the love of one's enemies, now became a way of life for Martin Luther King Jr. Practising it, he would change the face of the American south.

As yet, however, he was still a student. Graduating from Crozer in June 1951 (with the 'most outstanding student' award) he won a scholarship to Boston University School of Theology where he would study for a doctorate. He was reading widely in philosophy now, trying to find a philosophical base for his newly discovered social gospel of nonviolence. Eventually he found it in the gentle doctrine of personalism, the belief that a personal God is at work in the universe and in the depths of every heart, giving to every human being an incalculable dignity and value. The divine spark in all men made them capable of coming together in peace and brotherhood.

When King married Coretta Scott in June 1953, it seemed as though he had everything he wanted. The world (or at least the part of it that was black) lay at his feet. With a doctorate in systematic theology, he found any number of academic doors open to him. But he was a divided self. While part of him longed to settle for the cloistered life of the academe, another more insistent part felt that his destiny lay among the negroes in the south. Receiving a firm offer from Dexter Avenue Baptist Church in Montgomery, Alabama, he went along there to preach a trial sermon. In March 1954 he was appointed pastor there, with the unusually high salary of $4200 a year.

He found it hard to explain such a decision. Commonsense might have kept him in Boston. After all, he was used to the city, happy in it. Why should he leave its relative tolerance and return to the ugly discrimination of the south? Why indeed should he subject his new bride, Coretta, to such a fate when she had grown accustomed to something better? But something was driving him. Here was his opportunity to put Gandhi's ideas to the test. It would only be for a few years, he had consoled himself; after that he could return north, to the peace of the academic life. Half believing himself, he had written to Dexter and accepted the appointment.

2

In Montgomery, Alabama, during that May of 1954 when Martin Luther King came to live there, the white people were distinctly unhappy. A United States Supreme Court decision had just overturned the sacred doctrine of separate schools for blacks and whites, declaring segregated schools to be illegal. The ruling was a frontal attack on *apartheid* and the southern way of life; and after the first shock, the white south was rallying to defend its values, Ku Klux Klan and all. Confrontation was in the air when the new young pastor arrived in the city that had been the birthplace of the slave-based Confederacy.

At Dexter he cared conscientiously for his flock, trying to

talk them into a non-violent and conciliatory approach to their domestic problems, insisting that mutual understanding was the very best way to sort out differences. He made his mark as a preacher. Each week he would spend fifteen hours or so researching and writing his sermons, but in the end he would throw away his notes and speak extempore. It was not long before he realised that the emotionalism that he had despised in his father's church was somehow essential to a negro congregation. The intellectual approach did not satisfy them. So he reconciled himself to the traditional negro practice which allows the congregation to pepper the sermon with 'Amen', 'Hallelujah', 'Praise the Lord' and 'Yeh, man'.

Before long the young preacher involved himself in local affairs. He was elected to the committee of the Dexter branch of the National Association for the Advancement of Coloured Peoples (NAACP) and joined one of the rare inter-racial groups, the Alabama Council on Human Relations. On the whole the races did not mingle and the rigid caste system of the south accentuated the differences between them. There was an undercurrent of negro discontent, but as yet it was vague and undifferentiated. Most negroes, either from habit, fear or the desire to keep out of trouble, acquiesced in the system, degrading though it was.

In any case, the whites were determined that nothing was going to change. White Citizens' Councils were set up, to ensure that the new anti-segregation laws would have no effect. The whites feared integration, and fear bred violence in a city where the white man's law was guaranteed to protect him. The smallest negro crime was savagely punished, but the white man could torture, lynch or rape a negro, bomb or burn his house, set fire to his churches, and be found not guilty.

On the buses, the humiliation of the negroes was almost a local sport. Very few of the blacks had cars, so they were heavily dependent on public transport. Yet, though they took their money, the drivers (all white) lost no opportunity of abusing and tormenting their black passengers. A large 'WHITES ONLY' sign banned the negro from the first four rows of seats, even when these were empty. If they were full, and more whites got on the bus, the negroes further back would be ordered to give up their seats. Fines and even imprisonment were the penalties for non-observance of the rules. The negroes were not allowed even to walk past the sacred front rows. Having paid their fare at the entrance, they were made to get off and walk round to the rear door, while quite often the driver would drive off before they got there. It was great fun for the drivers, shouting out 'niggers', 'black cows' or 'black apes' with impunity.

Resentment festered. Protesting voices were sometimes heard, but their owners always ended up in the city jail. There were dark mutterings about a boycott of the buses, but nothing was done. Until, that is, Friday 2 December, 1955. On that historic day Mrs. Rosa Parks, a 42-year-old seamstress in a Montgomery department store, decided that enough was enough. Ordered to give up her seat to a white man, she refused point blank. She'd had a hard day, she was tired, and her feet hurt. She stayed where she was. The driver called the police, and Mrs. Parks was 'booked' for breaking a city law.

Negro fury knew no bounds. Martin Luther King called a meeting in his church and fifty civic leaders and preachers attended. Rising above their normal timidity, they all agreed on a bus boycott. At least it would be preferable to the blood-bath some of the younger hotheads were threatening. King himself did not use the word 'boycott'; he preferred the more Gandhian 'non-cooperation': with an evil and inhuman law.

Those were heady days. Thousands of leaflets urged negroes not to ride the buses 'to work, to town, to school or any place' on Monday 5 December. Sixty or seventy drivers from Montgomery's eight negro taxi companies agreed to pack their cars with negro passengers at ten cents a head. And when the first buses rolled into the city on the Monday morning, they were empty. Students thumbed lifts, their elders used the taxis, a few came into town on mules and donkeys. But the vast majority walked, often a round trip of twelve miles before and after a hard day's work. Not a single negro travelled by bus on that memorable day.

That afternoon a permanent committee was set up to run

the boycott. It was called the Montgomery Improvement Association and Martin Luther King was unanimously elected president. This meant that from now on, the rage and resentment of the whites would be directed principally at him. At a mass meeting on that Monday evening there was not an empty seat to be found. King, who had lacked the time for his usual research and phrase-polishing, launched into an impromptu speech of great clarity and power. His moment had come and he knew it. It was now that, with all the oratory at his command, he must win his fellow negroes to action without violence.

That night he held them in his hand and they listened to him spellbound. He told them what they already knew, that they were sick and tired of being kicked around, that they had had enough and wanted an end to injustice. But, he warned them, it could not be right to counter violence with violence; the blacks must not become another variant of the Ku Klux Klan; their cause was just and they must pursue it justly; they must persuade not browbeat; love not hate. Jesus, he reminded them, had said 'Bless them that curse you, do good to those who persecute you.' As followers of Jesus, it was not for them to become bitter and turn to hating their white brothers. As Booker T. Washington had said, 'Let no man pull you so low as to make you hate him.'

If we protest courageously and yet with dignity and Christian love, when the history books are written in the future, somebody will have to say: 'There lived a race of people, of black people, of people who had the moral courage to stand up for their rights. And thereby they injected a new meaning into the veins of history and civilisation.' This is our challenge and our overwhelming responsibility.

Here was the master word-spinner. Never had he spoken more eloquently, never were his hearers more transfixed by that powerful voice. No one doubted that here was a natural leader. It was as though every person in the hall had been reborn, each one suddenly aware of his own dignity as a human being. A watershed had been reached: there would be no turning back.

Under King's guidance, the MIA submitted a list of demands to the bus companies: that negro passengers should be shown elementary courtesy; that they should have the same right to a seat as the whites; that negro drivers should be used on mainly negro routes. Until these demands were met, the boycott would remain in force. It was little enough that the negroes asked; the miracle was that they had summoned the resolve to ask anything at all. As King was later to say: this was the day 'when fifty thousand negroes became willing to substitute tired feet for tired souls'. In the place where slavery had once flourished, a new freedom was about to be born.

But mild though the demands were, they were too much for the city fathers, who rejected them out of hand. In fact the whites hardly took the boycott seriously, believing it would soon collapse from lack of steam. But as December wore on and the negroes continued to trudge to work in the rain, the officials changed their tune. It was the work of Communist agitators, they declared – which gave them a good excuse to hit back.

First they banned the taxis. But that had little effect, since the negroes simply replaced them by a volunteer car pool of around three hundred cars. Many of them in any case preferred to keep walking. When King heard an old lady say, 'It used to be my soul was tired and my feets rested. But now my feets is tired but my soul is rested,' he felt that the words were a miracle in themselves.

He began to hold twice-weekly classes in the theory of non-violence. 'It is not passive non-resistance to evil,' he explained, 'it is active non-violent resistance to evil.' Freedom, he told them, is never given away free; the oppressor never willingly relinquishes his hold; he will do so only if forced to by the oppressed. But the forcing must not be violent.

To meet hate with retaliatory hate would do nothing but intensify the existence of evil in the universe. Hate begets hate, violence begets violence, toughness begets a greater toughness. We must meet the forces of hate with the power of love; we must meet physical force with soul force. Our aim must never be to defeat or humiliate the white man but to win his friendship and understanding.

Gently he asked them to be willing to shed their own blood, but not to take the life of another. The blood that would flow would be negro blood, for undeserved suffering always had the redemptive power to transform both the oppressor and his victim. 'Along the way of life, someone must have sense enough and morality enough to cut the chain of hate. And this can only be done by projecting the ethic of love to the centre of our lives.'

King's oratory was persuasive, and the negroes agreed to give non-violence a try. By contrast the whites 'fought dirty', circulating rumours that King had used MIA funds to buy cars for himself and Coretta; doing everything they could to split the negro preachers and make the others jealous of their leader. A campaign of police harassment followed. Negro drivers from the car pool were arrested and threatened with losing their licences or insurance cover. King himself was arrested and even jailed for a minor traffic offence, a fact which caused him far less disquiet than the daily stream of obscene hate mail that poured through his door. Death threats to himself and his family were a regular occurrence. At times he felt so afraid that he was tempted to give up. How could he submit his wife and children to such mortal danger? In despair he turned to prayer and begged for guidance. It seemed to him that an inner voice answered him: 'Stand up for righteousness, stand up for justice, stand up for truth and God will be at your side for ever.' At once his fears disappeared.

The experience brought him a new calm. Shortly afterwards, after an enraged crowd of whites had tried to blow up his house and the blacks had gathered around in ugly mood, King quietened the negroes. 'I want you to go home and put down your weapons,' he urged. 'We cannot solve this problem through retaliatory violence. We must love our white brothers, no matter what they do to us. We must make them know that we love them. Jesus still cries out across the centuries: "Love your enemies" – and this is what we must live by.' Whatever his own feelings were, as he looked at the wreck of his house, he forced himself to understand that the whites did not know the evil they did; their cultural, social and historical traditions all led them to believe that their attitudes were right. As the angry black crowd slowly drifted away, a white policeman was heard to exclaim in relief: 'If it hadn't been for that nigger preacher, we'd all be dead now.'

Still the boycott dragged on. In February the white authorities dug up an obsolete state law which declared boycotts to be illegal. An all-white jury indicted eighty-nine negro leaders on a charge of violating the law. Whereupon all eighty-nine (King included) turned themselves in. This was not at all what the authorities had had in mind, and they were very embarrassed. King's trial took place in a blaze of publicity, with black people picketing the court house, black crosses on their chests inscribed with the words 'Father forgive them'. In spite of the fact that he was fined $500 plus costs, King drove away from the court house in a state of euphoria. For he had got what he wanted: the whole nation was now aware of the happenings in Montgomery, Alabama.

Exploiting this sudden nationwide interest, King spoke with his usual eloquence to a television audience. Overnight he became a national figure. That spring and summer he embarked on a coast-to-coast lecture tour, the crowds flocking to hear him wherever he went. The negro, he told them, was weary of 'the pagan peace' which exploited and abused him; he wanted his freedom. 'And so we must straighten our backs and work for our freedom. A man cannot ride you unless your back is bent.' Again he uttered the sombre warning that negroes must suffer in the cause of freedom, perhaps even be killed. But only thus could America regain its soul.

Human nature being what it is, the negroes were growing weary of the boycott, weary of all the walking, weary of the vicious white backlash. On the day that the Montgomery authorities threatened to ban the car pool, King saw defeat staring him in the face. Then the unbelievable happened. Into the court house, where the city's lawyer was demanding heavy damages and the closing down of the car pool, came the

amazing news that the US Supreme Court had declared
Alabama's segregationist laws to be unconstitutional. The
ground seemed to open up before the incredulous whites; and
an old black man shouted 'God Almighty has spoken from
Washington DC.'

At the celebrations that night, King returned to his theme.
There was to be no bragging about a negro victory. This was
not a victory over the whites, but a victory for justice and
democracy. 'Don't go back on the buses and push people
around,' he implored. 'We are just going to sit wherever
there's a seat.'

At last the Montgomery negroes could hold their heads
high. Later that night fifty car-loads of Ku Klux Klansmen
drove through the negro quarter in all their terrifying regalia;
but the negroes did not, as they usually did, go into the house
and bar the doors. They stayed outside and behaved as
though the Klansmen were invisible.

It was a whole month before the federal order could reach
Montgomery, and all that time the White Citizens' Council
were promising a blood-bath when desegregation eventually
came into force. King used this time to hold seminars on
non-violence, encouraging the negroes to act out potentially
violent scenarios on the buses, teaching them how to reply
courteously to insults. From within the MIA he acted as host
to a newly founded Institute of Non-Violence attended by
both blacks and whites from all over the country. Addressing
them, King reminded the delegates that they were living
through 'one of the most momentous periods of history', in
which the possibility of human brotherhood could actually be
glimpsed.

When the Supreme Court Order eventually came through,
the mayor of Montgomery proclaimed that he would abide by
it. Whereupon King announced the end of the boycott and
appealed for restraint, saying: 'As we go back to the buses, let
us be loving enough to turn an enemy into a friend. It is my
firm conviction that God is working in Montgomery. With this
dedication we will be able to emerge from the bleak, desolate
midnight of man's inhumanity to man, to the bright and
glittering daybreak of freedom and justice.'

On 20 December, 1956, Martin Luther King and Glenn Smiley, a white minister, sat together on the first-ever integrated bus in Montgomery. The two men sat in the all-white section of the bus, and the skies did not fall. The boycott had lasted a year; its cost had been enormous; but what had been gained was out of all proportion to the cost.

Negroes in three other southern cities – Birmingham, Mobile and Tallahassee, Florida – undertook a similar bus boycott. As the expected white backlash took shape, as the Klansmen marched, and as dynamite rocked black houses and churches, King began to plan a negro organisation with its roots in the negro Church, which would cover the whole of the American south. The first Southern Christian Leadership Conference met in Atlanta on 10 January. Negro leaders from ten southern states pledged themselves to reject segregation, but also to reject violence as a way of overcoming it. Unanimously they elected Martin Luther King as their president.

3

'Give us the ballot,' cried the negro preacher, 'and we will no longer plead – we will write the proper laws on the books. Give us the ballot and we will fill the legislatures with men of goodwill. Give us the ballot and we will get the people judges who love mercy . . . Give us the ballot and we will transform the salient misdeeds of the bloodthirsty mobs into the calculated good deeds of orderly citizens.'

It was 17 May, 1957. On that day 37,000 people, including 3,000 whites, took part in a Prayer Pilgrimage for Freedom in Washington. At the Lincoln Memorial, Martin Luther King had taken up the mantle of the former President and made an impassioned appeal for the right of negroes to vote. When the Prayer Pilgrimage was over, a New York newspaper described him as 'the number-one leader of the 16 million negroes in the United States.' Victory was being won on the buses, but there were still many other fronts on which to make a stand for negro civil rights. The question of the negro vote was the most outstanding.

It was obvious that the die-hard conservative south would not change except in response to federal pressure. But in this respect President Eisenhower was a disappointment, since he was unwilling to exert the pressure required. In the south, as a result, the process of desegregating the schools was obstructed while negro voting rights were relentlessly voted out. (In principle the negro had the right to vote, but in practice his rights were hedged about with so many provisos and property qualifications, that very few could exercise them.)

In September 1957 Governor Faubus of Arkansas used National Guard troops to keep nine new negro students away from a desegregated school at Little Rock; and President Eisenhower could no longer maintain his detachment. The moral conscience of America was aroused, and he was forced to take action. Federal troops were sent to escort the negro children to school, and as Americans watched the drama unfold on their TV screens, they began to get an inkling of the great injustice being done to the blacks all over the south.

On Lincoln's birthday the following year, King spoke on the subject of negro voting rights at a rally in Florida – one of twenty-one mass meetings held simultaneously in southern cities. 'We must and we will be free,' he cried. 'We want freedom now. We do not want freedom fed to us in teaspoons over another hundred and fifty years.' Why must they be so apathetic, he entreated his negro audience; why could they not become aware of the injustice under which they lived, and take steps to remove it? They ought, for example, to register for the vote.

Sermons, lectures and rallies all over the nation left him no free time; yet somehow he managed to write his first book, *Stride Towards Freedom*, part autobiography and part appeal for non-violence. 'Today the choice is no longer between violence and non-violence. It is either non-violence or non-existence.' He went to New York to promote the book on radio and TV. One afternoon, as he sat in a department store autographing copies, a well-dressed but deranged woman stabbed him in the chest near the heart. As soon as King recovered consciousness, he asked about his assailant, saying urgently, 'She needs help. She is not responsible for the violence she has done me. Don't punish her; don't prosecute her; get her healed.'

Prayers went up for his recovery. When the media reported King's doctor as saying that if he'd so much as sneezed, it would have meant his death, a white student wrote to him: 'I'm glad you did not sneeze, and that God spared you to continue to do good.'

The enforced pause at least gave him a breathing-space in which to take stock of his progress and his future plans. Unwillingly he recognised that, like Gandhi, he must be prepared to suffer for his convictions. 'This is not the life I expected to lead. But gradually you take some responsibility, then a little more; until finally you are not in control any more. You have to give yourself entirely . . . I have reached that point now. I have no option any more about what I will do. I have given myself fully.'

For three years now he had been unable to give to his congregation at Dexter Avenue the attention they deserved. Regretfully he decided to resign, and to return to Atlanta as co-pastor at his father's Ebenezer Church, where he would be near the headquarters of the Southern Christian Leadership Conference, and have more time to give to civil rights issues.

Dexter's loss did not appear to the blacks in Atlanta as their own unmitigated gain. In fact the negro leaders were suspicious of King, afraid he might upset the delicate relationship which existed between them and the white authorities. Of course desegregation would have to come, but it must do so gradually; they certainly did not want an excitable outsider like King to come in and force the pace.

Elsewhere, in North Carolina and Tennessee, the negroes were far less cautious and conservative. When four students in Queensboro', N. Carolina, sat down at a (segregated) lunch-counter and refused to move unless they were served, they triggered off a chain-reaction in the whole south, with hundreds of black and white students staging their own lunch-counter sit-ins by way of support. Many of the students carried posters reading, 'Remember the teachings of Gandhi and Martin Luther King.' (When the SCLC offered to train the students in non-violent tactics, a new organisation, the Students' Non-Violent Co-ordinating Committee, SNCC, was born.) It was during these demonstrations that the students adopted as their anthem the old negro hymn, 'We Shall Overcome'. Before long it would be heard at every march and protest rally in the land.

As the south crawled painfully along the road to integration, the sit-ins continued. In May 1961 the area of protest grew wider, to include the segregated bus stations of the south. Two racially mixed groups boarded two separate buses in Washington DC and made a test journey to New Orleans. King and the SCLC did not join them, but offered sympathy and help. Flashpoint occurred on 14 May when one of the Greyhound buses arrived in Anniston, Alabama, to find an armed mob waiting. Hooligans smashed the windows of the bus, threw grenades inside, and beat up the passengers as they tried to escape. Forewarned, the second bus went on to Birmingham, Alabama, where the police appeared to have become suddenly blind and deaf, standing by as a Ku Klux Klan gang attacked the bus's occupants with lead pipes and bicycle chains.

For the majority of the Freedom Riders, enough was enough, and they continued the journey to New Orleans by aeroplane. But a small nucleus of student activists gathered in Birmingham and swore to continue the struggle. The Attorney General, Senator Robert Kennedy, was sympathetic to their cause and with his help they acquired a bus and set off for Montgomery. Not unexpectedly, their arrival was greeted by a furious, howling mob armed with clubs and lead pipes. Just as at Birmingham, the police stood by and made no attempt to control the crowd.

King rushed to Montgomery and addressed an assembly of twelve hundred mixed blacks and whites in Ralph Abernathy's First Baptist Church. Outside, angry whites rioted and hurled stones through the windows of the church. As the congregation prayed and sang 'We Shall Overcome', the rampaging mob outside the walls set fire to every vehicle parked in the vicinity. Cars blazed all night long; and not until daylight, when 600 Federal Marshals arrived on the scene, were the people inside the church able to emerge and return home.

The Freedom Rides were a success. At Robert Kennedy's request, regulations were issued ending segregation in interstate bus stations after 1 November, 1961. Southern negroes, though the majority of them were still sunk in the apathy of centuries, had made a significant stride into freedom.

4

Birmingham, the richest city in Alabama, was the most thoroughly segregated in the whole country. Most of its white inhabitants, including its mayor and police chief, were passionately opposed to any kind of integration at all, and in 1962 they voted George Wallace into the state governorship with a slogan 'Segregation Forever'. Only ten thousand of the eighty thousand black citizens were registered voters, and anti-negro sentiment in the city ran high. Over the previous five years negroes had been intimidated, viciously assaulted, even murdered; their homes and their churches set on fire or blown up. 'All the evils and injustices the negro can be subjected to are right here in Birmingham,' commented King. It was time that something was done. Time, too, that the ordinary American should be made aware of what was happening in Birmingham.

The Rev. Fred Shuttleworth, a negro pastor in Birmingham who had suffered a great deal at the hands of the whites, was head of the Alabama Christian Movement for Human Rights. He now suggested that King's SCLC should join forces with them in a combined assault on the status quo in the city. King went to Birmingham with a group of colleagues, and a plan was worked out. First among their targets were Birmingham's large stores, with their segregated lunch-counters and restrooms, and their refusal to employ negroes on the staff. If the city's negroes could only be aroused to boycott the stores, and to back up the boycott by protest marches and demonstrations, there was a chance of forcing an end to their discriminatory practices.

Long ago, King had recognised the power of the media. He knew that if Americans could see what was happening, Congress might be driven to legislate for the desegregation of public facilities. Birmingham's Commissioner of Public Safety, 'Bull' Connor, who had sworn that blood would run in the streets before he would allow Birmingham to desegregate, was just the type of blinkered boor Americans most love to hate. If Connor could be seen in action, the nation's hackles might well rise.

Exactly one hundred years after Lincoln's Proclamation of Emancipation (as King did not hesitate to point out) Birmingham's negroes were about to lay claim to that long-deferred hope of freedom. On 3 April, 1963, King issued a 'Birmingham Manifesto' which went straight to the heart of the matter, with a demand for lunch-counters, rest-rooms and drinking fountains in down-town stores to be desegregated; for negroes to be employed in local stores and factories; and for a mixed-race committee to investigate other areas in which grave injustice was being done.

On the first day a mere sixty-five negroes staged sit-ins at five department stores. Bull Connor's police arrested twenty of them. The media arrived, waiting for events to hot up.

But the Birmingham negroes were an apathetic community. Many of them resented King and his friends trying to stir things up. He had to work hard to make any impression on them, particularly on the preachers who were still content to preach about the glories of heaven and leave the miseries of earth to sort themselves out. Exerting the full force of his powerful magnetism, King pleaded with them to join in the struggle. 'The bell of man's inhumanity to man does not toll for one man,' he cried ringingly, 'it tolls for you, for me, for all of us.' Somehow the miracle happened; somehow he pierced their mistrust and changed it into enthusiasm. Before a week was out, volunteers were pouring into his non-violent army, 'that would move but not maul, . . . sing but not slay'. Willingly they handed over their weapons and offered themselves for training in the techniques of non-violence, in which a determination to win through was matched by a refusal to be overcome by hatred and anger. Every volunteer had to sign a

Commitment card. One of the rules written on the card was 'Walk and talk in the manner of love, for God is love.'

A farcical situation now developed. As fast as Bull Connor jailed the protesters, the movement's leaders would bail some of them out and send them back onto the streets. There were demonstrations every day, until the city officials obtained a state injunction banning them. King declared that he would break the injunction, and prepared himself to go to jail, even though the movement had run out of cash and the courts would no longer accept bail guarantees. Friends tried to talk him out of his decision, but King was set on making a public act of witness.

Good Friday was the day he chose to make his act of faith. Speaking in Zion Hall Church just before the march, he said that injustice in Birmingham was so bad that only 'the redemptive influence of suffering' could unseat it. Then he came down from the pulpit and set off marching with fifty volunteers, while the rest of the congregation followed clapping. The police were soon on the scene, and the marchers came up against a barricade. Face to face with Bull Connor, King and his friend Ralph Abernathy fell to their knees in prayer. At a signal from Connor, policemen grabbed the two preachers by the seat of their pants and flung them and the other marchers into the station wagons waiting to take them to jail.

King was in prison for eight days, during which time he wrote his inspired 'Letter From A Birmingham Jail', in response to a group of Christian and Jewish preachers from Alabama, who had called his protest unwise and accused him of being a publicity-hungry agitator. The letter was written on scraps of toilet paper and on the margins of old newspapers. It was his apologia, a complete rationale of the cause of nonviolence. 'I am here because injustice is here,' he explained his presence in Birmingham. 'Injustice anywhere is a threat to justice everywhere. We are caught in an inescapable network of mutuality, tied in a single garment of destiny. Whatever affects one directly affects all indirectly.' He referred to 'the ugly record of brutality' which had afflicted the negro, the broken promises, the humiliations, the blighted hopes. 'We had no alternative,' he assured the white ministers, 'except to prepare for direct action whereby we would present our very bodies as a means of laying our case before the conscience of the local and the national community.' Only direct action could highlight these issues to the point where they could no longer be ignored. 'We must see the need for non-violent gadflies, to create the kind of tension in a society that will help men rise from the dark depths of prejudice and racism to the mystic heights of understanding and brotherhood.'

Perhaps, he conceded, the present action was 'untimely'. But would there ever be a 'timely' time? Privileged groups never willingly gave up their privileges. The oppressed had to summon up the courage to demand what they needed. There would always be those who counselled caution, but in their vocabulary, 'wait' usually meant 'never'.

Were they law-breakers? he asked, reminding the ministers of Augustine's verdict that 'an unjust law is no law at all'. Any law which degraded human personality was by nature unjust, and all segregation laws were unjust, because 'segregation distorts the soul and damages the personality.'

Finally he tried to explain that the present tensions were not of the negroes' making. What they had done was to bring long-hidden and festering sores to the surface where they had the possibility of cure. Non-violence offered the negro a creative channel for his discontent, the chance of putting into practice Jesus's law of love.

The white ministers did not reply to the letter.

Meanwhile the steam seemed to be going out of the protest in Birmingham. An infusion of energy was needed. At this moment a brainwave occurred to the black Christian leaders: they would use the school-children. The black children were eager to play their part, but the decision to send them out on marches was bound to come under fire, both from whites who would see it as an unsavoury gimmick and from blacks who feared that harm would come to their children.

Despite all the objections, the children's crusade was launched on 2 May, when over a thousand youngsters aged six and upwards marched two abreast in downtown Birmingham singing 'We Shall Overcome'. Automatically the police moved in on them and carted over nine hundred off to jail – in school buses.

Next day a repeat performance took place, but with more children. Over 2,500 children marched. Beside himself with fury and apprehension, Bull Connor over-reacted, as King had always hoped he might. He ordered his men to turn the fire hoses on the children; and television audiences watched in horror as negro children were knocked to the ground or swept up against buildings while the powerful jets of water ripped the clothes from their backs. It was too much for some of the negroes standing by, who started to hurl bricks and bottles at the police. And then Connor made his biggest blunder; he ordered the dogs to be let loose. As Doberman Pinschers rushed among the children, snapping and snarling, there was understandable panic. In the chaos at least three children were badly bitten by the dogs, as the crowd scattered in terror. The march was over. But, depending on one's point of view, the battle was already won (or lost). America was shocked as never before and a storm of moral outrage was about to be unleashed.

King kept up the pressure, and the demonstrations grew in number and scale. Not just children now, but all sections of the black community laid aside their fears and reservations and joined in the marches. Connor continued to counter the negroes' aggressive non-violence with fire hoses, police dogs and even armoured cars. History had unkindly thrust him into the role of oafish villain, while, in the opposing role of hero, King captured the attention of the nation with one of the most moving and eloquent orations ever heard:

We must say to our white brothers all over the south who try to keep us down: 'We will match your capacity to inflict suffering with our capacity to endure it. We will meet your physical force with soul force. We will not hate you. And yet we cannot in all good conscience obey your evil laws. Do to us what you will. Threaten our children and we will still love you . . . Say that we're too low, that we're too degraded, yet we will still love you . . . Bomb our homes and . . . our churches . . . and we will still love you. We will

wear you down with our capacity to suffer. In winning the
victory we will not only win our freedom. We will so appeal
to your heart and your conscience that we will win you in
the process.'

This moving exposé of the politics of non-violence was dramatically illustrated on the following Sunday afternoon, when a
group of Baptist clergymen at the head of a crowd of three
thousand youngsters knelt down in front of a police barricade
and prayed. Then they calmly rose to their feet and moved
forward. Connor ordered them back, but they moved re-
solutely on. 'Turn on the water! Loose your dogs! We ain't
goin' back. Forgive them, Lord.' Connor was distraught.
'Turn on the hoses, dammit,' he yelled. But his men were
unnerved by the courage of the unarmed blacks and they fell
back, allowing the group of negroes to pass by unharmed.

'It was one of the most fantastic events of the Birmingham
story,' exulted King. 'I saw there, I felt there, for the first
time, the pride and the power of non-violence.'

In fact, though the marches continued and the jails were
full to bursting, it was really all over. The heart had gone out
of the opposition. In any case, King could afford to sit back
and let the American conscience take over. Telegrams
poured into the White House, excoriating Connor and demanding justice for the negroes. Years ago King had said: 'I
hope to subpoena the conscience of the nation to the judgment seat of morality.' Here at Birmingham that is what he
had done.

What could the business and civic leaders do now but agree
to talk with the negroes? Talks started on 7 May. When the
meeting adjourned for lunch, the strength of the negro cause
was dramatically underlined by a massive turn-out of
marching, singing, clapping negroes in the streets of the city.
King no longer had cause to despair of their apathy;
thousands had marched from the outlying districts to give an
impressive display of solidarity. 'There were square blocks of
negroes, a veritable sea of black faces,' rejoiced King. 'They
were committing no violence, they were just there and singing.'

Three days later the whites accepted the terms which King had demanded before the trouble started. There would of course be a backlash, but King was prepared to call off the campaign and accept the risk of white violence. 'The city of Birmingham has reached an accord with its conscience,' he announced to a press conference. 'Birmingham may well offer for twentieth-century America an example of progressive racial relations; and for all mankind the dawn of a new day.'

The logic of Birmingham was obvious, and conclusions were quickly drawn. If injustice could be righted in such a place it could be righted anywhere. Within a few months nearly one thousand cities had followed suit, as black people took their destinies in their own hands, banding together to outface official brutality. Nearly one million negroes demonstrated on the streets that summer without violence. With them were many whites.

President John Kennedy himself bowed to the force of events when in 1963 he proposed a Civil Rights Bill which Congress passed a year later. 'I shall ask Congress,' promised Kennedy, 'to make a commitment it has not fully made in this century – to the proposition that race has no part in American life or law.

5

Civil rights had come a long way, but this was no time to let its momentum slacken. Instead the black leaders called for a massive, peaceful march on Washington.

Around 100,000 people were expected: over 250,000 came, by car, by bus, by train, by plane, and even on foot, from all over the American continent. About one quarter of them were white. They marched down the Mall from the Washington monument to the Lincoln Memorial, to hear Martin Luther King make the most memorable address of his life. As his wife Coretta has written: 'Abandoning his written speech, forgetting time, he spoke from his heart, his voice soaring magnificently out over that great crowd, and over to all the world. It seemed to all of us there that day that his words

flowed from some higher place, through Martin to the weary
people before him. Yea, heaven itself opened up and we all
seemed transformed.'

I have a dream (he said). It is a dream that is deeply rooted
in the American dream. I have a dream that one day this
nation will rise up, live out the true meaning of its creed:
'We hold these truths to be self-evident, that all men are
created equal.'

His dream was of freedom and justice and of the day when
freedom would dawn. Transfixed, the huge crowd was caught
up into his far-ranging vision, sharing for these few moments
the dream that had the power to save them:

When we allow freedom to ring from every town and every
hamlet, from every state and every city, we will be able to
speed up that day when all of God's children, black men
and white men, Jews and Gentiles, Protestants and Catholics, will be able to join hands and sing in the words of the
old negro spiritual, 'Free at last, free at last, great God
Almighty, we are free at last.'

When the magnetic voice finished speaking, the applause
crashed out. Everyone recognised his own deepest hopes in
what King had just said. Of that inspired day the negro writer
James Baldwin was later to say: 'That day, for a moment, it
almost seemed that we stood on a height and could see our
inheritance; perhaps we could make the kingdom real,
perhaps the beloved community would not forever remain
that dream one dreamed in agony.'

Beyond any shadow of doubt, Martin Luther King was now
the voice of America's conscience, the moral leader of the
nation. Yet there was a paradox here, for King's private
conduct fell far short of his public image. All his life he had
had a weakness for women; and marriage had not saved him
from his appetites. To J. Edgar Hoover and the Federal
Bureau of Investigation, who were deeply alarmed by King's
impact on the nation and by the way he was reshaping public

attitudes ('the most dangerous negro of the future in this nation'), the discovery of such weakness was a cause for rejoicing. Here was a potential scandal which they could exploit to the full. Tapping King's phones and bugging the hotel rooms where King stayed, Hoover easily obtained damaging evidence of sexual misconduct with both black women and white. Copies of an eleven-page monograph indicting King as an unprincipled moral degenerate were sent from Hoover's FBI to the Attorney General, the White House, the CIA, the military, the Secretaries of State and of Defence. Robert Kennedy, the Attorney General, was shocked by the revelations but maintained that private misdemeanours did not affect a man's public integrity. On Kennedy's instructions, Hoover reluctantly retrieved all the copies of the document. But this temporary setback only served to fire his determination to expose Martin Luther King as a fraud and a scoundrel. From now on Hoover became obsessed with his hatred of King and with the desire to destroy him.

King was far from proud of his conduct. His conscience was uneasy about his frequent sexual transgressions, and about the comfort in which he now lived. Over and over again he would resolve to take a vow of poverty and to stay faithful to Coretta, but always the flesh proved stronger than the spirit. Unhappily he confided to friends that his was a split personality, that 'the Martin Luther King the people talk about seems to be somebody foreign to me.' In sermons he came perilously near to confession. 'Each of us is two selves,' he proclaimed, 'and the great burden of life is always to try to keep the higher self in command. Don't let the lower self take over.' That he himself often lost the struggle against his lower self, he was ready to admit. 'Every now and then you'll be unfaithful to those to whom you should be faithful. It's a mixture in human nature.'

But if he was under no illusions about his own flawed character, he had no doubts whatsoever about the reality of his mission 'to save the whole of mankind'. He had to come to terms with his fallibility; he had to learn to accept the ever-increasing risk of violent death: the one thing which was paramount was his sense that God was using him to lead not only negroes but the world onto a saner path.

At thirty-five he became the youngest-ever recipient of the Nobel Peace Prize. In that year, 1964, the award amounted to $54,000, which he divided between the SCLC, the Congress of Racial Equality, the SNCC, the National Association for the Advancement of Coloured Peoples, the National Council of Negro Women and the American Foundation of Non-Violence. In Oslo he accepted the award with 'an abiding faith in America and an audacious faith in mankind'. Humanity, he warned, must turn its back on hatred; only love could bring a peace that would 'transform our imminent cosmic elegy into a psalm of creative fulfilment.' He would refuse to accept, he said, 'that man is mere flotsam and jetsam in the river of life which surrounds him. I refuse to accept the view that mankind is so tragically bound to the starless midnight of racism and war that the bright daylight of peace and brotherhood can never become a reality.'

Hoover was understandably furious at the attention being lavished on the man he considered to be 'the most notorious liar in the country', a degenerate and a Red. As King continued to be foolishly indiscreet in his behaviour, the FBI arranged for an updated version of the previous year's monograph to be leaked to the press. In this version he was accused of Communist sympathies and financial malpractice as well as sexual misbehaviour.

King was quite accustomed to being called 'Communist'; it was the expected term of abuse for anyone involved in civil rights activities. A charge so demonstrably false did not upset him. But the charges of embezzlement worried him very much. He had always been proud of his honesty in handling public funds, but here was Hoover accusing him of directing SCLC funds into Swiss bank accounts. The only thing he could do was meet Hoover and have it out with him: a 'summit meeting', in fact.

The two men came face to face on 1 December, 1964. They did not refer to King's personal life, only to the other charges. King swore that he was honest and denied that he was a Communist. Communism, he told Hoover, was 'a crippling totalitarian disease', not at all compatible with Christianity. Hoover must have been in some measure convinced, for after this meeting, some, though by no means all, of the heat went out of the FBI's attacks on Martin Luther King.

6

New York gave him a hero's welcome when he returned from Oslo with the Peace Prize. But he had no time to linger there. 'For the past few days I have been on the mountain-top,' he told a negro congregation in Harlem. 'I really wish I could just stay on the mountain. But I must go back to the valley . . . I must go back, because my brothers and sisters down in Mississippi and Alabama can't register a vote. I've got to go back to the valley . . . There are those who need hope . . . There are those who need to find a way out . . . I go back with a faith. And I still have a dream.'

By Christmas 1964 plans were completed for Project Alabama, the direct action campaign designed to win southern negroes the unqualified right to vote. In parts of the south, the registration of black voters was proceeding at a reasonable pace; but not in George Wallace's State of Alabama.

Selma was chosen for the confrontation, a middle-sized town in Dallas County, deep in Alabama's black belt between Montgomery and Birmingham. Previous attempts to secure black registration here had foundered on the rocks of white opposition and black apathy. In Selma only 333 out of 15,000 eligible blacks could exercise their right to vote. Martin Luther King planned to bring about a situation in Selma in which the federal authorities would be forced to intervene. What he wanted was a federal law for negro voters, a law that could be rigorously enforced.

Why were there so few black ('nigger' in Selma language) voters? The Dallas County Board of Registrars met only twice a month and seemed to specialise in rejecting negro applicants, dismissing them for such trivial reasons as failing to cross their t's on the application form. The Civil Rights movement was gaining momentum, watched carefully by police chief Wilson Baker, a subtler man than Bull Connor, and determined to avoid the mistakes that Connor had made. Unfortunately for Baker, there were plenty of Connors around, plenty of people who believed that the only way to deal with would-be desegregators was to string them up or shoot them. Chief among these was Sheriff Jim Clark, an insensitive man who was soon to oust Bull Connor from his role as America's most hated man.

King was invited to take charge of the civil rights movement in Selma. Arriving there in December, he addressed an assembly of negroes at Browns' Chapel, making his intentions quite clear:

> Today marks the beginning of a new, determined, organised, mobilised campaign to get the right to vote everywhere in Alabama. If we are refused, we will appeal to Governor Wallace. If *he* refuses, we will appeal to the legislature. If *they* don't listen, we will appeal to the consciences of the Congress . . . Our cry to the state of Alabama is a simple one: Give us the ballot . . . We are not on our knees begging for the ballot. We are demanding the ballot.

The cheering, stomping crowd went wild with delight at such fighting words. Then they returned home to wait in patience for the next registration day, still a few weeks away.

On 18 January the day came. King and his followers marched to the court house and formally asked Sheriff Clark to register the negroes for the vote. Clark, as they had expected, turned them out, swearing that if the 'niggers' came near his court house again, he'd arrest every goddam one of them. Next day King called his bluff by sending fifty volunteers along. Clark was true to his word: as reporters watched, he arrested them all.

At the end of the month, King and Ralph Abernathy led 250 blacks and 15 whites to the court house, and they too were all arrested. Some were released later on bail, but the two leaders insisted on going to jail. From his cell, King continued to direct the campaign, passing instructions to his executive director, Andrew Young. The volunteers kept on coming, until the town's jails were accommodating 3,000 negroes.

News reporters and camera-men streamed into Selma, and King judged the time to be ripe for a 'Letter from Selma Jail', which duly appeared in the 5 February issue of the New York Times. In it he explained what the fuss was about.

> Why are we in jail? Have you ever been required to answer one hundred questions on government, some of them abstruse even to a political science specialist, merely to vote? Have you ever stood in line with over a hundred others and after waiting an entire day seen less than ten given the qualifying test? THIS IS SELMA, ALABAMA. THERE ARE MORE NEGROES IN JAIL WITH ME THAN THERE ARE ON THE VOTING ROLLS.

That same day he accepted bail and held a press conference at which he announced that he would ask President Lyndon Johnson to sponsor a Voting Rights Bill for southern negroes. Then he lunched with a visiting party of congressmen, giving them a great deal to think about.

It was Clark who sent the temperature soaring. On 10 February the sheriff with a posse attacked a group of young student marchers, running them a mile out of town at the double, beating them with billy clubs and giving them electric shocks with cattle prods. 'You wanted to march,' they yelled. 'So, march.'

Selma's negroes were infuriated. King led 2,800 of them on a protest march, and called for night marches in all the adjacent districts. During one of these a young man called Jimmie Lee Jackson was shot in the stomach by state troopers, while trying to protect his mother and grandfather. As he lay dying, the trooper colonel callously served him with a writ for 'assault and battery with intent to kill a police officer'. King preached the eulogy at the boy's funeral, announcing afterwards that he would lead a fifty-four mile march all the way from Selma to Montgomery, beginning on 7 March. When the marchers arrived in Montgomery they would present a petition to the Governor, George Wallace. 'I can't promise that it won't get you killed,' he told the crowd at Brown Chapel, 'but we must stand up for what is right.'

In his heart he was sure that the marchers would get no further than the Edmund Pettis Bridge on the outskirts of Selma, for the police would be waiting there to arrest them. As he himself wished to avoid being arrested so early in the campaign, he did not intend to join the marchers right at the start. So, on what came to be known as Bloody Sunday, 525 people, some of them white, left Brown Chapel carrying sleeping bags and blankets. Beyond the bridge waited Sheriff Clark, Colonel Al Lingo of the Alabama Highway Patrol and sixty state troopers standing three deep across all the lanes of Highway 80, wearing gas masks and wielding clubs.

The marchers were ordered to halt and given two minutes in which to disperse. But the troopers' blood was up. After only one minute, they moved in on the defenceless negroes, clubs swinging. Twenty people were trampled underfoot in the first charge. The troopers then attacked with tear gas, while white spectators jeered, shouting 'Kill the SOB's'; and Sheriff Clark added the refrain of 'Get those goddam niggers.' Clark's men came to the aid of the troopers, lashing the negroes with bullwhips and rubber hoses, or chasing terrified men, women and children with electric cattle prods all the way back to Brown Chapel. Old people vomited at the roadside as troopers charged right over them. Dropping their bedrolls and picnic lunches, the negroes retreated weeping and in a state of shock.

Clark, oblivious of the cameramen and news reporters, was triumphant, raring to move in for the kill. He encouraged his men to run amok in the 'nigger' sections of town, laying about them with sticks and clubs. Around 140 negroes were hurt, seventy of them needing hospital treatment.

King's grief and remorse spurred him to an inspired decision. Sending telegrams to all the religious leaders across the nation, he urged them to come to Selma for 'a ministers' march to Montgomery' on 7 March. As most of these men and women had watched in horror as the Selma outrages were perpetrated, the telegrams galvanised them into action. Over 400 ministers, rabbis, priests, nuns, seminarians, lay readers – black and white – headed for Selma to join Martin Luther King. 'Agitators', howled the state authorities in Alabama, preparing to ban the march. King ignored the ban. 'We've gone too far to turn back now,' he declared at Brown Chapel. 'We must let them know that nothing can stop us, not even death itself . . . I do not know what lies ahead of us. There may be beatings, jailings and tear gas. But I would rather die on the highways of Alabama than make a butchery of my conscience. There is nothing more tragic in all this world than to know right and not to do it. I cannot stand in the midst of all these glaring evils and not take a stand.'

And so, 1,500 people, half of them white, marched out of Selma on the appointed Tuesday. Among them were a handful of nuns and 450 clergymen. There was a dramatic moment at the bridge when the tensed and glaring troopers ordered them to halt. All 1,500 fell to their knees and prayed.

A point had been made. For the present it was enough. King was afraid that if the march continued there would be bloodshed, so, amid general consternation, he ordered the marchers to return home.

That night, the fury of the white extremists spilled its bounds. One of the visiting white ministers, James Reeb, was killed by Klansmen as he dined at a negro restaurant with two friends. Over 2,000 people of both races and all denominations attended the funeral, and President Johnson made a historic speech to Congress which was broadcast to the whole nation:

At times (said the President) history and fate meet at a single time in a single place to shape a turning point in man's unending search for freedom . . . So it was last week in Selma, Alabama . . . What happened in Selma is part of a far larger movement which reaches into every section and state of America. It is the effort of American negroes to secure for themselves the full blessings of American life. Our mission is at once the oldest and the most basic of this country – to right wrong, to do justice and to serve man. Their cause must be our cause too. Because it is not just negroes, but really all of us, who must overcome the crippling legacy of bigotry and injustice. And we *shall* overcome.

It was an address worthy of King himself, and in the course of it Johnson assured the listening millions that the Voting Rights Bill would have top priority on his list of proposed legislation. With that, the barriers fell away as though by magic. The march to Montgomery was given federal approval and Alabama state officials were ordered to leave the marchers alone.

On Sunday 21 March, two weeks after the infamous Bloody Sunday, Martin Luther King marched in triumph out of Selma at the head of about 5,000 blacks and whites. Jeers and obscenities from the onlookers left them unmoved. Eight miles beyond the bridge, the numbers thinned to about 300, all of whom intended to walk the whole distance to Montgomery.

Wednesday found them camped on the outskirts. All through the night bus-loads, train-loads and plane-loads of supporters joined them from every race, religion and class. 'We have a new song to sing to-morrow,' exulted King. '"We *have* Overcome".'

Next day, like Moses leading his people towards the Promised Land, King led the crowd of 25,000 through the streets of Montgomery, the heart and heartland of the old slave-based Confederacy. At Confederate Square, with tears drenching their faces, they stood and sang:

> Deep in my heart, I do believe
> That we have overcome today.

Martin Luther King's eloquence matched the historic occasion: standing in triumph on a trailer he cried:

> They told us we wouldn't get here. And there were those who said we would get here only over their dead bodies. But all the world today knows that we are here and that we are standing before the forces of power in the state of Alabama, saying, 'We ain't gonna let nobody turn us around.'

Sounding more than ever like an Old Testament prophet, he continued:

We are on the move and no wave of racism can stop us. The burning of our churches, the bombing of our homes, the clubbing and killing of our clergymen and young people will not deter us . . . My people, my people, listen. The battle is in our hands . . . there are difficult days ahead. We are still in for a season of suffering. But we must struggle on with faith in the power of non-violence. Our aim must never be to defeat or humiliate the white man but to win his friendship and understanding. We must come to see that the end we seek is a society at peace with itself, a society that can live with its conscience. That will be a day not of the white man, not of the black man . . . That will be the day of man as man.

It was Martin Luther King's finest hour, the nearest he ever came to seeing his dream fulfilled.

7

When King turned his attention to the ghettoes of the north, after 1965, his touch was less sure. Northern negroes had the vote but were the victims of discriminatory practices and unequal schooling. Sensing their unrest, King was anxious to channel the rising anger into non-violent forms of protest.

But they did not understand. When, in August 1965, Los Angeles erupted into violence, the rioters in the suburb of Watts naively believed that victory was theirs. In reality, the emergence of the negro as violent and lawless did incalculable harm to the civil rights movement in America, causing white citizens to recoil in fear and loathing.

All this made King determined to preach the gospel of non-violence more loudly than ever in the north. In a sermon at the Riverside Church in New York 1965 he affirmed his commitment: 'We will return good for evil. We will love our enemies. Christ showed us the way and Gandhi showed us it could work.' He would have nothing to do with Black Power or any kind of black separatist or anti-white hate movements. He hoped to neutralise the power of such ideological groups by pointing out the blessings of integration as opposed to separatism. King wanted improved economic conditions for the negro within, not outside the present system.

In Chicago he tried to convince Mayor Daley of 'the seething desperation of the black ghettoes'. He organised sit-ins, camp-outs, boycotts, demonstrations; but the Chicago gang-leaders set more store by shoot-outs. To the followers of Stokely Carmichael and Frantz Fanon, who believed that only violence could liberate the oppressed blacks, he repeated again and again: 'Darkness cannot drive out darkness; only light can do that. Hate cannot drive out hate; only love can do that.' Where Fanon wanted a new man with hatred in his heart, King sought a new man who prized justice and humanity. 'A dark, desperate, confused and sin-sick world waits for this new man and this new kind of power. The real revolution must be based on hope, not hatred.'

As the black community drifted steadily away from his influence, King wrote *Where Do We Go From Here?*, a moving attempt to stem the tide of violence, to keep dissent positive and creative. Meanwhile, his country's involvement in the war in Vietnam disturbed him greatly, driving him to take an ever stronger line against the war, thus alienating President Johnson. 'I can't be silent,' he cried. 'Justice is indivisible . . . The bombs in Vietnam explode at home: they destroy the hopes and possibilities for a decent America.' America was not ready for such sentiments. 'Martin Loser King', they called him now, as moderate and liberal sentiment swung sharply away from him.

While coals of fire were being heaped on his head, he launched a campaign which would bring thousands of unemployed blacks to Washington in April 1968. In this new great march on Washington, he wanted to confront the federal government and expose the racial basis of economic injustice. Almost everybody was against the march, believing that it would provoke a blood-bath. Even King's closest advisers warned that he was playing with fire. The voices of doom and disaster were so insistent that he became moody and apprehensive, fearful of the ever more numerous death threats.

On Sunday 4 February, 1968, he spoke to his congregation in Atlanta about his own funeral service. There must be no long, sweeping eulogy, he said; no admiring talk of his degrees and diplomas, of his Nobel Peace Prize. It was as a man who had tried to spend his life serving others that he wished to be remembered.

Before ever the Washington march could take place, Martin Luther King Jr. was dead.

It happened in Memphis, Tennessee. In Memphis the – mostly black – rubbish collectors had asked the city authorities for better wages, better conditions and official recognition of their union. The authorities refused; the dustmen went on strike. When the police broke up their protest marches with sticks and stones, the whole black community was aroused and took to the streets in protest. Martin Luther King was invited to lead a big march on 28 March.

Unfortunately he was poorly briefed on the situation in Memphis. Nobody had seen fit to tell him that Black Power was strong in the city, that many of the black youths simply scoffed at the idea of a peaceful protest. The omission was disastrous. Too late King discovered, as the procession moved off, that militant youngsters at the back of the column were running berserk. The police weighed in and all hell broke loose. When at last the smoke cleared, 155 shops had been looted and smashed up, sixty people were injured. And the police had shot and killed a sixteen-year-old black youth.

King was devastated. For the first time men of violence had seized control of one of his protests; it might well spell the end of non-violence. But he was determined to try again, to show the world that non-violence could still prevail. To this end he announced that in early April he would return to Memphis to lead a peaceful demonstration. If protest in Memphis could not be peaceful, what chance did the march on Washington have?

On the morning of 3 April there was a bomb scare on the plane carrying Martin Luther King to Memphis. He arrived tired, restless and apprehensive; and the lashing rain and threatening storm seemed tailored to his state of mind. When he went down that evening to address a crowd at Mason Temple, the thunder was already crashing out over the city.

It was as though he knew that this would be his last address, as though he had a definite sense of his impending death. He spoke of the great issues of the time, of the bus boycott, of the Freedom Rides, of Birmingham, of Selma, and of the day he had stood at the Lincoln Memorial to tell the world of his dream. Man's very survival was now at stake, he warned; if something were not done soon to rescue the poor people of the world from their poverty, then the world was doomed. It had been his privilege, he assured them, to lead the black people of America in their historic twentieth-century struggle out of darkness. But now his days were numbered; there were so many threats to his life. For all of them the way ahead was clouded with uncertainty.

> But it really doesn't matter with me now (he went on), because I've been to the mountain-top. Like anybody I would like to live a long life . . . But I'm not concerned about that now. I just want to do God's Will. And He's allowed me to go up to the mountain. And I've looked over. And I've seen the Promised Land. And I may not get there with you. But I want you to know tonight that we as a people *will* get to the Promised Land. So I'm happy tonight . . . I have a dream this afternoon that the brotherhood of man will become a reality. With this faith *I* will go out and carve a tunnel of hope from a mountain of despair . . . With this faith, *we* will be able to achieve this new day, when all of God's children – black men and white men, Jews and Gentiles, Protestants and Catholics – will be able to join hands and sing with the Negroes in the spiritual of old, 'Free at last, Free at last, Thank God Almighty we are free at last.'

Less than twenty-four hours later he was dead. At six p.m. on 4 April, as he stood on the balcony of his hotel, a bullet tore at his throat, scything through his jaw and neck, fracturing his spine. He fell in a pool of blood, and died shortly afterwards on his way to the hospital. That haunting voice had been stilled for ever.

The assassin was a white man, James Earl Ray, an escaped convict, and there were dark (never proved) suspicions that he was part of a conspiracy to do away with King. Some indeed rejoiced in his death; but for the most part Americans were dazed with horror. President Johnson proclaimed a day of national mourning on 7 April, and all over the country flags fluttered at half mast, while thousands marched, prayed and sang in his memory. The following day, Coretta and her older children led nineteen thousand through the streets of Memphis. No violence was offered them.

At his funeral in Atlanta, a recording of King's last sermon in Atlanta was played, to stand as his epitaph:

I want you to say that I tried to love and serve humanity. Yes, if you want to say that I was a drum major, say that I was a drum major for justice. Say that I was a drum major for peace. That I was a drum major for righteousness. And all the other shallow things will not matter. I won't have any money to leave behind. I won't have the fine and luxurious things of life to leave behind. But I just want to leave a committed life behind. And that's all I want to say.

3.
Maximilian Kolbe
1894–1941

Auschwitz itself remains inexplicable. The most profound statement yet made about Auschwitz was not a statement at all but a response.

The query: 'At Auschwitz, tell me, where was God?' And the answer: 'Where was man?'

Sophie's Choice, William Styron

We who lived in concentration camps can remember the men who walked through the huts comforting others, giving away their last piece of bread. They may have been few in number, but they offer sufficient proof that everything can be taken from a man but one thing: the last of the human freedoms – to choose one's attitude in any given set of circumstances, to choose one's way.

Man's Search For Meaning, Viktor Frankl

The vision of naked humanity is not at all a figment of the imagination of a sick mind. It could become reality sooner than we might expect. If this should happen, who will man be on an over-populated, barren and poisoned earth? A rat insane from terror and hunger, or still a man?

From an article on Kolbe in *Twórzość*, 1972, by Jan Józef Szczepański

1

On 11 October 1982, the day after Maximilian Kolbe had been proclaimed saint in Rome, Pope John Paul II addressed a large number of his Polish compatriots in the Nervi audience hall at the Vatican. Saint Maximilian, martyr of Auschwitz, he told them, was indeed uniquely Polish, expressing in his own life and death all the suffering and hope of twentieth century Poland. Yet his significance was not for Poland alone but for the world; St. Maximilian stood out as one of the 'signs of the times', a witness, a prophet for our times; his story belonged to the history of twentieth century man, especially European man; the raw material of his sanctity was no less than the great central, deeply painful human condition:

> That difficult, tragic period marked by a terrible contempt for human dignity gave birth in Auschwitz to its sign of salvation. Love showed itself to be more powerful than death, more powerful than the inhuman system. Human love won its victory there, in that place where hatred and contempt appeared to triumph. In this victory for love at Auschwitz we can see in a special way the victory of Golgotha. Men saw the death of their fellow-prisoner, not as a final defeat for man, but as a sign of salvation, a sign for our time, for our century.

*   *   *

The second son of Julius and Marianna Kolbe was born on 8 January, 1894, in Zdunska Wola, a village outside Łódź, in that part of Poland which was ruled by Czarist Russia. (Since the eighteenth century, Poland had been partitioned between Austria, Russia and Prussia.) On that same day the baby was baptized and given the name Raymund.

Julius was a poor weaver and an ardent patriot who dreamed of freedom for his country and played an active part in various underground freedom movements. His wife Marianna had earlier wanted to become a nun, but as that was not possible in Russian-occupied Poland where the convents were suppressed, she had settled for marriage with Julius. They were both devout Catholics with a particular, very Polish, devotion to the Blessed Virgin. (In the Polish up-risings, mothers would arm their sons with a huge medallion of Our Lady of Częstochowa or of Ostra Brama as they went off to fight; and legend has it that enemy bullets simply ricocheted off them.) Every day, like other Polish families, the Kolbe family knelt together in prayer before a statue of the Virgin, and often they walked in pilgrimage to her national shrine at Częstochowa.

When Raymund was still a baby, Julius, in search of work, moved his family first to Łódź, the textile centre of Poland and then to Pabianice, where he opened a small weaving shop. Marianna, though untrained, found work locally as a midwife in order to eke out the inadequate family income. In Russian Poland there were no free schools so Julius taught his sons to read and write himself. (A census taken in 1897 revealed that illiteracy in this part of the country was as high as 70 per cent.) Later on, Julius managed to pay for the elder boy, Francis, to attend a school, but Raymund had to stay at home and help in the shop or in his mother's kitchen. But the parish priest soon discovered that he was a bright boy and undertook to teach him Latin, a task later taken over by the local pharmacist. Raymund made such progress in the subject that his parents felt duty bound to have him educated along with his older brother; and so he too was given his chance. The school of course was Russian, with the lessons given in Russian and concerned only with Russian history and culture. All things Polish – including, until 1905, the language – were banned. Fortunately for his sons, however, Julius Kolbe was a book-lover and spent hours reading aloud to them from patriotic Polish books. For their part, they used to assert their Polish-ness by drawing white eagles on the walls or playing at being knights in a Polish legion.

The boys – another son was born after Raymund – were brought up strictly, Marianna not being one to stand any nonsense. Raymund appears to have been a healthily naughty small boy, with a talent for exasperating his mother. One day when he had driven her beyond endurance, she wondered aloud whatever would become of him, and seven-year-old Raymund was stricken by her distress. The story (told by Marianna only after his death) is that he rushed in tears to the church where he put the same question about his future to the Virgin Mary. What happened then he would reveal only to his mother, and only because she became as alarmed by his sudden gravity as she had previously been by his unruliness. Mary had appeared to him, he told her, holding two crowns, one white, one red, offering him a choice. The white one signified life-long purity, the red promised a martyr's crown – and Raymund told the vision that he would take them both.

From time to time members of various religious orders from the more relaxed Austrian provinces would cross over into Russian territory to recruit young men for the seminaries. In this way, when Raymund Kolbe was thirteen, he and his older brother Francis were invited to join the junior seminary in Lwów, run by the Franciscans. Both boys were keen to go, and in the end Julius and Marianna agreed.

Raymund did well at the seminary, acquitting himself brilliantly all round, especially in mathematics and physics. He had dreams of becoming an engineer or an inventor, but finally set his heart on joining the newly formed Polish Legion, yearning, as St Francis of Assisi had done, to fight tyranny and injustice on the field of battle. So taken was he by the idea of crusading for the Virgin Mary in her role as Queen of Poland that by the time he was sixteen he had firmly decided to leave the seminary and enlist in the army.

He was actually on his way to tell the Rector of his decision, when a loud knocking was heard on the friary gate. The visitor was Marianna, his mother, bursting with news: as all their sons had now left home, she and Julius had both decided to enter the religious life, Marianna with the Benedictine sisters at Lwów, Julius with the Franciscans at Craców.

The coincidence of his mother's arrival at that precise moment overwhelmed Raymund, who took it as a clear message that he must give up his dreams of joining the army, and stay where he was. When he saw the Rector, he made no mention of his earlier plans, asking instead to be admitted as a novice Franciscan. With the rough brown habit, he was given a new name, Maximilian, after a third-century Roman citizen from Carthage who had been executed for refusing to serve in the Roman Legion. 'I am a Christian, I cannot serve,' he had insisted. (The martyr's namesake must have perceived a certain irony in the choice of name.)

A year later, after taking temporary vows, he was sent to Craców to study philosophy. And from there he went to Rome, to pursue his studies and widen his horizons. At the Gregorian College and at his own Franciscan College, the professors were impressed by the young Pole's varied talents. 'A rare natural genius', one of them called him. Fascinated by the exciting new idea of space travel, the young man produced a paper on the possibilities of inter-planetary and inter-stellar travel, backed by calculations and detailed drawings. He even designed a prototype jet plane for the space traveller, causing Professor Gianfreschi, the eminent Jesuit physicist at the Gregorian, to prophesy a brilliant future for him in this branch of science. But by now Maximilian wanted only one thing: to become a priest.

It was in Rome that the first signs of tuberculosis began to appear: the poor circulation, haemorrhages, headaches and intolerable tension that would plague him for the rest of his days. It was also in Rome that he discovered his life's work. Maximilian was distressed by the aggressively anti-Catholic behaviour of the Italian Freemasons who in 1917 were celebrating their two-hundredth anniversary in Rome. They had marched in procession to St. Peter's Square, their black banners showing Lucifer with a defeated Archangel Michael under foot and the legend, '*Non Serviam*': I will not serve. Other banners were just as specific: 'Satan Must Reign in The Vatican'; 'The Pope Must Be His Slave'; and supporters thrust virulently anti-clerical pamphlets at the bystanders.

Maximilian was horrified that his fellow Catholics dismissed the affair so lightly. He himself would have welcomed a showdown. Like Francis of Assisi, his patron and model, he was incapable of doing things by halves. Just as Francis had once rushed off to try to convert the Sultan at the height of the Crusades, Maximilian was all for setting off to convert the Masonic Grand Master. When friends dissuaded him from such an extreme course, he began to plan a different kind of counter-attack. From now on the young friar's conversation was salted with military expressions: 'routing the enemy', 'the engines of war'; and 'bringing up the heavy artillery'. 'In the face of such strong attacks by the enemies of the Church,' he earnestly asked, 'is it enough to complain and weep? No, each of us has a sacred obligation to build a trench and personally hurl back the assaults of the enemy.' The soldier lurking in Maximilian's heart had found a cause worth fighting for: a new crusade was in the making.

It was about this time that he began to consider Mary's role in combating the evils which threatened to destroy a world now in the grip of war. He began to perceive Mary – the human being who had been divinely chosen to be the mother of Christ – as the instrument by whom Christ would heal the human race. This conviction of the power of God working through Mary was to become the mainspring of his life, the source of his limitless love for her, and the explanation perhaps of his otherwise inexplicable strength. She was his Queen, he her Knight.

Remembering, no doubt, his earlier dreams of enlisting in the Polish militia, he now asked permission to launch a militia of his own, to win the world back to God, opposing the Freemasons' 'I will not serve' with the obedience of the faithful knight. 'We have three fronts to conquer,' he declared. 'We must first conquer ourselves. This is the most vital battlefront of all, because without it we have no chance of winning the remaining two. The second front is our immediate neighbour; the third is the whole of humanity.'

The young Franciscan, still a year away from being ordained priest, was allowed to do as he wished. With six other friars who expressed an interest, he formed his militia. By one of those strange coincidences with which Maximilian's life was filled, the seven young men held their inaugural meeting in Rome on 16 October, 1917, on which date, sixty-one years later, Maximilian's compatriot and disciple, Karol Wojtyla, would be elected to the Papacy. The new knights pledged themselves to unite the world in love, to 'convert sinners, heretics and schismatics, particularly Freemasons';* to sanctify all men under the protection of the Virgin Mary. Against what they saw as the forces of division

---

* European freemasonry was much more aggressively free-thinking and anti-clerical than its more philanthropic counterpart in Britain.

and hatred in the world, they were raising the standard of the only human being (if one excepts Christ himself) whose Yes to God had been made without qualification or reserve.

2

At last, in November 1918, Poland was free; after a century and a quarter of Partition, the occupying powers were in disarray. Austria and Germany had been defeated in the war, Czarist Russia thrown into turmoil by revolution. The Treaty of Versailles restored Poland to the world's maps as an independent state. Bloodied by the war, her frontiers still to be secured and her economy in ruins, Poland nevertheless rejoiced in her longed-for freedom.

So it was to a changed Poland that Father Maximilian (he was ordained in April 1918) returned, to teach philosophy and church history in the Franciscan seminary in Craców early in 1919. It was the very seminary to which his father Julius had come. But Julius had met a tragic death in the meantime. Not finding fulfilment with the Franciscans, he had, after a time, joined Pilsudski's army and fought against the Russians. When he was wounded and taken prisoner by them, he knew that, as he was still officially a Russian citizen, he could expect no mercy. They hanged him as a traitor.

Maximilian mourned his father, but it seemed likely that he would soon be joining him. His health had deteriorated so badly that he was given only three months to live and was packed off to a sanatorium in the mountain resort of Zakopane. He had just enough time to launch his militia before he went, inspiring many people religious and lay with his own infectious enthusiasm, though just as many had no patience with him at all.

One lung had collapsed completely, the other was hopelessly damaged. Frequent haemorrhages made it difficult for him to breathe and his movements were slowed to a snail's pace. Some of his more unsympathetic confrères mocked his sluggishness, but he did not complain, of either the pain or the taunts. In true Franciscan spirit he embraced

'Sister Suffering', and when, the crisis having surprisingly
passed, he returned to the friary, he spoke of suffering as 'the
fire in which all gold is purified', as the only real school for
love. 'We shall achieve much more if we are plunged into
exterior and interior darkness,' he prophesied, 'filled with
sorrow, weakened, exhausted, without consolation, persecuted at every step, exposed to constant failure, abandoned
by all, ridiculed, scoffed at, as was Jesus on the Cross;
provided that we want to draw them to God . . . We must not
grieve if we do not see here below the fruits of our works;
perhaps it is the will of God that we should gather them after
our death.'

Although physically slowed down, mentally he was racing
ahead with plans for a monthly magazine which would take
the Gospel to millions. With some reluctance his superiors
gave him the go-ahead; though many of the friars thought the
project crazy, especially at a time when Poland was in the grip
of a severe economic depression. All over the country newspapers were going into liquidation, so what hope could
Maximilian have? They scoffed at him for an unpractical
dreamer.

Without any financial backing, with no help in writing,
proof-reading or composition, and with little or no moral
support from the brethren, Maximilian went ahead, forcing
himself to beg from house to house and on the streets, going
into debt to buy supplies and equipment for the first issue.
The friars looked on in horror, expecting that they would
soon be asked to bail him out.

They need not have worried. In January 1922 five thousand
copies of the magazine, *Knight of the Immaculate*, were
printed, a sixteen-page issue written mainly by Maximilian
himself. Its aims were those of the Militia: to combat the
growing secularisation of society and to lead men back to
God. Believing the causes of this secularisation to be pride,
selfishness and the pursuit of pleasure, Father Maximilian set
himself to encourage asceticism and to shed as much light as
possible on Catholic teaching. Although one of *Knight*'s main
aims would be to convert others, it must attempt this task with
tolerance and 'without racial, national, cultural or social

prejudice'. Only by offering understanding and friendship could it truly reflect the love of Christ, which was the source of happiness. Indeed the contemporary search for happiness was the theme of this first issue: 'If the heart of man is not satisfied with riches, sensual pleasure and the smoke of a passing glory, then it must look for the supreme good which is limitless and unending – God Himself. To be happy, one must strive to be holy, and to be holy is to love God *beyond* the limit of one's resources.'

Maximilian distributed the copies free. Then, with more faith than realism, he started work on the next issue, wondering where the money was to come from to pay the printers' bills. Somewhat desperately he knelt to pray at the altar of the Virgin Mary in the Franciscan church; and as he rose from his knees he spotted a small envelope on the altar. He picked it up, noticing the words written on the outside: 'For you, O Immaculate Mother'. Inside was the exact sum that he owed his creditors!

But miracles did not happen every day, and the difficulties of printing almost overwhelmed the inexperienced friar. Even when money came in – and he was now asking for a contribution from those who could afford to buy a copy of the magazine – devaluation of the currency rendered it almost worthless overnight; rising costs and frequent strikes forced him to change printers five times in the first year. All this restless activity in the friary upset the Craców brethren, and they were not sorry when Maximilian and his entire operation were moved to Grodno at the eastern end of Poland. Maximilian too was pleased, for though the friary in Grodno was ramshackle, he would have there two assistants, three rooms to work in and a printing-press of his own, an ancient, manually operated press known affectionately as Granny.

Operating the press was back-breaking work. For each edition of *Knight* Granny's handle had to be turned 60,000 times. Maximilian shouldered his share of the work without complaint, working by day in the parish and frequently all night on the magazine.

Within the first three years *Knight*'s circulation increased dramatically from 5,000 to 45,000 per issue, enabling Maximilian to place an order for a modern type-setting machine. The friars ridiculed Maximilian's fondness for new machinery and suggested that it would make more sense to invest the profits, a notion which Maximilian rejected as un-Franciscan. 'Our greatness is not to be found in amassing material things,' he chided them, 'but in freeing ourselves from them.'

All this over-work and excitement proved too much of a strain on Maximilian's health. Nobody was surprised when he collapsed once again with a raging 105° fever and was sent back to Zakopane for several months. It was frustrating – especially at a time when the work was prospering so greatly – but he accepted the inevitable with his usual calmness. Other friars had come along to join the publishing enterprise, so despite Maximilian's absence, *Knight* continued to flourish.

In fact, when the circulation figure soared to 60,000, it was clear that Grodno in its turn had been outgrown. Maximilian began looking for a new site. On his return from Zakopane he was functioning on only one quarter of one lung, but far from flagging his energy seemed to have redoubled. Searching around he came upon the ideal site, a six-acre plot of land on the Teresin flats outside Warsaw, with a railway station nearby. There was just one snag, but it was a big one: he lacked the money to buy it. Maximilian, however, was not easily deflected. Discovering that the land was owned by a young Catholic nobleman, Prince Jan Drucki-Lubecki, he decided to ask the prince to give him the land. To underline his claim, he placed a large statue of the Virgin Mary in the centre of one of the fields. The astonished prince attempted at least to impose one or two conditions but was quietly out-manoeuvred. Recognising defeat, he gave way with good grace, offering the land to the Franciscans as an unconditional gift.

The friars arrived on the site in the autumn of 1927 with ambitious plans for a great friary. 'The monastic spirit will flourish here,' declared Maximilian, 'we shall grow in obedience and be poor in the spirit of St. Francis.' They named the place Niepokalanów, which means 'place of the Immaculate One'; and they built their friary with bare hands throughout a freezing Polish winter. Cutting down timber they built a chapel, sleeping quarters, equipment sheds, workshops and offices, working cheerfully, Maximilian along with the others. For he would accept no concessions to his quarter-lung, insisting on mixing cement and carrying bricks like everyone else, his only shelter a rough hut exposed to the biting winds.

The arrival of the new machinery – the finest that modern technology could provide – caused great excitement among the friars, who gave the machines names like Sister Motor or Brother Press, much as St. Francis would have done. Where machinery was concerned, Maximilian was years ahead of his time: these were the tools of his mission to spread the Gospel of Christ. For themselves, the friars must live in poverty, sharing even their boots and overcoats; but for the work of God no expense must be spared.

Maximilian was in his element – planning, organising, bringing something out of nothing by sheer determination. Many of the visitors to Niepokalanów were astonished at the change in him. 'And to think he used to be so hide-bound,' exclaimed one of the Craców friars. Others, especially among the older friars, continued to think him mad. But his own Niepokalanów friars loved him and looked on him as a second St. Francis, because he was gentle and kind and cared for them greatly. Young men were now queueing up to join the Order, some of them lured by the fame of the new machinery which Maximilian would allow only Franciscans to operate. The original community of two priests and seventeen lay brothers, who had arrived in 1927, grew within ten years to 762 friars, of whom thirteen were priests. It was the largest religious community in the world, with every one of its members some kind of specialist. Among them were doctors, dentists, farmers, mechanics, tailors, builders, shoemakers and cooks. They made their own clothes, farmed their own land, sold their own produce; they built a friary, a college, a novitiate, a hundred-bed hospital, an electric sawmill, a food-processing plant and even a fire station. As for the publishing house, the nerve centre of Niepokalanów, it had become one of the most up-to-date in the whole of Poland.

In the midst of so much success, Maximilian was anxious to make sure that his friars kept their priorities straight, reminding them constantly that their central task was the imitation of Christ. 'All progress is spiritual,' he taught, 'or it is not progress. The true Niepokalanów is in our hearts. Everything else is only secondary.'

3

On a train one day Maximilian met a group of young Japanese students who charmed him with their kindness and courtesy. Suddenly it seemed to him intolerable that young people like these should have no opportunity of knowing Christ and his Gospel. Acting on impulse, he asked his superiors to send him to Japan to establish a friary there. Rather to his amazement they agreed.

Before he set off for Japan, someone asked him what he was going to do for money. 'Money?' he echoed in surprise. 'Oh, it will turn up somehow, Mary will see to it. It's her business – and her Son's.'

With this unquenchable faith he left, taking four companions with him. On the way they started to learn the characters of the difficult Japanese language, but when they arrived in Nagasaki in March 1930 they were still almost as ignorant of the language as they were of the law, customs or culture of the Japanese people. Given that they were destitute and that Maximilian was a desperately sick man, it is obvious that only a total faith in the eventual success of their mission could have sustained them.

As always in the past, their faith was justified. The Archbishop of Nagasaki, who at first refused Maximilian's bizarre request to publish a magazine in Japanese, warmed towards him on discovering that he had two doctorates. It was agreed that in exchange for a licence to publish, Father Maximilian would teach philosophy in the diocesan seminary.

It was hard going. The Polish friars' only shelter was a wretched hut whose roof and walls threatened to fall in. They slept on what straw they could find, covering themselves with coats – and one night the roof actually did fall on them. They cooked inadequate meals on a camp fire, using a rough plank as a table. But despite the hardships, on 24 April, 1930, exactly one month after their arrival, a telegram was despatched to Poland: 'TODAY DISTRIBUTING JAPANESE *KNIGHT*. HAVE PRINTING PRESS. PRAISE TO MARY IMMACULATE.'

Critics did not fail to point out that the new magazine left a lot to be desired. The Brothers had set the type themselves, struggling clumsily with the unfamiliar Japanese characters. But the miracle was that it had been done at all, and on the whole the response was encouraging. Sufficiently so for Maximilian to risk looking for a site on which to build a friary, a printing establishment and a junior seminary – another Niepokalanów, in fact.

He found what he wanted on the slopes of Mount Hikosan, land that had once been used as a cemetery and was thought to be haunted. Maximilian liked it and resolved to build there, haunted or not, disregarding the Cassandras who believed him crazy to build on a mountainside sloping away from the town. (In 1945, when the atomic bomb reduced Nagasaki to rubble, Mugenzai no Sono, the Japanese Garden of the Immaculate, was virtually unharmed.)

Slowly the friary took shape, as Maximilian and the others once again approached the herculean task of building it. The courage and simplicity of the friars attracted both Christian and non-Christian Japanese. Young men came to join the Order and within four years the initial little group of four had grown to twenty-four. Within six years there were twenty Japanese studying for the priesthood in the seminary built by the friars. All was going well and when Maximilian returned to Poland in 1936 for the general meeting of the Franciscan community, he was able to report on much progress in Japan and the possibility of further extending his work to India.

But his already precarious health was getting worse. Violent headaches and chronic abscesses plagued him. When his superiors saw the state he was in, they decided that he must not return to Japan. They sent him instead back to Niepokalanów.

* * *

In view of the many serious charges of anti-Semitism laid against Father Kolbe at the time of his canonisation in 1982, and as at least some of the mud has seemed to stick, it is perhaps necessary at this point to pause and consider the background to those charges.

The first Jews settled in Poland in the fourteenth century and over the centuries their numbers steadily increased, until in 1918, when Poland became independent, there were over two million of them, a much higher percentage per head of population than anywhere else in Europe. Then, as one and a half million Jewish refugees from the Russian Revolution poured into the country, the number was almost doubled. Ten per cent of the thirty-two million inhabitants of Poland were now Jewish.

This massive influx of strangers with an alien lifestyle, coming at a time when the Poles were impoverished by the war and desperately trying to stave off economic collapse, was a recipe for intense national resentment; especially as Jews already controlled much of the industrial and commercial life of the country and were dominant in professions such as medicine and law.

While Marshal Pilsudski was still alive, the Jews received relatively sympathetic treatment. But his death in May 1935 coincided with a changed political climate not only in Poland but throughout Europe. As economic conditions became more painful, the traditional tolerance of the Poles became strained. Outbursts of anti-Semitism, deplored by many but approved by others, became all too common. Access to the professions and to the universities was made more difficult for Jews (and other minorities), while boycotting Jewish shops and businesses became an accepted feature of Polish life. As a result of these pressures and, in the case of the refugees from Russia because of their unrelenting poverty, 400,000 Jews opted to leave Poland. Their reasons were entirely comprehensible, although, as Isaac Cohen of the Anglo-Jewish Association was later to point out, 'Jews who imagined that they were maltreated in Poland did not have long to wait for conditions which made Poland look like Paradise.'

The political party with most animus against the Jews and

other minorities was the 'Poland for the Poles' party of the National Democrats. But though they ardently advocated economic penalties for the Jews, they stopped well short of a pogrom and were by no stretch of the imagination in the same league as the Nazis. Nevertheless they detested the Jews, and it is undeniable that they received a good deal of support from various prominent Church leaders. When, following the death of Pilsudski in 1935, the Polish bishops invited the Franciscans at Niepokalanów to produce a national daily paper to combat the nation's 'drift to chaos', the result was *Mały Dziennik* (Little Daily) whose editor, Father Marian Wojcik, was a sympathiser with the anti-liberal, anti-Jewish views of the National Democrats. Whether it was, as a critic claimed, 'the voice of extreme anti-Semitism, sowing hatred and contempt' is open to doubt; but it most certainly produced anti-Semitic articles and expressed anti-Semitic sentiments over the years.

As he was in over-all control of the entire publishing operation, to that extent Father Kolbe may be blamed for its unacceptable utterances. But it must be remembered that when the tone of *Mały Dziennik* was being set, he was several thousand miles away in Japan. It therefore seems a little hard that he should be held responsible for the paper's editorial policy. In any case it is on record that he urged the friars at home to adopt an altogether gentler, less polemic approach. From Nagasaki on 12 July 1935 he wrote:

As for directives I am too far away at present to suggest a policy. But I will offer some advice. Contributors should write in the spirit of salvation . . . avoiding all unnecessary branding of peoples or parties or other nations. When talking about Jews, I would be very careful not to stir up or deepen hatred towards them in people who are already sometimes ill-disposed or openly hostile.

And as regards the 'Don't buy Jewish buy Christian' campaign in *Knight*, which many Jews understandably construed as anti-Semitism, Father Maximilian had this advice for his colleagues:

Generally speaking I would pay more attention to the development of Polish trade and industry than to the condemnation of the Jews.

Whatever his private, Polish reservations about the Jews, those are not the words of the 'rabid, racist anti-Semite' depicted by Father Kolbe's present-day enemies. It is said that in 1939 he refused to enter a parish house from which a priest had recently expelled a Jew. Later that same year, surely he passed the most acid test of all. For when the Jewish calvary began in earnest, few people did more to aid and succour the Jews than Father Kolbe and his fellow Franciscans.

*   *   *

In the printing establishment at Niepokalanów more technologically advanced equipment had been installed, including three machines capable of producing 16,000 copies of *Knight* in an hour. New techniques made it possible to meet the ever-growing demand for more and more publications, for books as well as newspapers and magazines. Maxmilian's presses were offering no less than nine different publications, ranging from a spiritual magazine for priests in Latin to an illustrated *Sporting Journal*. *Mały Dziennik* now ran to eleven daily editions, with a staggeringly high circulation (by European standards) of 230,000. *Knight* was approaching the million mark, and with its wide international following kept sixty-five friars busy in its correspondence section alone.

Within Poland itself Father Maximilian's influence seemed to be enormous, scarcely a Catholic home being without its copy of one or other of his productions. Priests in parishes all over the country reported an upsurge in religious practice, which they attributed to the literature coming from Niepokalanów. A campaign against abortion in a 1938 issue of *Knight* brought people of all classes and professions into the Militia.

True, he made little impact on secular circles or on Polish cultural life. There were many who ridiculed his naivety and derided his passion for the latest in technology. While he was still in Nagasaki, he had written of his dream of 'a friar in patched habit and well-mended shoes flying an aeroplane of the latest design.' Maximilian had not long been back in Poland before he acquired a radio station and in 1938 Radio Niepokalanów took to the air, with an orchestra of friars playing the Lourdes hymn ('Immaculate Mary') as their signature tune. He planned to make films, in which he would use the best actors in Poland; and just before the outbreak of war he had drawn up plans for an airfield and had already sent two of the brothers to train as pilots. The satirical press in Warsaw ran a cartoon which showed the friars piloting their own planes, loaded with their own publications. Though the laughter was on the whole benign, this mixture of science and holy simplicity was felt to be curious, to say the least. What would Father Kolbe be up to next?

Maximilian himself had no illusions about the future. If he always seemed to be in a hurry, it was because there was so little time. Ever since his return he had been warning the Brothers to expect the worst, predicting an appalling cataclysm ahead. But, he consoled them, 'whatever happens, no one nor anything can do us real harm. Suffering, whether of the body or the spirit, can only serve to make us holy. Suppose they kill us . . . well, that will mean a free passage to heaven . . . And would it not be the supreme honour if we could seal our faith with our own blood?'

Just before the floodtide of barbarism engulfed his country, Father Maximilian gathered his friars together and spoke to them of the three stages of the spiritual life: the preparation for life's task; the fulfilment of the task; and the suffering that must necessarily follow.

For my part (he told them), only now do I pass to the third stage. Where? How? She alone knows. What happiness it would be to die as a soldier, not in bed but on a post of execution, with a bullet through the heart; to seal our love for the Immaculate with our own blood; to pour out the last drop in order to speed the conquest of the whole world for Christ, through her. That is what I wish for you, my sons, and that is what I wish for myself.

4

Armageddon finally arrived at dawn on 1 September, 1939 when, in a hell of armoured tanks, Panzer troops and aircraft raining bombs from a clear blue sky, Germany invaded Poland. Maximilian promptly sent many of the Brothers back to their homes or to join Red Cross units. He said goodbye to them one by one, knowing that they would probably never meet again. He had always foretold that he himself would not survive the war.

Only thirty-six friars remained, and they were stretched beyond capacity, caring for the homeless refugees who now crowded into the friary. Poland had not stood a chance. Within forty-eight hours of the invasion her gallant airforce was wiped out, and within two weeks her military resistance was almost at an end. Refugees, civilian and military, fled blindly eastwards, carrying everything they could hold. And then came the next devastating blow. On 17 September, while the Germans still besieged Warsaw, the Red Army attacked from the east and Poland was caught in a giant nutcracker intent on her total destruction.

Two days after this, a German motorised unit arrived at Niepokalanów and ordered the Brothers out. 'Take courage, my sons,' Maximilian consoled them, 'we're setting off on a new mission – and we're having our fares paid for us. What a stroke of luck.'

They were driven in trucks to Rawa Mazowiecka and next day passed through Częstochowa, (where people threw food for the hungry friars to eat), and eventually, by way of Lamsdorf in Silesia, reached Amtitz, near the border with Germany. They were cold and hungry, and they had to sleep on the ground in a huge military tent where there were already 300 internees, many of them wounded, some of them dying. Father Kolbe moved among them, praying, consoling, listening to them, distributing his supply of Miraculous Medals and urging his own Brothers to endure their situation without complaint.

Warsaw held out against inhuman odds until 28 September, when the city had to surrender. On that date the Polish army's resistance collapsed: Poland was finally defeated. The freedom she had won at the Versailles Peace Treaty of 1919 had lasted a mere twenty years, and now the old enemies were back in force.

From Amtitz the friars were sent northwards to a camp outside Poznań. (The mania for transferring people from one camp or prison to another was characteristic of the Nazis all through the Occupation.) Here they were housed in a cellar and put to work in the kitchens. Most of their fellow prisoners had been captured in random street round-ups and were due for deportation to Germany. Maximilian made friends with them and organised readings or study groups to keep their minds off their immediate future.

Suddenly, on 8 December (the Feast of the Immaculate Conception) the friars, without any explanation, were released. They returned to Warsaw, to find it in ruins and swarming with German troops. Making their way back to Niepokalanów, they discovered that it too had been vandalised, though the buildings were still intact. The friars now begged Father Maximilian to seek safety in another friary, but he would not entertain the idea of leaving them. Instead he set to work to repair the damage and to do the best he could for the masses of refugees seeking asylum there.

About 3,000 refugees and deportees passed through his hands, among them about 2,000 Jews. The friars shared everything they had with these poor wretches: 'We must do everything in our power to help these unfortunate people who have been driven from their homes and deprived of even the most basic necessities,' said Father Maximilian. 'Our mission is among them in the coming months.'

Irrepressible as ever, Maximilian asked the German authorities for permission to continue the publication of *Knight*, though most of his machines had been put out of action or sealed with lead. At first the Germans refused, but he wore them down. Reluctantly they gave permission for a single issue, for the Warsaw area only. So 120,000 copies were printed and the friars distributed them all by hand on 8 December, 1940. The date was significant. Once again it was the Feast of the Immaculate Conception, a year ago to the day since their sudden and unexplained release from the camp at Poznań. Realising perhaps that the intervening year had been one of respite and that the real testing-time was now at hand, Maximilian put pen to paper and soared to prophetic heights in the last editorial he was ever to write:

No one in the world can change Truth. What we can and should do is to seek Truth and serve it when we have found it. The real conflict is within. Beyond armies of occupation and the hecatombs of the extermination camps, two irreconcilable enemies lie in the depths of every soul. And of what use are the victories on the battlefield if we are defeated in our innermost personal selves?

Maximilian would never know that inner defeat. He must have sensed that with those words of open defiance, he was signing his own death warrant. It could surely not be long now before the Gestapo arrived. For the moment, however, he was being pressed to sign the Volkslist. Poles with German names (Kolbe was a Germanised variant of the Czech name Kolber) were offered the chance to buy immunity by renouncing Polish citizenship and claiming German nationality. To save themselves from the concentration camps, there were many who yielded. But Father Maximilian was not of their number, insisting that, in spite of his German-sounding name, he was Polish to the core.

They came for him on 17 February, 1941, and he made no attempt to avoid arrest. A friend had slipped him an advance warning, but he did not try to escape. The previous evening, contrary to his custom, he had asked if he could share supper with some of the older friars; and next morning he had risen early and made the rounds of all the Brothers who were sick. Only later did they understand that he had been saying goodbye. After Mass he optimistically dictated an article on a theme that preoccupied him: the relationship of the Blessed Virgin to the Trinity. Mary, he argued, was the visible manifestation of the Holy Spirit for the Church, the sure means by whom all men might be brought to Christ.

Promptly at nine thirty the Gestapo arrived and he went out

calmly to meet them. Taking with him a small attache case and his overcoat, he said goodbye to his brethren with the words, 'The Immaculate will take care of you.' When they had recovered from the shock of his departure, twenty of the friars hastened to sign a petition offering themselves in his stead, and they delivered it in person at Gestapo head-quarters. But such would not have been Maximilian's way – and, for quite different reasons, it was certainly not the Gestapo's.

It was to Pawiak that they took him, the infamous prison in the centre of Warsaw. By now the terror was in full flood; thousands of Poles were being shot and thousands more were rounded up from their homes or on the streets and sent to places like Pawiak to await transportation to somewhere even worse. One of the SS guards was aroused to fury at the sight of the Franciscan priest who was now handed over to him. He tore at the rosary which girdled the priest's waist and thrust its crucifix at his face. 'Do you believe in that?' he shouted contemptuously. When the Franciscan answered 'I do,' the guard struck him a vicious blow in the face. He repeated the question and, receiving the same reply, he began to rain blows upon the priest's head and shoulders. A fellow prisoner, Edward Gniadek, later witnessed to Father Maximilian's calm self-control. 'Don't be upset for me,' the priest whis-pered to this man when the SS man had finally made off. 'You have enough to worry about, and, in any case, it is all for Mary Immaculate.' 'He behaved,' said Gniadek, wonderingly, 'as though nothing untoward had happened.'

For the last time he wrote to the Brothers at Niepokalanów: 'Pray much, all of you; work well and do not worry. Nothing can happen without God's knowledge and will.'

On 28 May, with over three hundred other prisoners, Father Kolbe was herded into a cattle truck without food or water, and sent to Auschwitz concentration camp. As the trucks moved off on their long journey, his voice could be heard leading the others as they sang a hymn – to Mary Immaculate.

5

Auschwitz had not yet become identified with the genocide of the Jews; the infamous Final Solution was still on the drawing-board. In that first year of its existence, only the Poles came there, condemned for their unflagging resistance to the despoilers of their country. Auschwitz was an entirely new kind of concentration camp, more barbaric than existing camps in Germany – Dachau, Sachsenhausen or Buchenwald, for example. An experiment in systematised terror and deliberate degradation of its victims, Auschwitz was 'a new society based on the absolute expendability of life' (William Styron: *Sophie's Choice*). The cynical legend, *Arbeit Macht Frei* (Work Liberates) over the entrance gates, might with far more truth have read, 'All Hope Abandon . . .' As it was, the smoking crematoria soon conveyed the message.

In this terrifying incarnation of Dostoievski's 'world without God', human values were overthrown and human beings reduced to the level of mere objects, to be exploited, terrorised, starved, tortured and killed at whim. And all in the name of a nightmare view of the world in which an elite race of Nordic supermen claimed to have inherited the earth. Non-Aryans were *Untermenschen*, sub-human; vermin to be crushed underfoot without a qualm. But to destroy the body was not enough; the Third Reich's moral crusade was to throw out the whole soft Judaeo-Christian nonsense of human value, human solidarity and human brotherhood. Love, compassion, mercy had no place in the vocabulary of National Socialism. In their place were enthroned arrogance, hatred and contempt. Might was right, and Auschwitz was living proof of it.

They had chosen the site with unerring instinct: Auschwitz was a desolate, marshy spot not far from Craców. What did it matter that men would not long survive such a place, since it was near to a railway line, and fresh reinforcements of slave labour could be constantly supplied?

On 14 June, 1940, the day that Paris fell and a miasma of despair settled over Europe, the first transports of Poles arrived in sealed cattle trucks for delivery to Auschwitz. As each one passed through the gates, he was issued with a shapeless blue and white pyjama suit and branded on the forearm with a tattooed number. From this moment on, he (and later, she) was no longer a person, no longer a name. Henceforth he was a slave, performing meaningless work at the random behest of his masters, 'at the double', urged on by kicks and clubs. Here he would find what sleep he could, packed solid with other unfortunate wretches on a straw-covered bunk, unable even to turn; here he would queue daily, on his knees, to have his tin mug filled with watery soup and for the three slices of sawdust bread which were his daily fare; here he would be cold and filthy; here he would be constantly humiliated – for even his necessary visits to the latrines would be supervised and timed in seconds. Here, where the dank, venomous mists rose from the marshes and poisoned all human life he might, as thousands did, die of a chill or of pneumonia. If, that is, he did not die, like the majority, from the loss of hope.

Father Maximilian was branded with the number 16670. If Franciscan poverty meant being stripped of all material things, then he was now even poorer than St. Francis had been, for not even his name was left. With the other Polish priests he was assigned to the 'Babice' section, under the direction of a German ex-convict, Heinrich Krott, an arch-sadist, known to the inmates as 'bloody' Krott. Priests in Auschwitz were singled out for especially vicious treatment and every effort was made to brutalise and de-humanise them. 'Priest-swine', the SS called them. 'These men are layabouts and parasites,' pronounced Commandant Hoess, handing them over to Krott. 'Get them working.' Nothing loath, Krott forced the priests to cut and carry enormous logs. All day long, whatever the weather, the priests worked, without a break, carrying the heavy logs over rough, stony ground, always 'at the double', always kicked by the guards when they stumbled or fell.

Father Maximilian did not complain, and was often heard to whisper 'May God forgive you' to Krott. Infuriated by the priest's calm, Krott was determined to break him. He rained blows on the Franciscan when he fell, forcing him to his feet.

The priest would not allow any of his companions to come to his aid, for that would only have meant a beating for them too. 'The Immaculate helps me,' he gasped. 'I will hold on.'

One day, seeing the Franciscan barely able to crawl along with his load, Krott went berserk. Personally selecting the heaviest logs he could find, he loaded them onto the priest's back and ordered him to run. Father Maximilian staggered one or two steps and then collapsed. Whereupon Krott kicked him in the face and groin, screaming, 'So you're too lazy to work, parasite. Just wait, I'll show you what work is.'

That evening, as the men queued for their starvation rations, Krott summoned Father Maximilian from the queue and ordered him to lie face down on a pile of logs, while a couple of SS men gave him fifty lashes. When the priest lost consciousness, Krott flung him contemptuously into the mud, covered him with a scattering of twigs and left him for dead.

Only much later, under cover of dark, could his companions return to take him to the Revir, the makeshift camp hospital. He was bleeding freely, the flesh of his back hung in ribbons and he was running a high fever. All around him, in the Revir, men were breathing their last, dying three or four to a bed, with little or no medication.

Father Maximilian asked to be placed near to the door. 'From there,' he explained, 'I shall be able to see the dead carried out and can pray for them.'

Slowly he recovered his former strength and, for the two weeks that he stayed in the Revir, set himself to bring some sort of consolation to the sick prisoners. For himself he would accept no privileges: when the Polish infirmarian (also a priest) smuggled him a cup of tea in the middle of the night, he would not drink it: 'The others have no tea; why should I be different?' All through the night, the sick men came to him, one at a time, and he listened to their confessions and tried to calm their fears. God was suffering with them, he assured them gently. Whatever happened, they must stay sure that love was stronger than hate. 'Hatred is not creative,' he whispered. 'Our sorrow is necessary that those who live after us may be happy.' Father Maximilian cradled the dying prisoners in his arms, and everyone marvelled that he seemed never to think of his own needs. 'He was black and blue from the beatings,' recalled Fr. Konrad Szweda, the infirmarian, 'yet he consoled me and raised my spirits.'

As his wounds began to heal, Father Maximilian was transferred to the convalescent block, exempt from hard labour but entitled only to half rations. He often gave away his share, or allowed it to be taken from him by some half-starved prisoner, saying cheerfully, 'You are hungrier than I.' When food was brought to the hut and everyone struggled to get ahead in the queue before the food ran out, Maximilian stood aside, so that frequently, when his turn came, there was none left. Asked whether such self-abnegation made sense in a place where every man was engaged in a desperate struggle for survival, he replied: 'Every man has an aim in life. For most men it is to return home to their families. But my desire is to give my life for the good of all men.' He had no doubts about his own fate, and a young man recalls him saying: 'My son, I will not survive the camp. But you and the other young ones, you *must* survive.'

Prisoners were allowed to write censored letters home every two weeks – but only in German. Father Maximilian, who knew the language well, helped the other prisoners with this task, and he himself had time only once to write to his mother, Marianna. The letter was short. 'Be calm, Mama,' he wrote, 'and do not worry about me or my health. God is everywhere. He watches over everyone and everything with His love.'

When he left the convalescent hut and returned to Block 14 he was put to work building roads. His reputation had gone before him, and soon the other prisoners were seeking him out, begging him for words of hope. Sometimes he would say Mass in secret for them, using his own daily bread for the Host, so that the words of consecration, 'Take this all of you and eat, for this is my Body, which will be given for you,' acquired a new and agonising poignancy. Often he would preach a homily. Those who heard him will never forget the sermon he preached shortly before his death. It was on his favourite theme of Mary, 'the masterpiece of creation', the human embodiment of the Spirit of God. He spoke of her total and flawless 'yes' to God, and of how in her, God's love for a creature and that creature's love for God had fused into one and been made fruitful by the Spirit. As they listened, a survivor has recalled, 'desperate and doomed men were suddenly set free from fear and hatred and transported into a world where love triumphs eternally.'

It happened one evening that a prisoner, Joseph Stemler, was ordered by an SS man to report to the hospital in order to remove the day's tally of corpses to the crematorium. One of the bodies was that of a young man who had quite obviously been cruelly tortured before death. Stemler almost fainted, and the SS guard began to scream curses at him. 'Then,' he says, 'I heard a voice say quite calmly: "Shall we take him together, my brother?" When we had finished carrying the bodies, reporting their numbers to the SS, and piling them on top of the huge mountain of corpses waiting to be incinerated, I was at the end of my tether. My companion edged me gently to the door, and when I heard his whispered "requiescat in pace", I knew it was Father Kolbe.'

Already men spoke of him as a saint. Another survivor, Fr. Zygmunt Ruszczak, was very much aware of him: 'Every time I saw Father Kolbe in the courtyard, I felt within myself an extraordinary infusion of his goodness. Although he wore the same ragged clothes as the rest of us, with the same tin can hanging from his belt, one forgot this wretched exterior and was conscious only of the charm of his countenance and of his radiant holiness.'

6

Every day a few desperate prisoners would hurl themselves onto the electrified wire fence which surrounded the concentration camp. Every day men drowned themselves in latrines or were hanged from meat-hooks or taken away to be shot.

The Austrian psychotherapist, Viktor Frankl, himself a survivor of the Nazi camps, has explained why so many succumbed to the intolerable pressures and became less than human:

Under the influence of a world which no longer recognised the value of human life and human dignity, which had robbed man of his will and had made him an object to be exterminated; under this influence the personal ego finally suffered a loss of values . . . and [man's] existence descended to the level of animal life.

It seemed as though the Nazi perverts would pronounce the last word on human nature. For where is man's humanity when he tears at the throat of his brother for the sake of a crust of stale bread? In this place, where human nature at its worst had seized control, was there no flickering spark of humanity to give it the lie? Was man indeed incapable of rising above his external fate? And did that prove the Nazis right, that the Judaeo-Christian message was a hollow sham?

One broiling hot day – either the last of July or the first of August 1941 – the wailing camp sirens announced the escape of a prisoner. The sound struck terror into the hearts of all who heard it: with the iniquitous rule of collective responsibility, for every man who escaped ten of his fellows must die. And this was the most terrible and the most feared way of death: a long, slow starvation, buried alive in specially constructed airless concrete underground bunkers.

That evening the prisoners were summoned as usual to the Appel (the twice-daily roll call that meant hours of standing under a merciless sun or exposed to bitter winds). Lined up in the passageway between Blocks 14 and 17, the prisoners learned that three men – one of them from Block 14 – had escaped. (One of them was found later, drowned in a latrine.) Everyone knew what that meant, and few could have slept that night.

Early in the morning they stood again on the Appel ground. All day long they stood at attention, without food or drink, each one dreading what might be in store.

At seven p.m. the camp's deputy commandant Karl Fritzsch appeared, accompanied by Gestapo chief Gerhardt Palitzsch. Two archetypal, jack-booted Nazi supermen: Fritzsch had personally supervised the first mass murder of prisoners by means of the Cyclon B gas which had originally been manufactured for the extermination of vermin; while Palitzsch, a torturer of some renown, proudly boasted that he had executed 2,500 prisoners with his own hands.

Slowly, wordlessly, they passed down the lines, their elegant uniforms contrasting starkly with the scarecrow rags of the men. Fritzsch pointed a finger, an SS man pushed a hapless man out of line, Palitzsch noted the man's number in his book, while another SS man began to form a new line of victims.

Seven . . . eight . . . nine. As the ninth man was selected, he uttered an agonised cry: 'My wife, my children, I shall never see them again.' His choking sobs pierced the silence, while the scarecrows looked at him unmoved. For them the ordeal was almost over. Nine down, only one to go. They held their breath.

For what happened in the next few minutes we have the sworn testimony of several witnesses, and their accounts are remarkably consistent. Suddenly a small, slight figure detached itself from the ranks, walked briskly towards the group of SS men and stood to attention before Fritzsch. The man removed his regulation cap as he did so. It was number 16670 – a prisoner whose cheeks had an unhealthy flush and who wore round spectacles in wire frames.

Something like animation stirred at last among the men. This was unheard of. That anyone should dare to step out of line during an Appel was unthinkable. Surely the crazy fool would be kicked senseless or shot out of hand by the Gestapo. They watched and waited.

The moment passed. The crazy fool remained alive. Perhaps Fritzsch's sheer astonishment inhibited his usual responses. 16670 pointed to the distraught man who had cried out, and asked, very calmly, in correct German, if he might take his place. The prisoners gasped. Perhaps Fritzsch gasped too, for he asked in amazement: 'Who are you?' (He did not normally enter into conversation with sub-humans.) 'A Catholic priest,' came the reply, as though that was all that needed to be said.

Incredulously, and indeed incredibly, Fritzsch nodded assent, gestured to the reprieved man, one Franciszek Gajowniczek, to return to his place in the line. Palitzsch replaced one number by another, ordered the condemned men to remove their shoes, and sent them off, to be stripped of their rags and buried alive. Next to the last in line went Raymund Kolbe, Father Maximilian, number 16670. As he was flung naked onto the concrete floor of that grisly cell, did he recall that centuries ago St. Francis had asked one of his friars to lay him naked on the bare earth to die?

The really incomprehensible thing is that Fritzsch agreed to the exchange. It would have been more in character to send both Gajowniczek and the priest to die. One thing is certain: Fritzsch could not have foreseen the far-reaching consequences of his decision. It would not have occurred to him that, in the memorable phrase of Szczepański, 'by this one act the world of violence was lost.' Even if he had understood the tremendous significance of 16670's act, he must have presumed that very shortly there would be no witnesses left. Everyone there was living on borrowed time; they were the living dead waiting for the crematoria to claim them. How could a man as morally purblind as Fritzsch have understood that he had just witnessed a classic victory of good over evil, a definitive routing of the ideology of hate. For with Maximilian's free and loving choice to undergo a horrible death for the sake of a total stranger, love had decisively conquered.

In the tense days that followed, the whole camp waited for news and prayed for the doomed men. For almost two weeks they waited, but not with the despair which might have been expected. With a kind of renewed hope. They had come perilously near to becoming dehumanised, to seeing themselves through the contemptuous eyes of their SS masters, without value or meaning. And then suddenly one man had revealed the truth that their degradation had hidden from them: that there is one human freedom that can never be taken away, the freedom a man has to choose his inner response to his fate, to soar above his own personal agony, to transcend himself. In Auschwitz, where life hovered always over the abyss of death, such things were understood. The effect of 16670's self-sacrifice was like a shaft of light in the darkness.

Down below ground, in Block 13, the jailers knew that this time was different. They were accustomed to screams, groans and curses, but in their place they now heard prayers and hymns. 16670, it seemed, had not only taken the place of one victim but was helping the other nine to die as human beings. Feebly but distinctly prisoners in other cells joined in the praying.

Bruno Borgowiec was an eye-witness of those dreadful yet luminous days, for he was an assistant janitor and an interpreter in those fetid cells. When there were no SS men around he did his best to comfort the dying men, though he could do nothing to ease their sufferings. But this time, he said, it was as though Cell 18 had become a church, as the prayers resounded through all the corridors of the bunker. 16670 led and the others made the responses. Often they were so absorbed that they did not even hear the tread of approaching feet. Only when the SS bellowed for the cell doors to be opened did they fall silent, and then indeed the poor wretches begged for water or bread, which they did not receive. When one of the stronger ones managed to get to the door, testified Borgowiec, he was kicked in the groin by the SS men and falling backwards onto the cement floor was instantly killed. Others were shot dead.

As death overtook them one by one, the voices grew feebler and the prayers descended to a whisper. 16670 had not once complained or asked for water, but had spent all his energies consoling the others. While they lay 'like heaps of rags', he was still to be found, at each inspection, propped against the wall, looking calmly into the faces of his persecutors. 'Lower your eyes,' commanded the SS. 'Do not look at us like that.' This man was beyond their comprehension, they were heard to admit; they had never met anyone like him.

Almost two weeks passed. Only four remained alive, and of these only Father Kolbe was conscious. The authorites were becoming impatient: they wanted the bunker for a new batch of victims and they were not disposed to wait. Bringing in the head of the camp hospital, a common criminal, by name Hans Bock, they ordered him to despatch the prisoners with an injection of carbolic acid. Seated on the floor, still moving his lips in prayer, Father Kolbe held out his left arm for the fatal injection. At this point the janitor Borgowiec could stand it no longer and fled.

When he returned to Cell 18, he found Father Kolbe 'still seated, propped up against the corner, his head slightly to one side, his eyes wide open and fixed on one point. As if in ecstasy, his face was serene and radiant.'

Who can doubt that Maximilian was aware of the date? It was 14 August, the day revered by the Polish people as the vigil of the great feast of the Virgin's Assumption into heaven. It was a date on which Maximilian would have wanted to die.

To the prisoners in Auschwitz camp news of his death came like the announcement of a victory. It had the force of an electric shock, arousing them to take a fresh look at their fate. 'The lunatic programme of the Nazis was defeated by military might,' Szczepański was to write, 'but the deepest essence of the meaning of humanity was liberated neither by armies nor by politicians. The definitive answer was given by a death in August 1941 in an underground cell in Block 13, the Block of Death, in Auschwitz concentration camp. It was given by a Polish Franciscan, Father Maximilian Kolbe, who gave an answer which no dialectic could ever provide.'

Friends tried in vain to save his body from the crematorium fires. It went up in smoke and his ashes were scattered over the surrounding fields. Years later, when his cause was being introduced in Rome, Karol Wojtyla, bishop of Cracόw, the future Pope John Paul II, was asked to send a relic of Father Kolbe to the Vatican. 'But I had nothing to give them,' he said sadly, 'nothing but a grain of Auschwitz soil.'

*   *   *

Father Kolbe's heroism went ringing through Poland and beyond. Against all reasonable expectation there were survivors, witnesses of that August afternoon in 1941. Among them was the man for whom the priest had given his life, Franciszek Gajowniczek. By a cruel irony he had returned home to the news that in the very last days of the war his two young sons had been killed on the street by Russian shells.

Newspapers all over the world began printing articles about

this 'saint for our times', 'saint of human brotherhood', and the demand for his beatification became insistent. 'The life and death of this one man alone,' the Polish bishops wrote to Rome, 'can be proof and witness of God's power to overcome the greatest hatred, the greatest injustice, even death itself.'

The beatification (first stage in the canonisation process) took place in 1971, a mere thirty years after his death. Following pressure from the Polish – and German – bishops, he was canonised as a martyr-saint eleven years later, in October 1982, by his fellow Pole, Pope John Paul II. Saint Maximilian was, said John Paul to the Poles next day:

> our countryman in whom contemporary man may discover a wonderful synthesis of the sufferings and hopes of our age . . . See what man can accomplish when he places an absolute trust in Christ, through the Virgin Mary! But in that synthesis there is also a prophetic warning. It is a cry directed to man, to society, to the whole human race, to systems which hold human life and human society in their hands. The man who yesterday was declared a saint came out of the very crucible of man's humiliation at the hands of his fellow-men . . . This martyred saint cries aloud for a renewed respect for the rights of men and of nations.

In one remarkable direction, Maximilian's death had begun its healing work: after the war he became as powerful a symbol in Germany as in Poland, and the Germans were as eager as the Poles for his recognition. On the day he was canonised a small miracle took place. Or perhaps it was a large miracle. That evening, in St. Peter's Basilica in Rome, Germans and Poles stood together for a service of reconciliation, and exchanged the kiss of peace with each other. In the congregation were Gajowniczek with many other survivors of Auschwitz and similar camps. Whatever their innermost thoughts at that moment, they were publicly acknowledging the truth for which Maximilian had died: that humanity will endure, as long as love can prove stronger than hatred.

4.
Janani Luwum 1922–1977

1

When Janani Luwum was consecrated as Anglican Bishop of Northern Uganda in January 1969, the scene was like a political rally. The huge Pece stadium in the administrative capital, Gulu, was filled with flowers; and among the galaxy of distinguished guests were President Milton Obote and his wife, together with many members of the government. Present also was the genial, former heavyweight boxing champion and one-time cook in the King's African Rifles, who was now the commander of the Ugandan Army and Air force. In her book, *Amin*, Judith Listowel has recorded this, her first sight of General Idi Amin:

> He was surrounded by soldiers – other ranks – drinking beer. His tie was loosened, his tunic unbuttoned, and a good deal of back-slapping was going on. He threw back his head and laughed uproariously, and the soldiers joined in, enjoying every minute of it . . . There was General Amin drinking and making merry with these men: making friends in the President's camp.

Exactly two years later Idi Amin seized power. Six years after that, on the afternoon of 16 February, 1977, Janani Luwum, by then Archbishop of Uganda, Rwanda, Burundi and Boga-Zaire, was summoned to speak with President Amin at the International Conference Centre in Kampala. That was the last time his friends saw him alive. In the evening Radio Uganda announced the arrest of Janani and two cabinet ministers on charges of plotting to overthrow the President. Next morning a banner headline proclaimed to a horrified nation: 'Archbishop and two ministers die in motor accident.'

It was a measure of the state of terror that existed by then in Uganda that nobody believed the official version. Everybody knew that murder had been done.

*   *   *

Janani's story really begins half a century before his birth, with the arrival of the first missionaries in Uganda in 1877. Until then this land-locked country in eastern equatorial Africa had been written off as too inaccessible and too remote. It was the explorer, Henry Stanley, who had changed all that. Arriving from the south into the rolling hill country of Buganda in 1875, he had discovered an earthly paradise of rare beauty, vibrant with brilliantly coloured tropical birds and butterflies; ablaze with blossoms of frangipani, bougain-villea and hibiscus. This delightful land was neither too hot nor too cold and its people were similarly well-balanced: intelligent, industrious chocolate-coloured natives, with courteous ways, a high degree of culture and civilisation, and a well-established hierarchical society led locally by chiefs, with a despotic (semi-divine) monarch paramount over all. Stanley was charmed by the king, or Kabaka, Mutesa, who had listened with interest to the explorer's account of his own country and of Christianity. In high excitement Stanley sent off a letter to the London Daily Telegraph declaring this matchless country to be ripe fruit for the missionaries.

The effect of the letter was electric. Donations poured in, preparations were put in hand. The first group from the (Anglican) Church Missionary Society arrived in June 1877, to be reinforced by six more volunteers in February 1879, just one week before the arrival of the Roman Catholic White Fathers from France.

Arab traders had reached Buganda more than thirty years earlier searching for slaves and ivory, bringing with them firearms, cheap cotton cloth – and the Muslim religion. Delighted to find that he could buy a musket in exchange for two male slaves and that one female was worth one hundred bullets, Kabaka Mutesa had welcomed the traders and even embraced their religion. As time went by, however, he wearied of them, coming to mistrust their influence over his chiefs. About his adopted faith he was lukewarm, and was pleased to welcome the Christians who would give the Muslims some competition and curb their ambition.

Stanley had been deceived about Mutesa: the Kabaka was not so much ripe for conversion to Christianity as adept at playing people off against each other, to his ultimate advantage. The missionaries were useful: they did not, it was true, bring firearms; but they had an impressive array of skills and equipment with which to excite the admiration of their hosts. Alexander Mackay, a 25-year-old Scots engineer, the first and perhaps the greatest of the missionaries, not only preached the Christian Gospel but placed his skills at the service of the Baganda,* introducing them to wheeled transport and to such modern magic as brick kilns, blacksmiths' anvils, printing presses, water pumps and magic lanterns.

At first there were few converts. The Kabaka himself blew hot and cold, veering like a weathercock from Anglicans to Catholics to Muslims and back again; increasingly confused by the hostility which the two groups of Christians showed towards each other; and finally returning to the Lubare, his own native gods. He died unconverted in 1884. Before that date, however, a few of the royal page boys had been baptized into the Anglican Church. On 18 March Alexander Mackay noted the fact of their baptism in his diary, adding: 'our earnest prayer is that these lads, all of them grown up to manhood, may be baptized not only by water but by the Holy Ghost and with fire.'

Had he been able to see into the future, he might have omitted that reference to fire. For it proved prophetic. Mutesa's successor, his son Mwanga, soon revealed himself as a degenerate tyrant who was determined to drive out the Christian missionaries. In 1885 he ordered the murder of James Hannington who was on his way to Buganda as the first bishop of eastern equatorial Africa; and this taste of blood

---

* It is useful to note the following: Uganda took its name from Buganda, its largest and most dominant region. Within Uganda, names of states often take the prefix Bu−; languages, Lu-; and persons, Mu-, with the plural Ba-; e.g. one Muganda belongs to the Baganda people who live in Buganda and speak Luganda.

seems to have shown him that the Christians could be attacked with impunity. A year later four royal pages who had gone on safari with Mackay were seized and made to march back to Mengo, the capital. One of them was later released to give the horrifying news that his companions were to be roasted alive. 'The Lord look mercifully on the agony of these poor black children,' Mackay confided to his diary.

The three youths, the youngest of whom, Yusufu, was only eleven, had their arms cut off before being thrown into the flames. Hundreds gathered to watch, and when they heard the boys refuse to deny their new faith and saw them die with a hymn of praise on their lips, the effect was magnetic. Far from being terrified by the sight, many found it inspiring; Baganda began stealing away in ones and twos to the mission hut at night, seeking baptism. Some went for instruction to the Anglican missionaries, some to the Roman Catholic. Under the shared stress of persecution, the two groups had drawn together for mutual protection and support. The first Catholic boy to die was Joseph Balikuddembe, a senior page and one of Mwanga's personal favourites. Balikuddembe had protested to his master about the brutal murder of Bishop Hannington, and he paid for the protest with his life.

At the end of May 1886 the Kabaka's paranoia burst the dams of reason. Returning one day from an unsuccessful hippo hunt, he found most of his pages in scattered groups reading the Bible. Beside himself with rage he summoned the boys, ordering them to choose between apostasy or death. The majority of them chose death. Mwanga had the boys tied together and made them march to the place of execution. On 3 June thirty-two young Africans, Catholics and Anglicans together, were trussed up in reed matting and placed in the centre of a slow fire. Not a sound escaped them other than the hymns they sang. When the executioner (who had been forced to burn his own son) reported to Mwanga, he marvelled that all the victims had gone to their deaths calling on God. God, shrugged Mwanga, did not appear to have taken much notice.

Mwanga's dementia lasted for almost a year, during which

time twenty-two Catholics* and twelve Anglicans had their limbs hacked off and were grilled alive. It was, as Roland Oliver wrote (in *The Missionary Factor in East Africa)*, 'a martyrdom as terrible as any in Christian history.'

Yet still the conversions continued. News of what was happening in Buganda was carried back to Europe and men began to wonder what kind of people these were who so cheerfully accepted a cruel death for the sake of their beliefs. As Bishop Festo Kivengere has recently written:

> Those early disciples in Uganda were young men set on fire by the message of the cross . . . When the Gospel reached Uganda the message penetrated Ugandans; they caught the vision. They said: 'Yes, there is a God who is not . . . a big mountain, who is not a big snake, but One who loved and died for all men in Jesus Christ.' When the early believers were filled with that, they could die for their faith in Him.

After a chequered few years of banishment and recall, the Anglicans had their triumph in 1890 when their branch of Christianity was established as the official religion of Uganda. For the Roman Catholics this represented defeat. The years of harmony, when the two groups had died together in the fires of persecution, had been replaced by a state of simmering mutual mistrust. This now erupted into open warfare, owing more to nationalism than religion, with the Anglicans looking to Britain for support, and the Roman Catholics to Britain's ancient enemy, France. In 1892, when Captain Lugard of the British East Africa Company, and Alfred Tucker, the first Anglican bishop, arrived together to take up residence, tensions rose so high that the two church parties engaged in a bitter and unedifying civil war. Captain Lugard, camped on the little hill known as Kampala, had to keep the peace between them. Fighting continued until in 1894 Uganda was declared a British Protectorate; and the churches retired to lick their wounds. But the enforced peace was only nominal; the wounds they had inflicted on each other con-

---

* The twenty-two Catholics were canonised by Pope Paul in 1964.

tinued to fester; and the relationship between them remained one of sour hostility for more than half a century. Symbolically the Anglican church built on Namirembe Hill and the Catholic one on Rubaga Hill went on glowering at each other from either side of the new city which was being built at Kampala.

2

Janani did not belong to the Baganda tribe, but the story of their boy martyrs was woven strong into his childhood. He was a northerner of the Acholi tribe, one of the Nilotic groups of jet-black warriors and hunters who inhabit the flat savannah lands. These warlike giants attribute their immense strength to a diet of millet and red meat, and they despise the smaller, paler, less aggressive Baganda who live mainly, they say, on mangoes and bananas.

Nevertheless young Baganda Christians had braved the hatred of these northern tribes, to bring them the message of love and forgiveness. It was an act of faith on the part of these educated southerners to leave their green and temperate land for the hot and dusty hinterland where unwashed natives in skins leaped about brandishing spears. Yet, although the new faith took root more slowly in these primitive parts, the missionaries met an enthusiastic response in the villages.

Janani's homeland in East Acholi, which borders on the Sudan, was one of the more resistant. When the Acholi people did at last succumb, it was initially not so much from conviction as from a sensible desire to learn the three 'R's from the missionaries. For the most part, they continued in their time-honoured animist beliefs, invoking the spirits, consulting the witch doctors and worshipping at their ritual shrines. The Acholi, said one Anglican bishop disapprovingly, were 'men without God'.

But it was into a true Christian home that Janani Luwum was born in 1922, for his father, Eliya Okello from Mucwini, was one of the first bona fide converts, a man who had dedicated his life to the service of Christ as a teacher in the local church. It was a poorly paid job; but the land around the family homestead – a cluster of thatched mud huts – was fertile, so the family always had enough to eat. There was always food cooking in the earthenware pot hung over the fire.

As a boy, Janani had to look after the family's cows, sheep and goats, protecting them from marauding neighbouring tribes. In his spare time he and the other village boys roamed the savannas, stalking wild animals or shooting small birds with their catapults, to supplement the family's diet. Sometimes they played the drums and performed the traditional tribal dances for which the Acholi were famous. Janani excelled at these: when he was older he taught the dances to the younger boys, accompanying them on the drums or on the lukeme, a locally made musical instrument.

He was ten years old by the time his father could afford to send him to primary school. Once there his keen intelligence and determination to learn soon enabled him to catch up with the others. His parents were proud of their clever son, and began to hope that one day he might become a tribal chief. They sent him to High School, eighty miles away in the regional capital, Gulu; and Janani walked the whole distance on foot at the beginning and end of each term, along unmade roads which were either muddy with rain or dusty with heat. Later on he went to the Boroboro Teacher Training College run by missionaries in Lira. Here too he did well, his name always among the top three scholars; proving himself an outstanding teacher and potential leader. When he had finished the course he took a job at the Puranga primary school not far from his own home in East Acholi.

Until this time, Janani had not become a Christian. He was twenty-six when it happened, and he was later able to give the day and the hour of his personal epiphany, 12.30 in the afternoon on 6 January, 1948. He became, in fact, a late convert to the popular revivalist movement which had taken East Africa by storm throughout the 1930s, turning passive Christians into aggressively committed ones. These born-again Christians became known as the *balokole* or 'saved ones'. Two of the *balokole*, Yusto Otunno and his wife,

Josephine, came to Janani's home village, Mucwini, to lead a mission. With dramatic results, for twelve people were 'saved' that day, among them eight members of Janani's family, including his brother, Aloni Okecho. During the meeting, Janani had three times broken into a heavy sweat, and at the end he had stood to give witness: 'Today I have become a leader in Christ's army,' he announced. 'I am prepared to die in the army of Jesus. As Jesus shed his blood for the people, if it is God's will, I will do the same.'

That night Janani and the other new 'saved ones' escorted the preachers home, a distance of six miles. On the way they prayed and sang:

> Glory, glory, hallelujah,
> Glory, glory to the Lamb,
> Oh the cleansing blood has reached me,
> Glory, glory to the Lamb.

Janani's conversion turned his life inside out.

When I was converted (he later said), after realising that my sins were forgiven and the implications of Jesus's death and resurrection, I was overwhelmed by a sense of joy and peace. I suddenly found myself climbing a tree to tell those in the school compound to repent and turn to Jesus Christ. From time to time I spoke in tongues. I stayed by that tree for a long time. Later on I discovered that some boys were converted due to a sermon I preached up that tree. The reality of Jesus overwhelmed me, and it still does.

While not precisely advocating that his pupils should climb trees and speak in tongues, he nevertheless became a fiery and demanding evangelist, preaching repentance to his pupils, using such a hard-sell approach that he soon found himself out of a job. The official Church in that area did not approve of the 'saved ones', viewing them as a disruptive and divisive influence. Janani was not deterred by being at odds with the authorities; on the contrary his evangelising activities reached such a pitch that he was arrested and charged with disturbing the peace.

At an open-air meeting he had spoken against the evils of drink and cigarette smoking, calling them works of the devil, challenging his hearers to abandon such practices and listen to the word of God. This did little to please the missionaries who in those days preferred to turn a blind eye to what the natives did. Janani was a stirrer, and he needed to be taught a lesson. It was at their instigation that Janani and eight fellow *balokole* were taken to Kitgum where they were thrown in jail, roughly treated and left without food for two days. When the prison warders returned and invited them to renounce their revivalism, Janani refused on behalf of the entire group:

> You are good people and our beloved brothers (he assured them earnestly). It is not you but your master, Satan, who is using you to torture us and leave us to go hungry. We love you, and our master, Jesus Christ, loves you too. The wooden bars at the window of this tiny cell cannot separate us from the love of God, nor stop us proclaiming his message of salvation through his son, Jesus Christ. All of us here are committed to Christ, even to death.

If the missionaries had hoped that the young men's ardour would be cooled after a taste of hardship, they were disappointed. Janani and the others came out of prison reinvigorated and preaching more relentlessly than ever. More trouble was inevitable. It happened that Yusto Otunno, the *balokole* who had converted him, was arrested along with Janani's brother, Aloni Okecho. When the two men were brought before the local magistrate, Otunno had obviously been beaten. Indignantly Janani rose to his feet. 'Have these people been beaten,' he asked, 'because they have preached in the name of Jesus Christ?' After a moment's pause, he informed the court that he too was a 'saved one', more or less daring them to arrest him too. The embarrassed magistrate charged him with contempt and sentenced him to a month's imprisonment or a twenty-shilling fine. Janani was all for going to jail and being a martyr, but the others urged him to pay the fine and stay in circulation while they were inside.

At the suggestion of the *balokole* Janani now decided to

abandon teaching and seek a full-time ministry within the
Church of Uganda – presumably in order to ensure a *balokole* presence there. A new chapter of his life was about to
begin.

3

Buganda, with its capital city, Kampala, was the nerve-centre
of British Uganda for politicians, merchants and missionaries
alike. All attempts to encourage the growth of an indigenous
Ugandan Church led by native African clergy focussed on
Buganda, where the political establishment was now markedly Protestant. Courses leading to the ministry were conduc-
ted in Luganda, the language spoken in Buganda. Inevitably
young men from the northern regions, who spoke a very
different language, found themselves excluded. But the
young northerners did speak English and, in 1949, against the
better judgment of some of the missionaries, a lay-readers'
course in English was set up at Buwalasi Theological College,
with Janani Luwum as one of its first students.

He was married by then, but for the first year of the course
he had to abandon his wife, Mary, and their three-year-old
daughter, leaving them at home under the care of Yusto
Otunno. They joined him for the second year, however, and
during that time Mary gave birth to their second child, a son.
When Janani obtained his certificate, the whole family returned to Acholi, where he had obtained a post as lay reader
at St. Philip's Church in Gulu, where he was also to train
catechists at the archdeaconry training centre.

Janani and Mary built a little house behind the High
School, and here at last he was able to indulge his talent for
making things; he was particularly good at chicken houses.
Janani was a family man, very domesticated, loving to do odd
jobs or help Mary with the cooking; a simple, cheerful man
who brought enthusiasm to everything he did. The Gulu
Christians were amazed by the zeal of their new lay reader
who arranged services, trained catechists, taught Sunday
school and organised groups of boys for building new class-

rooms and churches out of grass. Janani was a great success, so much so that the bishop packed him off back to Buwalasi with the family, to complete his ordination course. He was ordained priest in 1956.

These were the years when the first stirrings of Uhuru (freedom) began to be felt; and Africanisation of the country's institutions became a top priority. The missionaries were looking out for potential leaders, and Janani was an obvious choice. He was sent to England for a year to St. Augustine's College, Canterbury, before returning to Uganda to take charge of what his bishop regarded as the toughest parish in his diocese – Lira Palwo in East Acholi, a parish of twenty-four churches scattered over forty miles of scrubland; and only a bicycle with which to reach them.

Lira Palwo would have daunted a far more experienced man than Janani. His lack of success there was probably due less to personal failure than to the onward march of history. For by this time the fever of independence had spread to Northern Uganda and the whole process had leapt into sudden overdrive. The churches had no choice but to take a back seat, church commitment being expressed almost exclusively in terms of political parties based on the old tribal rivalries. Dr. Milton Obote spoke for the majority of northerners through the dominantly Protestant Uganda People's Congress, while the Catholics tended to support the Democratic Party led by a Catholic lawyer Benedicto Kiwanuka. The third contender for power in the race to freedom was the 'Kabaka Only' party which was traditionalist, monarchist and did not want a united Uganda. It too was Protestant in allegiance.

Lira Palwo shared in the national hysteria. Its fervour for Uhuru was far in excess of any religious fervour Janani might hope to instil. The people did not object to coming to church; but there the commitment ended. Janani tried everything he could think of, even introducing African music into the services. But he could not win their interest, and by the time the political hysteria had died down, Janani had been removed from Lira Palwo and sent, in 1961, to become Vice-Principal (and later, Principal) of his old College in Buwalasi.

With the help of the monarchists, Obote's UPC won the elections. When the Union Jack was hauled down at midnight on 8 October, 1962, and Uganda's flag flew triumphantly in its stead, Obote was firmly in the saddle. Soon afterwards Uganda was declared a republic with Kabaka Mutesa II (popularly known as King Freddie) as its President for a five-year term. Everything was being done according to the rules and in good order. There had been no blood-bath, as in the Congo (Zaire). In spite of the fact that the new republic was made up of tribes who hated each other, many were discreetly optimistic that democratic government would succeed. Others took a gloomier view: in their opinion, independence had come too soon and with indecent haste; by the premature removal of all civilising influences the way lay open to the ancient and bloody tribal rivalries.

It was not long before the alliance between Obote's UPC and the monarchist party broke down. Obote began to call for one-party rule in a bid to unite the unruly tribes into a single socialist state. He himself was one of the Langi, northerners like the Acholi, hostile to the more educated Baganda. It was a foregone conclusion therefore that the Baganda would be opposed to any move Obote made; to keep them docile he would need the backing of the army. Two virtually illiterate African NCOs from the King's African Rifles (renamed the Uganda Rifles in 1962) had been rushed at unprecedented speed up the promotion ladder, in order to be ready to take charge after independence. One of these had since married into the Baganda royal family, and so could not be relied on for present purposes. The other was Major Idi Amin, one of the Kakwa tribe from that region of the West Nile where Uganda merges indistinguishably into the Sudan and Zaire. It was to Amin that Milton Obote turned; and it was perhaps at this time that Amin's insatiable lust for power began to grow. He was the strong man on whom Milton Obote relied to keep Uganda stable.

Having made himself secure, Obote acted swiftly. In February 1966 he arrested five non-Nilotic ministers in the course of a routine Cabinet session. Within a month he had suspended the Constitution and declared himself President.

Idi Amin was put in control of the entire army. When the army attacked the royal palace in May, King Freddie narrowly escaped with his life. In a gesture of contempt which earned for Obote the undying enmity of the Baganda, the soldiers burned the almost sacred Royal Drums, then threw what remained of them onto the hill leading from the palace. The drums, of which there were more than fifty, were hundreds of years old, as old as the kabaka-ship which they symbolised. 'To touch them,' wrote King Freddie 'was a terrible offence, to look after them a great honour. A Prince is not a Prince of the Blood but a Prince of the Drum, his status determined by which Drum. They all had separate names and significance and can never be replaced.' (*Desecration of My Kingdom*, 1967.)

All pretence that Uganda was a democracy was dropped. Obote would tolerate no opposition. It seemed as though the Jonahs had been proved right: the hopes of paradise had after all been no more than a mirage. As the cost of living rose, the lot of the average Ugandan became worse than it had ever been under the British.

But in making himself dependent on the army (whose soldiers were now on double pay), Obote had made a noose for his own neck. Ahead lay danger, not least from the man to whom he had turned for protection, General Idi Amin. Aware of Obote's insecurity, Amin began to build up his own power-base within the army. His new recruits were men whose loyalty would be to himself: Kakwa tribesmen and the ruthless, lawless Nubians from the southern Sudan.

It was against this darkening backcloth of intrigue and power politics that Janani Luwum became Bishop of the newly formed diocese of Northern Uganda, a diocese which would include his own Acholi region and the Lango territory from which Milton Obote came. In the minds of the people these two successful sons of the North were becoming linked, a link which it suited Obote to exploit: hence his presence at the consecration. In the massive stadium, the altar was raised high in the centre of a brilliant red carpet; a police band played the hymns; and Radio Uganda carried the ceremony to the entire nation.

Whether this was a good or a dangerous opening to Janani's episcopate was open to debate. But he had had no choice: everything had been decided by the politicians.

4

The Church of Uganda was looking forward to 1977, the centenary of the arrival of the first missionaries. By that time they hoped that the Church would have become self-supporting, and to this end they launched a ten-year plan. Janani threw himself into the plan with enthusiasm, travelling round his diocese, urging the congregations to give generously to the Church. But in those northern areas the Church was still relatively weak, and many of his appeals fell on deaf ears. He faced an immense challenge: since independence, several of the native clergy had given up, churches had sunk into disrepair, others had simply collapsed; and nobody seemed to care. People contributed scarcely at all to the upkeep of their parish, and the pastors spent more time on growing food with which to feed their families than on providing spiritual nourishment for their flocks. 'Take the hoe out of your pastor's hands,' urged Janani. He would speak simply to these scattered congregations, convincing them of his own deep beliefs. 'It was as though,' commented a colleague, 'here was one very human person telling his friends what it was like to know Jesus Christ personally.' A born teacher, he found illustrations they could understand, making his point with wit and compassion. They were, he told them, like a man who had invited a friend to dinner; all the preparations were made, the house cleaned, animals slaughtered for the feast, other guests invited; but all the guest got to eat was the head of a chicken, and he went away sad that his friend had been so ungenerous. 'We are like that unloving friend,' admonished Janani. 'We give God so little. We buy new clothes, meat and other things. Our hearts are far away from him: we love ourselves more than we love God.'

The bicycle had given way to a car, in which he drove at terrifying speed over the rutted roads, sometimes getting bogged down in thick mud, at others almost blinded by clouds of dust. Janani was not the kind of bishop who would stay at home and concern himself with administrative problems; he was a practical man who liked to be in the thick of things. So he hurtled around the diocese, full of brave plans, opening here a farm centre, there a school, elsewhere a clinic. On one red-letter day, he had the joy of opening a sixteen-bedded ward for leprosy patients near Gulu, provided by donations from West Germany.

Not all his plans were successful, but the people loved him for his concern, and for his infectious enthusiasm. For his part, their lack of commitment saddened him. They were as indecisive as a hyena at a crossroads, he colourfully complained. Like the hyena they rushed first down one road, then back again and down another, always fearful that the sweeter meat was to be found on the road he was not on.

Hoping to encourage their weak faith, in April 1970 he held a mission week, inviting missionaries from all over the country to try to get through to his people, 'that they may return from darkness to light'. The initial response was disappointing, but as the week went on, interest built up. On the final day numbers were high and the whole congregation went in procession to Pece stadium, gathering others along the way. Here Bishop Luwum held aloft a huge cross, praying aloud that all who had found joy that day would be given the grace to stand fast in the faith.

It was a timely prayer; and they would soon have much need of grace. For far-reaching changes were in the air. Suspecting that General Amin was trying to assassinate him, Obote had been planning to replace him by Brigadier Okoya, an Acholi soldier. When Okoya and his wife were found murdered in January 1970, suspicion naturally centred on Amin, and Obote ordered an investigation with all speed. By the time he was ready to leave for the Commonwealth Conference in Singapore in January 1971, a strong case had emerged against Amin, made even stronger by charges of overspending and embezzling of army funds to the tune of £2½ million. From Singapore Obote issued a call for Amin's arrest. But the call was intercepted and, forewarned, Amin took prompt action. By dawn the following morning (26 January) he had carried out an almost bloodless coup. Kampala awoke to see tanks massed in the streets flanked by posters proclaiming 'Amin – our Christ'. That night his own soldiers declared him President of what he lost no time in proclaiming as the Second Republic. Milton Obote went into exile in Tanzania.

There were many who rejoiced, not least the Baganda, who danced in the streets with joy. It was not that they knew much about Amin, but they had loathed Obote who had expelled their king and dishonoured his name. Amin enjoyed himself, revelling in the sudden popularity, driving around the country delivering tub-thumping addresses – and promising the earth: hospitals, tarmac roads, free elections, reduced taxes, complete religious freedom for all and increased prosperity all round. (Promises that he had no intention of keeping – for within a month he had suspended all political activity and dissolved Parliament.) Radiating good will, he released political prisoners, going so far as to make one of them, Benedicto Kiwanuka, Chief Justice. Then, to ingratiate himself further with the Baganda, he announced that the body of King Freddie, who had died in London in November 1969, would be flown back for a state funeral. The Baganda were ecstatic, their hopes high that Amin would restore the monarchy and place King Freddie's son on the throne.

But the Acholi and Langi, the tribes most likely to be pro-Obote, went in fear for their lives. At the end of March, when the Kabaka's body lay in state in a glass-topped coffin in Namirembe Cathedral, for four days and nights mourners filed past, sobbing as though personally bereaved. Many Acholi went into hiding, fearing that the sight of the dead Kabaka would arouse the Baganda to violence. Even Janani was persuaded by his wife, Mary, to leave Gulu and seek the relative calm of his native village until the funeral was safely over.

A dark shadow hung over Janani's land of Northern Uganda. But it was not the Baganda, so much as President Amin's Nubian soldiers, that the people had to fear. These men were famed for their brutality and for their jealous hatred of the Acholi and Langi, who had always been given the top positions in the King's African rifles. For this the Nubians would exact a dreadful vengeance.

Soldiers and civilians alike fell victim, as the Nubians rampaged from village to village in the north, drunk with *waragi* – the banana gin which they bought cheap in the army stores – intent on revenge. Trucks filled with soldiers went rooting out Obote supporters, arresting some, shooting others, throwing the bodies into the Nile or leaving them where they fell. Deserters who obeyed Amin's call to return to barracks (with an implied pardon) were bayoneted and tossed into the Nile; as were fifty-six officers from a single barracks. Elsewhere thirty-two senior Langi and Acholi soldiers were driven into a room which was then blown up.

Everywhere Janani went he heard the lamentations of his people, wailing for their dead. Helplessly he comforted them, trying to persuade them to forgive their tormentors as Christ had forgiven his. Secretly he was afraid that they might stage a counter-coup, which would precipitate even greater blood-shed. He was full of fear, yet at the same time angry at the senseless massacre of his people. At his prompting, the bishops protested to Amin, to be met with a nonchalant shrug. The enemy had to be got rid of, the President ex-plained. The massacres went on.

5

That August (1972) President Amin announced the imminent expulsion of Uganda's eighty thousand Asians, many of whom had lived in the country for three generations or more. The Second Republic was in a mess and the Asians offered a convenient scapegoat. On the whole, Amin's decision pleased the Ugandans who resented the Asians – the bulk of the nation's merchants and shopkeepers, to say nothing of doctors and nurses – for their prosperity. Few people stopped to think that if the Asians were driven out there were not enough skilled Africans to replace them, and that therefore the economic plight of Uganda would become even worse.

Janani was attending a meeting of the World Council of Churches in Holland when he heard this news. With considerable courage (for the Security Forces at home would be bound to hear about it) he agreed to join a sub-committee of four which drafted a statesmanlike resolution expressing dismay at this latest violation of human rights and freedoms.

Superficially his relations with President Amin were amicable enough, though Janani was too honest and straightforward for Amin's taste. The President preferred men around him who did not criticise or ask awkward questions. Besides, he could never forget that Janani's name had once been linked in the popular mind with that of Milton Obote. That fact alone made it impossible for him to trust Janani. Fear of the exiled Obote, and of Julius Nyerere who had given him shelter in Tanzania, tormented Idi Amin, so he could not have been taken by surprise when, in mid-September, one thousand Ugandan guerrillas, under the command of an Acholi colonel, crossed the border from Tanzania. It was the expected counter-coup, which Janani had so dreaded.

Fortunately for Amin the invasion was badly planned and it was a disastrous failure. But it gave him an excuse for further butchery of the unfortunate Acholi, Langi and others whom he suspected of treachery to himself. In Ankole where the invasion had actually taken place, all the chiefs were put to death; in Mbarara, near the border with Tanzania, Amin's troops penetrated a hospital which had taken in three of the guerrilla forces. They shot one man on the operating table, the other two in the compound.

A death list was drawn up of offenders from all over the country. When Benedicto Kiwanuka (the Catholic leader of the Democratic Party whom Amin had so recently made Chief Justice) dared to call for a curb on the army's power of arrest, Amin had him dragged in broad daylight from the High Court and dismembered alive. His body was later identified with others dumped by a truck somewhere near the Zaire border.

It was estimated that in Amin's first two years between

ninety and one hundred thousand Ugandans were murdered on his direct orders or by his licensed thugs. In January 1973 Father Kiggundu, editor of the only Roman Catholic newspaper in Uganda, criticised Amin – and died 'in a car accident'. An autopsy revealed that he had been shot and strangled before the car had been set alight; whereupon the doctor who had performed the autopsy 'disappeared'. Father John Serwanika, who became the new editor, bravely continued his predecessor's editorial policy. He too was arrested; six weeks later he was said to have died in prison.

In the country areas large numbers of people were being arrested for so-called subversive activities. The Security Forces murdered at will. With grief in his heart (for apart from everything else one of his children had just died of a wasting disease), Janani went round his diocese, finding little of comfort. In other parts of Uganda, suffering made men turn to religion, to Christianity or to their native animism, to seek an explanation of their pain. But the northerners were more hard-headed and pragmatic. They knew where their suffering came from, and his name was Idi Amin. Whatever Janani urged, there was no question of their ever forgiving him.

Janani was depressed but not daunted: there were always a few who listened. Doggedly he persevered in the struggle for men's hearts and minds, preaching in the people's homes or under the mango trees for shade. In Gulu, where he had his office, people would come to see him to ask advice or just to talk, knowing him for a wise and understanding pastor.

It troubled him that as a bishop he had had so little success. In numerical terms his diocese was below par; churches were fewer and more run-down; funds were disgracefully low. There were no dramatic conversions: in fact some of the other clergy thought his sermons were far too low-key, too gentle, always more concerned with the forgiveness of God rather than with His anger. Then too there was the constant sparring that still went on with the Roman Catholics. Janani himself had a good relationship with the Roman Catholic bishop of Gulu, Bishop Kihangire, and as an active member of the Ugandan Joint Christian Council (formed in 1964 and the first in the world to include Roman Catholics as full members) he enjoyed a 'marvellous relationship' with more ecumenically minded Catholics. But at parish level the old rivalries persisted, with Church of Uganda pastors and teachers and Catholic missionaries sniping at each other over religious instruction in the schools or the siting of new churches. Matters reached such a pass that just before Easter 1974 Sister Claudia of the Verona Order (most of the missionaries in the north were Verona Fathers) complained to both Bishop Kihangire and Bishop Luwum that if Christians could not manage to pray together at Easter they might as well stop calling themselves Christians. The two bishops accordingly arranged a joint service for Maundy Thursday. Hundreds came along to pray for unity, and afterwards they set up small groups for shared Bible study.

Janani was not to reap the fruits of his labours in Northern Uganda. For in May 1974 the Anglican bishops meeting at Namirembe elected him as successor to the retiring Archbishop Erica Sabiti. Sad as he was to leave his diocese with so little achieved, he had to leave Gulu and move to Kampala.

His own Christians were both sad and proud. They loved Janani and did not want to lose him. But they were proud that he was leaving them to become a great chief, not understanding that in Janani's eyes it was not the task of an Archbishop to rule but to be 'the servant of the servants of God'.

He was installed in June with a simple ceremony, marked by none of the glamour attendant on his earlier consecration. President Idi Amin was not present in the cathedral at Namirembe.

*　　*　　*

With the departure of the Asians and with Amin's growing expenditure on arms, Uganda's economy had slumped dramatically. Even the most basic goods were in short supply, and everything – soap, sugar, salt, toothpaste, matches, petrol – had to be imported. Smugglers brought in quantities of these goods from Kenya and as a result there was a flourishing black market, and prices rocketed.

Hoarding became common. Janani pleaded with the Christians to share what they had and not to hide it away for themselves. He and Cardinal Nsubuga, co-operating to a degree which would have been unthinkable before independence, met to discuss means of helping their people through the present shortages. Both men were in contact with President Amin, who took pleasure in telephoning them in the middle of the night to ask their opinion of the situation, or sending a Mercedes to fetch one or other of them without delay to his presence. But in truth Amin had little use for the Christians. Ever since his meeting with Colonel Gaddafi, in Libya in February 1972, he had been resolved to turn Uganda into a Muslim State. The Western powers had disappointed this mercurial tyrant: they had thrown out his shopping list for Hawker Harriers and armoured cars with ground-to-air missiles, with which he hoped to attack Tanzania. So he had looked to the oil-rich Arab States for help. Colonel Gaddafi, calling Amin 'a second Mohammed', was quite prepared to give him money for Russian-made arms, in exchange for Uganda's conversion to Islam. King Feisal of Saudi Arabia had presented Amin with a golden sword, saying: 'With this sword make your country Muslim.'

Uganda was a predominantly Christian country, Christians making up 70 per cent and Muslims only 6 per cent of the people at the last British census. In his conversations with Gaddafi, Amin exaggerated the Muslim percentage, deceiving him into believing that Uganda was ripe for the plucking. Amin himself was Muslim, as were many of his Kakwa tribe. (Christianity had not reached those remote north-western regions where the Nile begins its four-thousand mile journey and where Uganda meets the Sudan). Christians now found themselves removed from office and replaced by Muslims, while Christian-owned businesses were handed over to Muslim ownership. Amin even had his army officers circumcised – under threat of being shot. Gaddafi's money bought radios, clothes, shoes and other luxuries by which Ugandans might be bribed to become Muslim. There is little doubt that some 'Christians' took the bribes, but they were few in number. When Colonel Gaddafi, on a visit to Makerere

University in Kampala in 1975, boasted that he was paying out money 'to eliminate the few remaining Christians and turn Uganda into a Muslim State' many of the students walked out on him.

Amin was angry when he discovered that the Archbishop was giving help to Christian government officials who had fallen from favour. But Janani calmly reminded him that in the Old Testament men fleeing from the wrath of those in power used to grasp at a leg of the Holy Table. 'In the same way, our Christians run to me,' he explained.

But by 1975 the persecution – and it was not only of Christians – had run out of control and the country was in the grip of terror. The Security Forces, belonging to the State Research Bureau or to the Public Safety Unit, were all Nubians, Palestinians, Libyans, or hired murderers from elsewhere, men who had no loyalty to Uganda and who cared even less about human rights. (It was said of Amin that he considered himself first a Nubian–Kakwa; secondly a Muslim; thirdly a West Niler; and lastly a Ugandan.) These men drove around in huge black cars, inspiring dread. Leading citizens simply disappeared or were executed on the spot. There was no right of appeal, no possibility of redress, and very little of survival after arrest. Bodies were found floating in Lake Victoria or caught in the papyrus reeds that fringed its shores; others were set alight or left to rot. The rancid stench of death hung over the swamps, while the crocodiles on the banks of the Nile were sleek and fat.

In despair, people turned to Janani to help find a missing husband, son, brother or lover. The Archbishop would make his way to the infamous State Research Centre, in whose dank dungeons 'countless hundreds, perhaps thousands, of victims were killed or died from beatings, sledge hammers or starvation' (George Ivan Smith: *Ghosts of Kampala*). He would make inquiries and plead, usually in vain, for the victims. If he drew a blank in that place, he would proceed to the offices of the equally unsavoury Public Safety Unit.

The churches in Uganda, whether Anglican or Roman Catholic, had no tradition of social criticism or opposition to the ruling powers, but they could no longer keep silent, in the face of such monstrous inhumanity and mass murder. 1976 was the year in which they found a voice.

In that year the Church of Uganda was making plans for its centenary year; but the joy which should have surrounded its efforts were markedly absent. Six actors who were rehearsing a pageant depicting the boy-martyrs were found murdered in a field; their crime, it was said, 'anti-government propaganda'. In June an attempt on Amin's life was followed by savage reprisals. One victim was Teresa Nanziri-Bukenya, the popular Catholic warden of Africa Hall at Makerere University. A girl student of hers had disappeared on her way home to Kenya and was said to have been assaulted by soldiers at Entebbe Airport. Mrs. Bukenya, recently married and eight months pregnant, refused to give evidence that the girl was 'a woman of loose morals'; a few days later her decapitated body was found floating in the Nile. In July a Catholic priest was taken away at gunpoint as he said Mass, his body later being found a few miles away. Anglicans and Catholics were once again dying together, as the early martyrs of their country had done.

July brought the hi-jacking of an Israeli aircraft and the subsequent daring rescue operation by Israeli commandos at Entebbe airport. Cheated of his big chance to demonstrate solidarity with the Arab world, Amin reacted with predictable fury. Soldiers roamed unchecked through the streets, committing unparalleled murder.

Reports from Ankole that Christians and Muslims had turned on each other and were burning each other's villages prompted the Catholic, Anglican and Muslim leaders in that province to sign a joint appeal to their followers, urging them to settle their differences peacefully, and to stop confusing politics with religion.

Perhaps it was this example of unity of purpose which encouraged Archbishop Luwum and Cardinal Nsubuga to further efforts. Calling together the bishops of both their churches at Lweza outside Kampala, they also invited representatives of the Orthodox and Muslim communities. Janani was in the chair. They talked about life in Uganda in all its aspects: about the lack of food and essential supplies; about corruption and racketeering; about the uncontrolled power of the Security Forces and the absence of even the most elementary justice for those who were arrested, tortured, executed. If civilians were to be arrested, they agreed, it should not be by military police but by uniformed civil police with an official warrant.

All those present signed the minutes. Then they requested an interview with the President. For answer he sent an angry reprimand to the Archbishop for holding a meeting without permission, and insisted on seeing a copy of the minutes. It is probable that from that moment Janani Luwum's fate was sealed.

Janani took his message to a police barracks in Nsambya. 'Uganda is killing Uganda', he told the men. 'We look to you to uphold the laws of our land. Do not abuse this privilege.' Some of the men came and thanked him for his words, but they had no power to do as he asked. They felt resentful of this regime which had effectively bypassed them and rendered them useless. Their animosity was shared by many sections of the army, for only the men of the West Nile stood any chance of promotion. Amin was well aware of this weight of resentment. Fearing treachery on all sides, his paranoia grew accordingly.

It must have baffled this man of low intelligence, without scruples or moral principles, that Janani refused to hate him. The Archbishop left him in no doubt about that. 'We must love the President,' he said frequently. 'We must pray for him. He is a child of God.' Janani's willingness to love a tyrant who was at once a killer and an incorrigible liar, offended some of his colleagues who accused him of being too lenient with the regime. Janani utterly repudiated the charge: 'I do not know for how long I shall be occupying this chair,' he answered his critics. 'While the opportunity is there, I preach the Gospel with all my might, and my conscience is clear before God that I have not sided with the present government, which is utterly self-seeking. I have been threatened many times. Whenever possible I have told the President the things the Churches disapprove of. God is my witness.'

When, at the end of 1976, groups of Ugandan exiles began

organising sabotage missions over the border from Tanzania, Amin's jumpiness increased. Once again the killer squads were let loose, charged with rooting out all potential opposition.

Christmas that year did not call for celebration. On Christmas Day Janani and his bishops prayed publicly for peace, pleading with the authorities to spare the land and its people from further suffering. Cardinal Nsubuga, making a similar appeal on Radio Uganda, was cut off in mid-speech. A Church deputation went to Amin begging for an end to repression and lawlessness. But the President chose to construe all these appeals as a threat of war: 'Some bishops are advocating bloodshed,' he proclaimed on Radio Uganda, and proceeded to threaten with a nameless retribution all those churchmen who persisted in 'preaching revolution'. In truth, Amin feared the extent of the churches' influence in the country, knowing that to most Ugandans religion was of paramount importance. It seemed to him that the more he cut down the Christians, the more of them there were.

Janani was a marked man. On Friday 28 January the countdown to his murder began. On that day he had gone to Bushenyi for the consecration of the first bishop of West Ankole. In front of a vast assembly of thirty thousand, gathered out of doors under a canopy of banana leaves, Bishop Festo Kivengere preached from a text in the Acts of the Apostles: 'But I do not account my life of any value nor as precious to myself, if only I may accomplish my course and the ministry which I received from the Lord Jesus, to testify to the gospel of the grace of God.' (Acts 20:24) The significance of the words was clear to everybody there. 'Remember,' cried Bishop Festo to the hushed crowd,

All authority comes from God . . . How are you using your authority? To uphold man or to trample him, to crush his face into the dust? God is going to judge how each one of us here is using his or her own authority. Judgment is not ours. It belongs to God.

It was brave to the point of being foolhardy. The words must have sounded like high treason to the Security Forces who were present at Bushenyi to hear them. As they sped back to Kampala, they had plenty to tell the President. Two days later Amin held an emergency meeting of his inner circle of advisers. Together they drew up plans for eliminating the opposition once and for all. Archbishop Janani Luwum's name was high on the list of those who were to be disposed of.

In the first week of February 1977, over one thousand people were arrested. As murder squads stalked the land, Milton Obote's home village was razed to the ground and many of its inhabitants slaughtered. In what the *Observer* (13.2.77) called 'the greatest single campaign of massacre on a colossal scale since the regime assumed power', once again it was the Acholi and Langi of the north who bore the full brunt of this renewed savagery. Amin's sick mind had now dreamed up a plot, in which he imagined that Obote and the Archbishop proposed to wrest power away from him and hand it to their two tribes.

Shortly after midnight on Saturday 5 February, a group of armed men forced their way into Archbishop Janani's house, allegedly in search of offensive weapons.

6

Hearing the noise of the fence being broken down, Janani looked through the window and saw a man he knew, one Ben Ongom, a tradesman from the north. 'We've come, Archbishop, we've come, let us in,' called the man, and believing him to be in need of help, Janani unbolted the door. The soldiers rushed in. Their leader, who spoke only Arabic, thrust his rifle into the Archbishop's stomach while the others demanded to see 'the arms'. Twenty-two cases had been brought into the country, explained the hapless decoy, Ongom; and half of these had already been discovered at his own house. The rest were still missing. 'Show us where they are hidden,' he pleaded, as the soldiers searched the house, the compound, even the chapel. 'If the arms are not in your house, tell us the location of any Acholi or Langi homes on Namirembe, so that they may be searched.'

The Archbishop was not to be tricked: 'This house is a house of prayer,' he told the gunmen. 'The only armament I possess is the Bible. I pray for the President. I pray for you, that you may learn to rule Uganda without destroying it.'

Finding no arms, the men moved off, ordering the gate to be opened for them. Janani's wife, Mary, angrily suggested that they should go out the way they had come, through the fence they had smashed. But Janani gently reproved her. 'No,' he said, 'we are Christians. We have clean hearts and, as a witness to our beliefs, we will open the gate for you.'

News of the attack on the Archbishop's house spread quickly, causing widespread alarm and dismay. Was nobody safe? Was nothing sacred? That same Saturday night, Bishop Okoth of Bukedi had been arrested, saying to the soldiers who came for him: 'If it is death for me, it is the gateway to the Lord. If life, I will continue to preach the Gospel.' When the soldiers failed to find what they were looking for, the bishop was released.

Incensed by these outrages, the House of Bishops protested to the President in the strongest possible terms. 'Every phrase must be like an arrow,' stipulated Bishop Festo, as they prepared the letter. Abandoning the relatively cautious officialese they had used at Lweza, they went straight to the point of their profound disquiet. The law had been replaced by the bullet, they firmly stated. 'The gun whose muzzle has been pressed against the Archbishop's stomach, the gun used to search the Bishop of Bukedi's house, is a gun pointed at every Christian in the Church.' The bishops deplored the crimes of the Security Forces: 'We have buried many who have died as a result of being shot, and there are many more whose bodies have not been found, yet their disappearance is connected with the activities of some members of the Security Forces.' They were in fighting mood. If the President wanted evidence, they asserted, he could have it, 'because widows and orphans are members of our Church.'

Nothing was omitted from the catalogue of the regime's crimes: the 'war against the educated'; the rampages of

Amin's licensed assassins; his attempted Muslimisation of the
Churches; his Arab entourage, his Russian advisers. Heed-
less of danger, they pursued the logic of their case, pressing
home the accusations:

> While you, Your Excellency, have stated on the national
> radio that your government is not under any foreign in-
> fluence . . . the general trend of things in Uganda has
> created a feeling that the affairs of our nation are being
> directed by outsiders who do not have the welfare of this
> country and the value of the lives and properties of
> Ugandans at heart. (The text of this letter was published in
> full in the *Observer*, 20.2.77.)

Had the Anglican bishops gone too far? Certainly the
Catholics thought so. Cardinal Nsubuga had gone to sym-
pathise with Archbishop Luwum, as soon as the attack on him
became known; and the Catholic and Anglican bishops had
hoped to work out a joint response. But when the Cardinal
received a copy of the Anglicans' letter he felt unable to sign it
unless it were considerably toned down and made less overtly
political. Janani and his bishops agreed to a few minor
changes, but they did not want to do more. With the assurance that the Catholics would send a separate letter of their
own lending all possible moral support, the fifteen Anglican
bishops signed the letter, sent it to the President and asked for
an interview. Nothing more was heard about a letter from the
Catholics.

For Amin the letter must have been the last straw. On
Monday 14 February he sent for Archbishop Luwum. Mary
begged Janani not to go, but he insisted. 'Even if he kills me,
my blood will save the nation.' Over a cup of tea at State
House, Entebbe, Amin accused Janani of plotting with Obote
to overthrow him, and warned that arms had now been
discovered near the Archbishop's house. Iain Grahame,
Amin's former superior officer in the King's African Rifles,
was a fellow guest that day and spoke to Janani and Mary on
the lawn. 'There are certain troubles,' he reports Janani as
saying, 'but I hope that they can be resolved.' As Janani and

his wife walked back over the lawn to the house, Amin turned to Grahame: 'Do not worry about the Archbishop,' he said. 'I will not harm him.'

What, then, went wrong? For within forty-eight hours Luwum was dead. Some reports claim that after the murder Amin told a fellow officer, 'I lost my temper. I have killed him.'

That may be the charitable explanation. But all the evidence suggests that the murder was premeditated, and that Amin had long since made up his mind that Janani Luwum was to die.

*   *   *

President Amin summoned the bishops for nine thirty a.m. on Wednesday 16 February. Members of the diplomatic corps, heads of government departments, and religious leaders were already assembled on the concourse of the Nile Mansions Hotel, next to the International Conference Centre in Kampala, when Archbishop Luwum and six of his brother bishops arrived. On parade were three thousand soldiers, and prominently displayed was exhibit number one, a large cache of arms: several suitcases filled with antiquated Chinese automatic weapons, hand grenades and rounds of ammunition. The sun blazed down mercilessly on the bishops as they stood surrounded by the soldiers and confronted by this apparent evidence of the Archbishop's guilt. When they attempted to move into the shade, the soldiers ordered them to stay where they were.

For two hours they stood in the blistering heat, as an (obviously tortured) prisoner was made to read out a lengthy memorandum alleged to prove an arms deal between Obote and the Archbishop. Janani shook his head in silent denial.

'They intend to kill me, but I am not afraid,' he whispered to Bishop Festo.

'What shall we do with the traitors?' shouted the Vice President, who was in charge of the 'trial'. The scene was so reminiscent of a trial that took place some two thousand years earlier in front of Pontius Pilate that it might almost have been stage-managed.

'Kill them, kill them,' screamed the soldiers.

'Put up your hands, those who want them shot in public,' demanded the Vice President, and a forest of hands rose into the air, without a single dissenter.

But in front of such a distinguished gathering, this was no time for allowing lynch law. The semblance of civilised behaviour must be preserved. The bishops were merely ordered into a side room inside the conference centre, while the rest of the assembly was dismissed. As they sat there, an official told Archbishop Luwum that the President wanted to see him in the next room. Janani rose to his feet and smiled at Bishop Festo. 'There is something I have not told you,' he said. 'Three days ago a girl came to warn me that I was number one on the Security Forces' death list. She had overheard some of the men talking in Swahili about it. She wanted me to escape, but I told her: I cannot. I am the Archbishop. I must stay.'

It was his farewell. Saying 'I can see the hand of the Lord in this,' he turned away from his friend and went calmly through the door. It was three thirty p.m.

When the other bishops had been sent home, Festo and Bishop Wani waited for Janani by his car. Just before five p.m. Bishop Wani went to make inquiries and was told that the Archbishop was still 'in serious discussion' with the President. The two men persisted. They were still clamouring for news when a Mercedes Benz passed them, driving at high speed. Festo had just time to see that the occupants of the car were two government ministers, Erinayo Oryema and Oboth Ofumbi, and Janani, before the soldiers forced him and Bishop Wani at gunpoint into their own car.

At six thirty that evening, Radio Uganda announced the arrest of the two government ministers and of the Archbishop. It is probable that by then all three were dead.

Next morning came the announcement that the three men had died 'in a motor accident', while trying to escape. 'No one in Uganda,' said Bishop Festo, 'not even a child at school, could believe that. We all knew, without a shadow of a doubt, that the Archbishop had been murdered.'

Hoping to claim the body for burial, Festo and two other bishops went to the hospital where they found many of the doctors and nurses in tears. The deputy superintendent was signing a death certificate with trembling hand, a security man standing at his shoulder. The bishops were not allowed into the mortuary. Later that day, a nurse who worked there told them she had seen the Archbishop's body, with two bullet-holes in the chest and his mouth full of blood. A doctor who had managed to see all three bodies while the guard was being changed, confirmed that they had all been shot.

A few details of the Archbishop's last hours were to emerge. He had been taken to the State Research Centre, stripped down to his underclothes and thrust into a large cell full of prisoners waiting for death. They recognised him at once and one of them asked for his blessing. When Janani agreed, the soldiers took him out and gave him back his cassock and crucifix. He returned to the cell, prayed with the prisoners and blessed them. A great peace and calm descended on them all, witnessed the only one of them all to survive. 'There is a rumour,' wrote Bishop Festo, 'that they were trying to make him sign a confession, which he would not do. We were also told that he was praying aloud for his captors when he died. We have talked to eye-witnesses who claim that they saw him shot, and with others who saw the bodies in the morgue with bullet wounds. The evidence suggests that they were shot at six o'clock (on the Wednesday evening).'

The bishops pleaded in vain for permission to bury the body next to that of Bishop Hannington, murdered by that other tyrant, Mwanga. Soldiers secretly took Janani's body north to Kitgum and forced the local (Acholi) Christians to dig his grave. Janani's mother and brother were brought along to identify the body. 'At least,' commented Bishop Festo, 'they did not throw his body to the hyenas.'

Radio Uganda ordered that there should be no prayers for the dead Archbishop, and a memorial service arranged for the following Sunday in Namirembe Cathedral had to be cancelled. Instead thousands came to the cathedral for Matins, and, as they came away after the service, voices in the crowd began to sing the hymn the martyrs had sung as they died:

> Daily, daily, sing the praises
> Of the City God has made . . .

In planning for the centenary, the Church had not foreseen that it would in the end be marked by the blood of a new martyr. Suddenly they all realised it. Margaret Ford, Janani's former secretary, was present at the service in the cathedral that day and recalls its remarkable climax:

> Then our eyes fell on the empty grave, a gaping hole in the earth. The words of the angel to the two women seeking Jesus's body flashed into our minds. 'Why do you seek the living among the dead?' Namirembe Hill resounded with the song that the balokole have taken as their own:

> > Glory, glory, hallelujah,
> > Glory, glory to the Lamb!
> > Oh, the cleansing blood has reached me,
> > Glory, glory to the Lamb.

> We came away from the service praising, healed by the revelation of the empty grave. We greeted each other, using the words of the old Easter greeting, 'Christ is risen': 'He is risen indeed'. Archbishop Sabiti spoke to me briefly as I was leaving: 'Why are we bothering about the body? Janani went straight to heaven.'

The 'Easter experience' which followed Janani's death breathed new life into the Church of Uganda. 'The uncommitted suddenly became committed,' says Bishop Festo (who left Uganda at that point, to avoid sharing Janani's fate, but who returned when Amin was expelled). 'Christians on the fringe felt that his death challenged them to assert their faith.' Among both Catholics and Anglicans a new spiritual fervour was born out of suffering.

But Janani had been mistaken in one thing, at least in the short term. He assured his wife that even if Amin killed him, 'my blood will save the nation.' So far it has not done so. Amin has gone into some limbo of his own, Obote has returned to power. And still the killing goes on, the Baganda now being the principal victims.

One lesson, however, has been learned. Though the present government is avowedly Anglican, (it has dismissed all the Roman Catholic civil servants); though religion is still confused with politics in the popular mind; though the once-hopeful Ugandan Christian Council has not met since the murder of the Archbishop and the disappointment over the absence of Catholic support: in spite of all those things, voices can be heard asserting that no Church today can afford to be identified with a political party. 'We have suffered enough to know better,' claims Bishop Festo. 'The Church cannot rely for support on a government, and remain a living, effective Church. And a living, effective Church is what we must be.' If that conviction gains ground, and if the Catholics also sub-scribe to it, then the way may be open for a renewed co-operation between them. And then perhaps the boy martyrs and Janani Luwum will not have died in vain.

5.
Oscar Romero 1917–1980

1

On the morning of Dr. Robert Runcie's enthronement as Archbishop of Canterbury on 25 March 1980, the news of Oscar Romero's murder in San Salvador aroused the horrified sympathy of the world. In his enthronement speech Dr. Runcie referred to his own feelings of shock at this murder which for him was 'a sober reminder that life and death for the Gospel are still the way Christians are called to change the world.'

Five days later the crowds gathered in San Salvador for the funeral. In the cathedral were bishops and government representatives from all over the world. They were to discover that violence is no respecter of death. Before the murdered Archbishop could be laid in his tomb, shots rang out, a bomb exploded and in the ensuing panic forty people were suffocated or trampled to death.

Had this man, then, been a firebrand, an inciter to violence, as his many enemies claimed? There were some, even within his own Church, who would have answered a resounding 'Yes'. Yet a Brazilian bishop called him Saint Romero of the Americas and Dr. Jorge Lara-Braud, a Protestant theologian, spoke for many when he told a hushed congregation:

Remembering how he lived and died, I have dared to say, 'Together with thousands of Salvadoreans, I have seen Jesus. This time his name was Oscar Arnulfo Romero. His broken body is broken with the body of Jesus, his shed blood is shed with the blood of Jesus. And as with Jesus, so it is with Monseñor, he died for us so that we might live in freedom and in love and justice for one another. His resurrection is not a future event. It is a present reality.'

Monseñor the people called him. Not Monseñor Romero: just Monseñor. It was a sign of their affection, and though he is dead, that is the name by which they still know him in El Salvador. He is their national saint. Yet in the beginning he was such unpromising material for a saint. Saints today, especially in strife-torn Central America, are not looked for in episcopal palaces at the heart of the establishment. And nothing in Oscar Romero's early life, as he steadily climbed the ladder towards position and power in the Church, suggested that on the eve of his sixtieth birthday and for the last three years of his life, he would come to a radically new understanding of the Gospel message, and by it would be transformed.

*   *   *

Oscar Arnulfo Romero y Galdámez was born in Ciudad Barrios, El Salvador, on 15 August, 1917. It was a small town which until the middle of the present century could be reached only on horseback or on foot. Once it was called by the Indian name, Cacahuatique, recalling the fact that the land had belonged to the Indians before the Spaniards wrested it from them in the sixteenth century.

The Romeros' house stood on a corner of the main square. Oscar's father, Santos, worked for a post and telegraph company, and the Romero children helped to deliver letters and telegrams in the town. Santos had bought a small property with his savings and he grew cocoa and coffee there to supplement his income. The family were not poor, but neither were they rich; there were no luxuries and the children had to share a bed.

Oscar was a serious child, studious and rather pious. He went to the village school and at thirteen was apprenticed to a carpenter. But secretly he longed to become a priest, and when the Vicar General of the diocese came one day to Ciudad Barrios, the boy confided his longing to him. One year later, despite the reluctance of his father, Oscar went off to a minor seminary in San Miguel, a journey of seven hours on horseback down a winding trail.

On 4 April 1942 he was ordained in Rome; and he celebrated his first solemn Mass at home the following month. He was a bright young man, marked out for promotion from the start. Over the next few years, first as curate, then as parish priest, he established a reputation as a fine preacher and as a dutiful, conscientious priest who, in addition to his parish work, visited the prisons and was chaplain at a girls' high school. A kindly, open man, he was popular enough with his parishioners in a routine sort of way.

The Vatican Council of 1962–5 – which brought the Catholic Church into the twentieth century – almost passed him by. He read the documents and reflected on them, but they did not elicit much internal response from him, and on the whole he was unsympathetic to the changes the Council demanded. In 1967 he celebrated his Silver Jubilee as a priest and received the courtesy title of Monseñor. This seemed to be just the first rung on the ladder, for a few months after this he left for the capital, San Salvador, to become Secretary General of the national Bishops' Conference; and a little later Executive Secretary to the Central American Bishops' secretariat. In 1970 Archbishop Luis Chavez of San Salvador asked to have him as his auxiliary bishop. He was ordained bishop in June of that year, in the presence of the President and army officials and with plentiful pomp and circumstance – much to the disgust and disappointment of the priests who were at loggerheads with the ruling classes in El Salvador and who were pressing for social change. In the new bishop they saw all the old traditional values being reasserted, all the things they felt were wrong with the Church. Here was a 'church man' if ever there was one, a career prelate, a dyed-in-the-wool conservative, a friend of the reactionary Opus Dei movement, a man who was about to take as his episcopal motto the sententious '*Sentire con l'Iglesia*' – 'to be of one mind with the Church'. They had little to hope from him. And for the next seven years Bishop Romero did nothing to make them change their minds.

2

Perhaps at this point we need to know something of the recent history of El Salvador, to explain why certain priests were so hostile to the ruling groups and why they were resentful of the new bishop. It would, in any case, be impossible to understand Oscar Romero without knowing something of his country.

El Salvador is the smallest republic in the Americas, no bigger than Massachusetts – or Wales. A poet once called it 'the Tom Thumb of America'. Five million individuals trying to be a nation – and prevented from doing so. Ever since the early nineteenth century the politics of El Salvador have been dominated by the economics of coffee. Coffee was first planted by the Spaniards in 1838 and the results exceeded expectation, with harvests yielding from 200,000 to one million pounds of coffee every year. Unfortunately for the inhabitants of El Salvador, the profitable growth of coffee for export required the placing of huge tracts of land under private control; and this inevitably meant the dispossession of the original tenant farmer. It was the Indians who owned the land; they held it in common and farmed it on a collectivist system. The men who now forced them off their ancestral land were almost all of European origin. By 1920 the new land-owning class, the fourteen ruling families of El Salvador, known as the oligarchy, was well established, and 70 per cent of the country's work-force were agricultural labourers, living in intolerable conditions and subsisting on black beans and maize pancakes. As well as his heritage, the Indian had seen his entire way of life absorbed into an alien culture, and because he was (inevitably) illiterate, he was allowed no vote by which to improve his status.

In the towns he fared even worse. Writing in the early 1930s, Major Arthur, the new US military attaché in Central America, has left us this description of San Salvador:

> One of the first things one notices is the abundance of luxury motor-cars driving through the streets . . . Nothing seems to exist between the dearest cars and the oxen cart

driven by a boy in bare feet. Practically no middle class exists between the enormously wealthy and the very poor . . . People with whom I have spoken tell me that approximately 90 per cent of the country's wealth is in the possession of 0.5 per cent of the population. Between thirty and forty families are owners of the entire country. They live as splendidly as kings, surrounded by crowds of servants and they send their children to be educated in Europe or the US and they squander money on their whims. The remainder of the population have practically nothing. I imagine that the situation in El Salvador today is similar to France before the Revolution, Russia before her Revolution and Mexico before hers. The situation is ripe for Communism and the Communists seem to have taken notice of that fact. (Letter to US Department of Defence, 1931. Quoted by Dermot Keogh)

When it came, in 1932, the popular insurrection was bloody. The revolt was led by Farabundo Marti in the capital, and by the Indian headmen in the rural areas to the west. It was doomed to defeat. Thirty thousand were killed, and the revolt was suppressed with savage brutality. In one place, where there was a heavy concentration of Indians, peasants were shot in batches of sixty.

And what was the role of the Catholic Church in all this? Before the revolt, the then Archbishop of San Salvador had appealed for better labour conditions and had pleaded with the President to stop the executions. But when Colonel Calderón marched back to the city after putting down the revolt without mercy, a Te Deum was sung in the Cathedral to celebrate this victory over the godless forces of Communism.

From that time on, the nation was ruled with varying degrees of severity by the armed forces, while the real power lay where it had always lain – with the oligarchy, the fourteen families of Spanish, Dutch or English stock, with a small sprinkling of very wealthy people of Irish extraction.

A series of soldier politicians were succeeded as President in 1956 by Colonel Jose Maria Lemus who consolidated his power by clapping all his political opponents into jail. By this

time the political opposition was showing open hostility to the
military regimes. In 1960 political rallies were banned, troops
invaded the University, smashed up classrooms and labor-
atories and beat up the students. The students took to the
streets and the troops opened fire on them.

In the reaction against violence that followed, the government was overthrown and a six-man junta came into power
promising moderate reforms. The junta in turn was succeeded by a civilian and military ruling council in 1961, with a
strong man, Colonel Julio Adalberto Rivera, in charge. The
Kennedy administration in the US gave this regime its backing on the condition that it would initiate some necessary
reforms. But the suggested reforms (farm and industrial
workers to be given Sundays free with pay, 30 per cent
reduction in rents, nationalisation of the central bank and
strict currency controls to prevent capital from leaving the
country) were strenuously opposed by the ruling élite and
they came to nothing.

However, as time went by the opposition was becoming
better organised. The Christian Democratic party was founded in 1960, but because of recurring electoral frauds, by 1968
it had still only 15 seats in the 54-strong national assembly.
Two other parties were formed in this period – the National
Revolutionary Party and the National Democratic Union.
All three were united in a rough coalition against the existing power structure and in 1971 they combined to fight the
presidential election for the following year. But in blatantly
crooked elections accompanied by violence and intimida-
tion, the election was 'won' by the military men's candidate –
Colonel Arturo Armando Molina. The rule of the military
seemed set fair to continue. El Salvador was to remain an
armed camp governed by men to whom the idea of 'national
security' amounted to paranoia, and to whom the very idea of
opposition was synonymous with treachery. The doctrine of
'national security' required the repression of all opposition,
the silencing of dissent by any means; and to enforce it, a
ruthless security police which would make mincemeat of the
government's opponents.

Sadly, in Latin America, the 'national security' state has

given itself the epithet Christian, and its adherents see no conflict between the claims of a monolithic state and those of the Gospel. Its leaders need the support of the powerful Roman Catholic Church, and traditionally they have received it. Right from the earliest days of the Spanish Conquest, there had always been a split in the Church between those who defended the rights of the dispossessed Indians and those who put themselves on the side of the conquerors. In the 'national security' state the conflict has been between those churchmen who were prepared, in the sacred cause of anti-Communism, to collaborate with the regime for the sake of preserving the Church's privileges (Catholic education in the schools, the official acceptance of the Church as the non-secular power in the land), and those who were not. A large number of priests, nuns and laymen were becoming radical, believing passionately that social injustice did not represent the will of God, that the poor must work and struggle for justice with God's help. For the poor of El Salvador were not poor through some natural immutable law; they were 'empobrecidos' – they had been made poor by the rapacious greed of their oppressors. Nor were they merely poor in the way Westerners understand the word: they had nothing at all. Half the people of El Salvador were living well below the breadline.

It was into this embattled area that Oscar Romero now stepped. The new auxiliary bishop of San Salvador did not accept the progressive views of the radical clergy, and he believed that peace and harmony should be sought at any cost.

3

His accommodating approach was made clear in his editorship of the archdiocesan newspaper, *Orientacion*. Whereas the previous editor had concentrated on social questions, Romero preferred the more anodyne topics of drugs, alcoholism and pornography, which fell more obviously into the Church's area of concern.

Before long, Romero found himself in the thick of controversy, and as always he came down heavily on the side of the established order. In the forefront of those within the church working actively for social justice, (at the Council of Latin American bishops at Medellin in 1968, the idea that the poor must undertake the struggle for a more just society was accepted by a majority of the delegates), were the Jesuits. And as the best schools and universities in the country were in their hands, the fact caused no little dismay among the secular and ecclesiastical authorities. The Jesuits had introduced discussions on the Medellin documents into their schools, and were holding evening classes to which boys from the poorer parts of the city were invited. Parents of the day pupils were up in arms and demanding action. Bishop Romero doughtily took up the cudgels in an editorial which, while it applauded Medellin's stance on behalf of 'liberating education' (i.e. making people become more aware of their situation), deplored the 'demagogy and Marxism' found in 'the pamphlets and literature of known red origin spread in a certain school'. The secular press took up the cry of 'Marxism' and latched on to the subject with the tenacity of bull terriers. Before the month was out the Attorney General had ordered an investigation and various Jesuits were summoned to defend themselves. They did so with ease, the parents were won over, bishops and priests likewise; and Bishop Romero faded into a discreet silence.

But one setback did not modify his real position. A document issued in 1973 claimed that *Orientacion* 'criticises injustice in the abstract but criticises methods of liberation in the concrete.' The magazine, it was said, 'defended the established order, was directed at a public "well satisfied with the existing situation", concealed the roots of national problems, and took a defensive attitude before the transformation of the nation.' The bishops, it was clear, still maintained an idea of church authority left over from the triumphalist days before the Vatican Council.

As time went by, the Jesuits became more clearly committed to the 'option for the poor'. But in 1968 they began cutting back on their educational institutions and decided to give up the major seminary in San Salvador, returning it to the bishop. The Jesuit provincial proposed one of his own theologians, Fr. Rutilio Grande, as Rector, but the bishops disapproved of him and chose a 'safer' Jesuit, Fr. Amando Lopez. But they were disappointed to find that Fr. Lopez continued the lax rule of his predecessors (allowing the seminarians to remove their cassocks while playing football, for example) and by 1972 the bishops voted to get rid of the Jesuits and replace them by Bishop Romero.

So he was now auxiliary bishop, editor of *Orientacion*, General Secretary of the National Bishops' Conference, and Rector of the San Salvador seminary. Perhaps it was not altogether surprising that as Rector he was not a notable success.

But Romero's ecclesiastical star was still in the ascendant, and in 1974, during the Synod of Bishops in Rome, he was named Bishop of Santiago de Maria, a diocese of some thirty thousand people, stretching from the border with Honduras to the Pacific Ocean. It was an area of coffee-growing highlands and cotton-growing coastal plains, which included his own birthplace of Ciudad Barrios. It seemed as though the wheel had come full circle; the local boy made good was going home.

At this time Bishop Romero still held to the rather simplistic belief that the Church was made up of the 'good rich' and 'good poor'; and he was accustomed to steer well clear of the extremes, the bad rich and the embittered poor. But events now began slowly to disillusion him.

On 21 June, 1975, the National Guard raided a hamlet called Tres Calles in Romero's diocese. The Guard attacked at one a.m., shooting and hacking to death with machetes five *campesinos* (peasants) and conducting a house to house search for concealed weapons. The bishop said mass for the victims, consoled the families and preached a sermon in which he condemned this attack on human rights. He remonstrated with the local Guard commander, who merely shrugged his shoulders and said the victims were evil-doers who had got what was coming to them. The bishop did not dispute the diagnosis but insisted that the *campesinos* had a right to elementary justice, no matter what they had done. Returning home he wrote a letter to President Molina, in which he expressed a courteous hope that there would be no repetition of such an incident. After which, he explained his conduct to his fellow bishops. Wishing to avoid a public protest, he said, he had lodged a private protest in the right quarters. After all, the Church was not really involved, and he could not even be sure of the real motives of the killers nor of the degree of guilt of the victims.

For the moment he was prepared to give the authorities the benefit of the doubt, believing, against all the evidence to the contrary, that they meant well but were cursed with trigger-happy subordinates. He clung to the hope that between them the Church and the civil authorities would reach a solution.

On a visit to Rome in 1975 he deplored the growing politicisation of the Salvadorean clergy and the spreading discontent at all levels within the Church. Back home again, on the country's national day (the Feast of the Transfiguration of Christ the Saviour) August 6, 1976, he preached of the dangers of the new theology and begged the warring sections of society to settle their differences and work together amicably. Even at this late date he believed that a little goodwill all round would work wonders.

Nevertheless, there were signs of change in him. He had begun to understand something of the desperate plight of the *campesinos*, trapped in their near-feudal helplessness. When he had to make a decision whether or not to close the centre run by Passionists at Jiquilisco for the training of *campesinos* as lay catechists, he decided to keep it open. Advanced ideas notwithstanding, at least the centre was a visible symbol of a caring Church.

Tension was rising steadily in El Salvador. A mild land-reform law passed in 1975 was emasculated and rendered gutless by the efforts of landowners and businessmen. President Molina conceded defeat on the issue, but the oligarchy were not content with mere words. They wanted to make sure there would be no further importunate demands, and they were determined to eradicate everything and everyone that threatened the status quo. There followed a violent repression especially in the rural areas.

Repression was in itself nothing new, but this time there was a new element. This time the Church was on the receiving end, as priests, nuns, laymen and Catholic institutions came under bitter attack. The *campesinos* had banded together in unions and their right to do so was endorsed by Luis Chavez, Archbishop of San Salvador, who for his temerity was viciously denounced in the press. The ruling classes were furious at the Archbishop's attitude, though it must be admitted that it was by no means an attitude shared by the whole Church. In general, the hierarchy frowned on any participation by the clergy in the increasingly politicised peasant unions.

But in 1977, Archbishop Chavez was on the point of retiring, and the choice of his successor was critical, a matter of political as well as Church concern. Would the man who followed Chavez be, like him, imbued with the concerns of Vatican II and Medellin? Would he, to be more explicit, understand the Church to mean 'the people of God', identifying therefore with the hopes and sufferings of the Salvadorean people, especially the poor and the oppressed? Would he consider that the Church's principal task was to establish a foretaste of Christ's kingdom here on earth, to bring about a new kind of society from which injustice, exploitation and oppression would be banished? Such a man would indeed be a subversive within a regime founded on the oppression of the many by the few.

The fate of the Church was hanging in the balance, and as the atmosphere grew more charged, many were the appeals sent to Rome – that the choice would alight on a man who could be trusted by the establishment, a man who would keep the 'Marxist' priests and grass-roots communities in their place, a man more concerned to keep the peace than to take the hazardous road into the wilderness of subversion. Rome listened and took the hint. They named Oscar Romero as the new Archbishop; and the oligarchy breathed freely again, believing that the future was assured.

4

The appointment was hailed by the press as a great conservative victory. On 10 February 1977 *La Prensa Grafica* of San Salvador published a brief interview with the future Archbishop, in which he stated his express desire to 'keep to the centre, watchfully, in the traditional way, but seeking justice'. At the same time, he put in a plea that the government 'should not consider a priest who takes a stand for social justice as a subversive element, when he is fulfilling his mission in the pursuit of the common good.'

Had he but known it, a new era of persecution was dawning for the church and people of El Salvador. It coincided with the beginning of his ministry in the archdiocese, a man of fifty-nine, more or less set in his ways, a man who had reached the summit of his ambition and might have been expected to rest there, immobile, as incapable of change as the country's progressive priests believed him to be. For the progressives were bitterly upset by Romero's nomination. All the indications were for a bland, traditionalist episcopate, dedicated to concern with fringe issues and compromise with the authorities on the major ones. Romero was a known admirer of the right-wing Catholic Opus Dei organisation and was, besides, a 'churchy' man, lover of rules and clerical discipline, friend of liturgical laws. His health was not good, and it was known that in his days as auxiliary he had been shunted on to more peripheral work. In fact the only thing in his favour was that he was honest, prepared to think for himself and dependably faithful to what he saw as his Christian commitment. With that the more progressive clergy and laity would have to be content.

Before Romero had been installed as Archbishop, the government seized the initiative. Assuming that the new Archbishop could be counted on, they began stepping up the harassment of the committed clergy. The campaign of vilification by means of press, TV and radio, reached unimaginable depths. Six clerics were arrested, tortured and deported to Guatemala. One of these, Willibrord Denoux, a Belgian priest known as Padre Guillermo, wrote to the retiring

Archbishop Chavez: 'Perhaps for the church of El Salvador the moment of trial, of the desert, has come . . . Finally the Church is where it always should have been: with the people, surrounded by wolves.' Grief-stricken, Chavez begged his successor to take over quickly. Romero agreed and on 22 February, in a brief, almost private ceremony, quite devoid of ostentation, he became Archbishop. A new presidential campaign was under way and the outgoing President Molina was not even aware that the ceremony had occurred. It had, said one commentator, taken place, 'just in time for the beginning of a new massacre of the people'.

The presidential elections were the catalyst for the massacre. It was well known that elections were rigged, and this one was no exception. Despite all the evidence of chicanery, on 26 February the government announced that the new President was General Carlos Humberto Romero (no relation), a man utterly committed to the status quo and suffering no inhibitions about repression of all dissenters.

What followed is history. About fifty thousand people staged a protest demonstration next day (Sunday) in the main square of the capital – the Plaza Libertad. After midnight troops opened fire on the two thousand or so who remained in the square and these people fled to a nearby church. During the day troops again fired on rioters and the government admitted to eight deaths, though others claimed that the number was anything from a hundred to three hundred. At all events, it was a day to remember. The priests of the archdiocese met to discuss the situation. It was Romero's first meeting with his clergy as Archbishop, and it was a true baptism of fire. He listened carefully and asked questions. Then, to everyone's amazement, he said: 'Let's stop talking. Go home, all of you, and take care of the people. Open your houses to any who think they may be in danger. Check to see if they really are being followed and, if they are, take them in and hide them.' To the clergy who were present at that meeting, it seemed as though a major milestone had been passed.

Events moved fast after that. On 12 March Fr. Rutilio Grande, a Jesuit priest and a friend of Romero's, was murdered, the first priest to meet his death in the new persecution. Fr. Grande was with an old man and a boy of sixteen when their jeep was shot at and they all three died. The Jesuit had worked tirelessly to bring new perspectives into the Church, to give practical expression to the guidelines laid down by Vatican II and Medellin. He had chosen to work in Aguilares, a remote country district where the main crops were cotton and sugar cane and where the majority of the inhabitants lived in squalid poverty. A month earlier, in a sermon regretting the expulsion of a priest-friend to Guatemala, he had said:

> It was a matter of being or not being faithful to the missions of Jesus here and now. And for being faithful there would be reprisals, calumnies, blows, torture, kidnappings, bombs and, if one was an outsider, expulsion. But there always remains the fundamental question: it is dangerous to be a Christian in our milieu. It is practically illegal to be an authentic Christian in our environment . . . precisely because the world which surrounds us is founded radically on an established disorder before which the mere proclamation of the Gospel is subversive.

Rutilio Grande had paid the price of his audacity. An article in the diocesan magazine, *Orientacion*, described his death as an attack on all those who desired the liberation of the people. 'And when we say liberation, we say it in the sense of breaking the bonds of sin which prevent the realisation of peace, justice and love in society. And the products of that sin are: poverty and hunger, undernourished children, broken families, abandoned children, unemployment, violence and deception of the people.'

As for Archbishop Romero, it was his moment of truth, the beginning of his road to Damascus. He is said to have spent some hours praying by the body of the murdered priest; then he said Mass and went out to demand an explanation. Gone was the deferential manner in which he had once addressed the secular powers. Aroused now, he buried the Jesuit and his dead companions without waiting for government permission; he excommunicated those responsible for their deaths;

he set up a permanent committee to monitor human rights in the country, closed all Catholic schools and colleges for three days, and cancelled all religious services on Sunday, 20 March except for a single Mass in front of the cathedral, which was attended by a hundred thousand people. Priests reported that many seemed to be returning to the Church from which they had long been estranged.

Romero had been appointed to put the brakes on the new militant Church; the death of Rutilio Grande changed all that. He saw that it was necessary to take sides, to be either with the poor or against them. In El Salvador there was no third way. He opted now for the poor, went to Rome to explain himself, and was encouraged by the Pope himself. '*Coraggio*,' said Paul VI taking Romero's hand in his own, 'be of good heart.'

He returned to find the press in full pursuit of a group of Catholic nuns accused of fostering sedition. The Sisters had been encouraging their pupils to reflect on the social conditions in their country, and on the implications of the death of Rutilio Grande. The inevitable cry of 'Marxism' had gone up, and though the fuss had died down a little, it was still simmering. Romero thought back to the days when he himself had attacked the Jesuits for just such 'liberating education'. Now, he realised, almost with a shock, he had changed sides.

In Rome the Archbishop had been working on his first Pastoral Letter to his archdiocese which his clergy had urged him to produce in time for Easter. It was the first time he had communicated in this way with his people, and since his appointment there had been the murder of Grande and the daily discovery of the bodies of dead catechists and lay workers. The Church, he said in the Letter, was living 'a paschal hour'. It was 'a renewed and powerful' Church, which knew that it did not live for its own sake. About this Church he was exultant rather than pessimistic: 'If I were to look for a word to describe this time of change in the archdiocese, I should not hesitate to call it a Resurrection.'

The outgoing President Molina asked for a meeting with the bishops to discuss the deterioration of Church–state relations. He complained about the participation of priests in

the demonstration on the Plaza Libertad, the confusing behaviour of Catholic school authorities, and the accusations by
the clergy that the government had connived at Rutilio
Grande's murder. Worst of all, an extremist guerrilla group
(Popular Liberation Forces, FPL) had now kidnapped the
Foreign Minister, Mauricio Borgonovo, and were demanding
as ransom the release of thirty-seven political prisoners.

Romero expressed genuine concern for the fate of Borgonovo, reiterating his outright condemnation of violence from
whatever source, and his desire for dialogue with the government. But he insisted that the government was itself responsible for the prevailing tension and said again that it was unjust
to pin the label 'Marxist' onto those priests who were trying to
live the Gospel as they understood it. The meeting ended in
stalemate.

On the evening of 10 May Borgonovo's body was found.
The people heard the news with fear and foreboding, knowing there would be reprisals. Romero said the funeral mass
and pleaded for peace, affirming yet again that the Church
unequivocally rejected violence.

Vengeance was swift to follow. That afternoon at five-thirty
four men forced their way into the priest's house at the
Church of the Resurrection in San Salvador and shot the
young parish priest, Alfonso Navarro, and a fifteen-year-old
parishioner, Luis Torres. The boy died the next day. Father
Alfonso died on the way to the hospital, saying 'I die for
preaching the Gospel. I know the people responsible for my
death. May they know that they are forgiven.' Such forgiveness was wasted on his murderers who lost no time in boasting
that they had killed him. The White Warriors Union (*Union
de Guerreros Blancos*, UGB), one of the many para-military
right-wing groups which were allowed to flourish, claimed
that they had struck Navarro down in revenge for the killing
of Borgonovo.

Archbishop Romero, who had buried Borgonovo one day,
buried Father Navarro on the next. Two hundred priests from
all over El Salvador came to concelebrate the mass with him.
The archdiocese's own radio, YSAX, carried his sermon
which began:

They tell how a caravan, guided by a desert Bedouin, was desperate with thirst and sought water in the mirages of the desert. The guide kept saying, 'No, not that way – this way.' This happened several times, until one of the caravan, his patience exhausted, took out a pistol and shot the guide, who, dying, still stretched out his hand to say: 'Not that way – this way.' And so he died, pointing the way. The legend becomes reality: a priest, pierced with bullets, who dies pardoning, who dies praying, gives to all of us who at this hour unite for his burial his message which we wait to receive.

And the message of Alfonso, continued the Archbishop, was that violence was not the way:

Violence is produced by all, not only by those who kill but by those who urge others to kill . . . (violence) even in those who merely do not do whatever is possible to uncover its origins is criminal. They are sinners as much as those who point the weapons of death. How is it possible that they be allowed to say this is only the beginning? How is it possible that they be allowed to take more lives?

It was all too possible. The hunt was up. Threats were multiplying. And already handbills were being circulated by the right-wing groups: 'Be a patriot, kill a priest.'

5

It was in truth 'only the beginning'. In Aguilares, parish of the late Rutilio Grande, the *campesinos* had taken over some land and planted a crop on it. (Legally this was forbidden.) On 19 May security forces occupied the village and forbade anybody to leave. A villager who tried to climb the church tower to sound an alarm bell was killed; every house in the village was searched; all possessors of Bibles or hymn books were arrested. Many were beaten up, shot or hacked to death. Four (foreign) Jesuits were dragged out of the church, tortured and dumped over the border in Guatemala. A Salvadorean Jesuit, Fr. Guevara, was handcuffed and thrown into a truck crammed with bewildered *campesinos*. They were imprisoned, and in between beatings the priest was tied to the bars of his cell.

The occupation of Aguilares lasted for a full month, and in that time everything in sight was destroyed. In the church the tabernacle was emptied and the communion breads scattered on the floor. Bishop Romero asked his people to open their homes to the refugees who had fled to the city and had nowhere to go. When he installed a new pastor at Aguilares in June he told the people: 'My job seems to be to go around picking up insults and corpses, and all that the persecution of the Church leaves behind.' He asked them to look for a redemptive meaning to their pain and suffering: those who took up the cross, he said, were following Christ. Forgiveness, too, was part of the Christian witness; there must be no hatred, no vengeful feelings. 'Let us pray for the conversion of those who struck us . . . of those who sacrilegiously dared to touch the sacred tabernacle. Let us pray to the Lord for forgiveness and for the due repentance of those who turned this town into a prison and a place of torture. May the Lord touch their hearts.'

Five thousand people applauded his words, their former doubts about the Archbishop forgotten. Two months later he was among them again and found a very different atmosphere, charged with tension and fear, the sense of being watched, of informers lurking everywhere. Yet in spite of everything the Christian communities were continuing to meet. 'The Church will remain faithful to its message,' Romero encouraged them, 'opposing brute force and psychological warfare with love and truth.'

Newspaper attacks on Archbishop Romero and his clergy grew more frequent and more venomous. As a sign of his disapproval of the government, Romero refused to attend the inauguration ceremony at which General Carlos Humberto Romero became President of El Salvador. The Archbishop went on radio to explain his action, but insisted that the Church had not broken off relations with the government.

The General, however, in his inaugural speech had spoken of 'small misunderstandings' with the Church. They were not 'small misunderstandings' at all, claimed the Archbishop. 'The Church preaches a just order and if it is not so understood but, rather, interpreted as subversion, then it is not a matter of minor differences but of something much more substantial.' Before there could be any dialogue between the Church and the government, continued Romero, there must be an end to the repression, an explanation of the murders of priests and laymen, and a return of those priests who had been summarily deported.

August 15, 1977, was the Archbishop's sixtieth birthday, and he marked the occasion by opening a coffee bar for his priests at the archdiocesan offices, where they could meet and discuss the latest developments in the country; and by leaving the episcopal palace. He went to live at the Divine Providence Hospital, a cancer hospital for the indigent poor.

The killings and torture continued, and thousands simply 'disappeared'. One day in December 1977, Bishop Romero said Mass for a group of mothers whose sons had done just that. His homily moved the women to tears: 'Like Mary at the foot of the Cross,' he said, 'every mother who suffers the outrage done to her child is a denunciation. Mary, the sorrowing mother before the power of Pontius Pilate who has unjustly killed her son, is the cry of justice, of love, of peace, of what God wills, in the face of what God does not will, in the face of outrage, in the face of what should not be.'

To preach thus, he insisted, was not politics but the denunciation of sin. 'This is what the Church is doing, crying out against the sin that enthrones itself in history, in the life of the nation, to say: let not the demon rule, let not hate rule, let not violence rule, let not fear rule. Let love rule, let peace rule in our homes, let what has caused distress return to calm.'

By now the audience for his sermons, broadcast each Sunday live on the Church's network YSAX, stretched beyond the confines of the archdiocese, far beyond the boundaries even of El Salvador. He came to be heard all over Central America and beyond, in Venezuela, in Colombia, even in Argentina. Romero commanded the largest audience of any programme in the country, and though many were afraid of the consequences of being caught listening to him (and many resorted to headphones so as to be less conspicuous), it was reckoned that 75 per cent of the *campesinos* and nearly 50 per cent of those in the urban areas tuned in each Sunday to hear the Archbishop's homily.

The explanation is simple. In a land where truth had long been degraded into propaganda, Oscar Romero spoke the truth. It was his way of joining in the struggle for justice. He was, says Jesuit theologian, Jon Sobrino, 'an impassioned teller of the truth'; and in speaking the truth he had a profoundly humanising effect on those who heard his words. He made it clear that truth was a basic necessity for any society, the basis of all personal and public relationships. Without it a society must collapse into ruin. Romero, says Fr. Sobrino, 'restored value to the silenced, manipulated, distorted word; and he made the word what it ought to be – the expression of reality.'

Always Romero sought dialogue with his people, and he involved them all in writing the sermons. Everyone contributed, priests, nuns, laity; they brought ideas, insights, information, illumination – and bald statistics. In the homilies the Archbishop would start with the scriptural readings for the day, and relate the words and experiences of Jesus to whatever was happening in El Salvador. He looked for new ways of bringing the Gospel to life for his people, of making them see its value in the light of their own lives. He spoke of the tortures they had endured during the week and was not afraid to confront the torturers with the Gospel. Romero was fast becoming '*la voz de los sin voz*' – the voice of those who had no voice.

With the poor taking to the streets in violence and the oligarchy blaming the Church, the scandal of division within the Church itself became more painfully acute. The clergy and religious of San Salvador had earlier in the year issued a statement of support for Romero: 'Whoever touches the Archbishop touches the heart of the Church.' But the bishops were another matter. He could count on the support of only one, Bishop Arturo Rivera Damas; the other four were utterly opposed to him, regarding him with distrust and distaste as a naïve Marxist, furious that their once 'safe' candidate was engaged in compromising the Church's independence by involving it in politics. Many ordinary Catholics shared the bishops' view; they saw the attack on the social order as an attack on themselves, and believed that men like Rutilio Grande and Romero had betrayed them. An editorial in *Orientacion* suggested that there were now two Churches: 'those who feel the assassination of a priest and those who don't. Those who suffer with their tortured brothers and the unjustly persecuted, and those who will not. Those who think and feel with the Pope and the bishops, and those who think they have the deposit of the true Faith.' (27.3.77)

Despite Archbishop Romero's attempts to heal the breach with his fellow bishops, their views could not be reconciled. The gap between them was emphasised in August 1978 when the two groups of bishops produced two separate Pastoral Letters. In theirs, Romero and Rivera were concerned to offer guidance about the mushrooming popular organisations. They defended the right of all people (laid down in the UN Charter as well as in the Papal encyclical *Pacem In Terris* and the Council Decree *Gaudium et Spes*) to organise themselves for their own protection and in furtherance of their own just aims. They pointed out that those organisations which supported the government were given complete freedom of action, whereas opposition groups were denied legal recognition and were terrorised by brute force. It was not that they intended to defend terrorism or anarchy: it had always been the Church's teaching 'that the end does not justify criminal means and that there is no freedom to do evil.' But it was fatally easy, they stressed, to confuse just demands with 'terrorism' or 'subversion'. This implied a tremendous challenge to the Church, which was required to serve the real needs of the people and to shed the light of faith, hope and love on their search for liberation. The two bishops were careful to explain what they meant by liberation:

It proceeds from a Gospel vision of man and is based on deep motives of justice in charity. It has within it a truly spiritual dimension and has as its final goal salvation and happiness in God. It demands conversion of heart and mind and is not satisfied with merely changing structures. It excludes violence, which it considers 'unchristian and un-evangelical', ineffective and unworthy of the humanity of the people.

The letter unreservedly condemned all forms of violence, the brute terrorism of the security forces and para-military groups on the one hand, the violence of revolution on the other. But Romero and Rivera underlined that the original violence in El Salvador, the root cause of the trouble, masqueraded as order. 'The institutionalised violence . . . (by which) the majority of men and women and above all children in our country find themselves deprived of the necessities of life;' the established system which depended on the majority being exploited by the privileged few. The monstrous fruit of such built-in violence was the repressive force used to extinguish the voice of protest. All the rest followed in a bloody sequence, violence breeding more violence in an unending spiral, with left-wing extremists claiming that violence was the only way to justice.

Did sentiments like these give too partisan a view of the situation? Certainly the other four Salvadorean bishops thought so, for they rushed into print with a Pastoral of their own containing a flat condemnation of the popular, Marx-contaminated organisations. While admitting that no one may deny the right of free association for just ends, they sternly insisted that Marxism was incompatible with Christianity. They warned priests of the danger of reducing the mission of the Church to its purely temporal aspect, of equating salvation with material comfort.

In fact, Romero too was wary of certain priests who had plunged recklessly into politics and were demanding that the Church identify itself publicly with the left-wing activists. The Archbishop continued to keep his distance from all purely political groups. His enemies could find no justification for their accusations against him: he was a severe critic of the unjust feudal laws and he was committed to the service of the poor. With him the Gospel always came first and he saw very clearly the dangers of immersing the Church in partisan politics. 'Just as with every human activity, politics requires a pastoral orientation. Our situation becomes grave when many Christians living in such a political milieu as exists in this country, take up a political position before they have found their Christian identity.'

The bishops did not give Romero the benefit of the doubt. It did indeed seem that there were two Churches. Unlike the conservatives, who wished to preserve some sort of influence within society and were radically opposed to any social change, Romero's Church wanted to proclaim the Gospel and live its message without fear and without self-interest, adapting it to the needs of the time and place in which they found themselves. The bishops, and the papal nuncio, found this intolerable and began to think up ways of removing this 'turbulent priest' from office.

Matters came to a head when Pope Paul died in August 1978, and the nuncio invited Archbishop Romero to an official reception to celebrate the inauguration of Pope John Paul I. Romero, who did not want to be seen (and photographed) chatting to top officials of the land with a cocktail in his hand, declined the invitation. A few days later he heard that the nuncio and Cardinal Casariego from neighbouring Guatemala were going to Rome, and had agreed with the President that they should advocate Romero's removal. Nor were they alone: the American and Salvadorean ambassadors to the Vatican were making similar requests on behalf of their governments.

Personal attacks on the Archbishop became more virulent. He was crazy, said one rumour; a political agitator, suggested another; the dupe of the Jesuits, insinuated a third. Pamphlets, cartoons, sickening caricatures abounded, the result of a million-dollar smear campaign launched by the landowners, entrepreneurs and the government. 'Marxnulfo', they called him, 'Oscar Marxnulfo Romero'. A new newspaper, dedicated to refuting the Archbishop's homilies, was financed, like the rest of the campaign, by limitless private funds and by voluntary donations. 'Give, to stop the bishop' the readers were urged. If such crude propaganda and such facile hatred were aimed at producing a nervous breakdown in the Archbishop, its perpetrators must have been disappointed. Romero, by all accounts a sick man before becoming Archbishop, always taking pills to soothe his nerves, had never felt better, although death threats, anonymous letters and obscene phone calls had become a part of his daily life, and he had to admit that at times he felt mortally afraid.

But if Romero had powerful enemies, he had many friends too. His reputation had spread to many different countries, including Britain. In November 1978, one hundred and eighteen members of the British Parliament nominated Oscar Romero for the 1979 Nobel Peace Prize. The consternation of the Salvadorean government and the conservatives in the hierarchy may well be imagined. That the thorn in their flesh, the arch-troublemaker, should be held up to the international gaze as a man of peace was a bitter pill to swallow. The award that year went to Mother Teresa of Calcutta. But the mere fact of being nominated gave Romero the encouragement, support and protection he needed for the difficult tasks that lay ahead.

6

One Friday evening in January 1979, a group of about thirty young Christians gathered for a weekend retreat sponsored by the parish of San Antonio Abad. Their meeting place was El Despertar (which means 'the awakening'), a rough brick building standing in a narrow unpaved street. With them was a Belgian nun and the 34-year-old conductor of the retreat, Father Octavio Ortiz Luna.

At six the next morning, while the retreatants were still asleep, security forces drew up in an armoured car. Battering down the iron gate leading into the yard, police and national guardsmen rushed into the house, rifles already blazing. Fr. Ortiz went downstairs to investigate, and was gunned down in the yard. (When his body was discovered, his face and one side of his head had been smashed in.) In the commotion that followed, four of the young men were shot dead, two of them fifteen-year-olds, the others around twenty-two. All the others were rounded up by the police, even the small children of one of the kitchen ladies.

In the security forces' report of these events, El Despertar was portrayed as a training centre for subversives and guerrillas. And that, protested the Archbishop, was 'a lie from beginning to end'. Octavio Ortiz was the fourth priest to be killed in the present wave of terror: in November, Father Ernesto (Neto) Barrera had been murdered in what the authorities alleged was a shoot-out with the security forces. But the killing of Fr. Ortiz was a direct frontal attack on the Archbishop, for the two men were known to be close friends. Ortiz was the spiritual director at the junior seminary in San Salvador, a man who was highly respected.

Over one hundred priests gathered next day in the cathedral for Romero's regular eight a.m. Mass. Outside a crowd of about fifteen thousand gathered, and an altar was set up outside the main entrance. It was Christian Unity week, and the Archbishop had invited Dr. Jorge Lara-Braud, representing both the US National Council of Churches and the World Council of Churches, to preach in his cathedral. Dr. Lara-Braud addressed the congregation on that morning, reflecting that 'Christian unity is never stronger than when it is sealed by the blood of the martyrs,' and going on to hope that the murder of Fr. Ortiz and the four young men had not been in vain. 'They have preceded us in the experience of the Resurrection,' he said, 'we honour them and our faith by living unafraid, by knowing that evil has no future.' The Archbishop followed his guest speaker. Denying the accounts put out by the government, he appealed for an end to the brutality of the security forces, and for a common effort to 'search for the root of our ills and bring about the daring and urgent changes that our society needs.'

Even in El Salvador where murder was an everyday occurrence, these latest killings produced a sense of outrage. An article entitled 'We've Had Enough' appeared in *Orientacion*:

This tragic and unjust situation forces us to shout with our Archbishop, ENOUGH. Enough of blood and assassination, enough of violence, enough of kidnappings and guerrillas, an end to repression . . . In no way do we want vengeance; we ask only for some justice that will awaken the hope of the people, a hope that – by non-violent means – will bring the day when one can openly enjoy human rights and the rights of the children of God. May no lie or calumny sully the bloody but pure sacrifice of these new Salvadorean martyrs. (28.1.79.)

Priests and nuns took to the streets with banners reading 'Enough, no more'. The phrase, in Spanish *Basta Ya*, became a slogan of defiance. But the repression continued, even though at that very moment the President was in Mexico, assuring questioners that in El Salvador there were no political prisoners, no 'disappearances', no police brutality, nothing resembling persecution.

Two days after the murders at El Despertar, Romero flew to Puebla in Mexico where the new Pope John Paul II was to address the assembled Latin American bishops. Would the spirit of Medellin be upheld? Or would the Church make a U-turn, as many of the bishops undoubtedly hoped? The arguments raged back and forth, but in the end the bishops at Puebla (perhaps a shade less enthusiastically than at Medellin), once again made 'the preferential option for the poor'. By which, they explained, they did not mean the exclusion of the rich, 'but rather, a call to the rich – to feel as their own the problems of the poor'. When Archbishop Romero appeared he received a standing ovation from the journalists present, and after the applause had died down, he told them the news which had just reached him – that a right-wing group had put out a contract on his life.

The murder of Fr. Rafael Palacios, on 20 June, 1979, brought the number of murdered priests to five in two years; whereupon the Archbishop called on the government to control 'these forces of hell and murder.' 'How long,' he asked, 'are we to endure these crimes without any just atonement?' Fr. Rafael, he said, was a victim of 'the structural sin built into, embedded in our society'; the young priest had paid with his life for denouncing that sin.

He needed now to explain to the people what had transpired at Puebla; and in August he announced that he had a fourth Pastoral Letter in view and would welcome any suggestions. The theme was to be 'The Mission of the Church in the Nation's Crisis'. As always, he tried to keep alive the dialogue with the people begun at the time of the third Letter. Questionnaires were distributed among the grass-roots communities and the Catholic organisations; and in the end he was able to say with justification: 'together we have written this Letter.'

But the comments on Puebla were his own. All that Puebla had said about social injustice was true of El Salvador, he told them. The Church must look to the liberating message of the Gospel and make its choice for the poor and oppressed, though its call must be to rich and poor alike. Puebla had called for new attitudes, a new awareness; and the Church must adapt its pastoral practice to its actual situation. He stressed, as he had often stressed before, that the Church must put its weight behind those Christians who had found their vocation in political activism. The apostolate of companionship, he called it, 'so that these Christians may feel that wherever they go they carry the germ, the word, the seed of salvation, the light of the Gospel.'

Meanwhile the economic situation in El Salvador was lurching from bad to worse, and the government was increasingly unable to cope. The organised movements among the poor gained in strength and momentum, and the country drifted steadily towards civil war. A sixth priest, Fr. Alirio Napoleon Macias was murdered, the Archbishop was continually harassed. But he would not accept any protection. 'The shepherd does not want security while security is not given to his flock,' he said.

Amid general scepticism President Carlos Humberto Romero told a press conference that he was ready to hold free elections and let the International Red Cross into the prisons to see that there were no political prisoners. He would allow the exiles to return, he promised, and would order an investigation into the murder of Fr. Macias.

Why, asked the Archbishop, did the President speak of necessary changes, yet continue to torture and kill anyone who actually sought such changes? He proceeded to read out the names of those who had 'disappeared' or been arrested in the preceding week, and produced a letter from a woman whose husband, son and brother had all been rounded up on the same day. 'This is the voice that is not heard, and that we must make heard. It would not be a true Gospel if we were indifferent in the face of such anguish.' And he voiced the fears of many that if (as was probable) the Red Cross did not find any political prisoners in the cells, then what had happened to those who had disappeared, and where were they?

In a homily preached in the following month, October 1979, Romero was more specific: 'The government has emptied the prisons of political prisoners,' he accused, 'but the cemeteries have filled with the dead.'

On 15 October, 1979, a group of young army officers staged a successful coup d'état. They set up a reforming junta which included civilians with impeccable credentials. The new leaders promised reforms, and Archbishop Romero was prepared to test their good intentions. The junta were reckoning, though, without the entrenched power of the landed élite. The latter were now recovering from the first shock of the coup and were beginning to fight back, organising street demonstrations and a publicity campaign in the media attacking the new junta. Their trump card was their control of the army, and when they restructured the army high command on 18 December they had in effect brought off a counter-coup and stalemated the junta. The military men now held the power and could dictate government policy. So a policy of alternate stick and carrot came into being. The army would allow some reforms but apparently reserved their 'right' to kill, beat, torture or arrest anyone they chose. Most of the junta, including all its civilian members, resigned in protest, leaving the military a completely free hand.

Archbishop Romero continued to hope against hope, and in so doing he lost the support of many of the popular organisations. In his 6 January homily, Romero reproached them:

No one has a right to sink into despair. We all have the duty to seek new channels together and to hope actively – as Christians . . . Using a comparison from today's Gospel, we might say that the star that must today guide the people, the government and the various sectors of society must be this: how to keep the march of the people towards social justice from becoming stagnant and atrophied; and how to preserve and further it.

In January 1980, when the Christian Democratic Party offered to form a new government with the military, it seemed as though Romero's hopes might be justified after all. The Christian Democrats demanded guarantees, such as an end to repression; but it soon became clear that the guarantees were worthless. As far as the military were concerned, the Christian Democratic connection would be merely a convenient facade behind which the repression could continue as before.

As the leftist groups sank their differences and began to co-ordinate their activities, they gradually became a coherent focus of opposition to the government. In his homilies of 13 and 20 January 1980, Romero analysed all three of the political options: the oligarchy, the government and the left. Reminding the oligarchs of John Paul's words at Puebla, – 'the Church does defend the lawful right of private property, but it teaches with no less clarity that all private property bears a social mortgage, to the common good' – he begged them to come to their senses. 'I call on them to hear the voice of God and joyously share their power and wealth with all, instead of provoking a civil war that will drown us all in blood. There is still time to take the rings from their fingers before they lose the whole hand.'

At the same time he urged the Christian Democrats to understand that as long as the oligarchy and the armed forces held the real power, reformist solutions were just not possible, and the Christian Democratic presence in the government served only to disguise the evil character of the regime: 'for their hands are red with blood as never before.'

On 22 January, 1980, on the anniversary of the 1932 peasant uprising, the left-wing organisations planned a large demonstration in the capital. But as the crowds assembled in the Plaza, riflemen opened fire, leaving twenty dead and 120 wounded. Immediately the government blacked out all radio stations, allowing only official accounts of the day's events. Romero hurried to open his archdiocesan offices to shelter the refugees from the attack. He was appalled by this senseless massacre of the people 'for taking to the streets in orderly fashion to petition for justice and liberty.' 'The cry for liberation of this people is a shout that rises up to God, and that nothing and no one can stop.' He reminded his hearers that human life did not end with the destruction of the body, and that full liberation could only be achieved after death. 'Temporal liberations are only worth struggling for in so far as they reflect on this earth the justice of the kingdom of God.'

Passionately he pleaded with all the warring factions, to leave the ways of violence; and he paid tribute to 'the maturity and good sense' of the popular organisations which had not allowed themselves to be provoked into counter-violence by the recent massacre. 'Making the revolution,' he cautioned them, 'is *not* killing other persons, because only God is the master of life. Making the revolution is not painting slogans on walls or shouting in the streets without thinking. Making the revolution is thinking out political designs that stand a better chance of building a society of justice and brotherhood.'

But by now the spiral of violence was out of control. The supporters of the leftist groups had learned the lesson that peaceful demonstrations would bear no fruit. From then on they would take care to be armed.

7

On 2 February, 1980, Oscar Romero received an honorary doctorate from the University of Louvain in Belgium. He attempted to convey to the audience in the hall and beyond, something of the reality of life in El Salvador, where the coup d'état had failed to put an end to the repression which now proceeded more bloodily than ever. El Salvador, he told them, was reliving the Crucifixion. 'The poor are the body of Christ today. Through them he lives on in history.'

From Louvain he travelled to Rome where he received a sympathetic hearing from Pope John Paul. All this was noted. The fact of Romero's growing international status and influence could only be interpreted at home as a threat to the reactionary government. And when, on his return from Europe, he drafted a letter to President Carter, begging him to reconsider a decision to send military aid to the government of El Salvador, that threat assumed alarming proportions. The letter attracted enormous world-wide attention and the government saw its very lifeline threatened. Romero had become dangerous.

Almost certainly Romero himself realised it. It is possible to read in his last pronouncements an awareness of his own approaching death. His final sermons are the most memorable of his life. On 17 February he preached on the Beatitudes: 'Blessed are the poor,' Christ had said, and his Church had to become incarnated among the poor, proclaiming the good news of salvation to them, as Jesus himself had done. But poverty is not just the lack of material goods, it is also a Christian virtue of complete openness to God, unhindered by attachment to worldly things.

> Blessed are you poor, for yours is the kingdom of God. You are the most able to understand what those who are on their knees before false idols do not understand. You who do not have those idols, you who do not trust in them because you have no money or power, you who are deprived of everything, the poorer you are, the more you possess the kingdom of God, provided you truly live that spirituality. The poverty that Jesus Christ here dignifies is not simply a material poverty, not just having nothing. It is a poverty that awakens consciousness, a poverty that accepts the cross and sacrifice – not out of conformity, but because it knows that that is *not* the will of God.

In the name of the Christian commitment to Christ in his poor, Archbishop Romero called on the Christian Democrats to leave the government. It was a profoundly shocking appeal. Next day a bomb destroyed the Church's radio transmitter at YSAX. The nation was stunned. Messages of support came in from an assembly of Latin American bishops in Brazil; and even the junta saw fit to deplore the attack.

The following Sunday was the first of Lent. Those who had them brought cassette recorders in order to record the homily, which on that day could not be broadcast. The Gospel reading told of Christ's temptations in the wilderness, his refusal of power and wealth. Instead, said the Archbishop, he had chosen 'a simple life, an ordinary life, to which he gave a meaning of love and of freedom. How beautiful our country would be if we all lived this plan of God, each one busy in his or her own job, not claiming to dominate anyone, simply earning and eating the bread that the family needs.'

That very week Pope John Paul had invited Catholics to mark the beginning of Lent by giving up their superfluous wealth in order to help the needy and disadvantaged of the world. Why, asked Romero, could not the oligarchy take heed of the Pope's request?

Let them share what they have. Let them not keep silencing with violence the voice of those of us who offer this invitation. Let them not keep killing those of us who are trying to achieve a more just sharing of the power and wealth of our country.

Lowering his voice, he continued, in a way that sent a shudder through the congregation:

I speak in the first person, because this week I received notice that I am on the list of those who are to be eliminated next week. But let it be known that no one can any longer still the voice of justice.

He was not in the habit of drawing attention to the many death threats that he received; this time he must have sensed that his enemies could no longer afford to let him live.

Time was running out. He was invited to rest in Nicaragua,

but he would not leave his people. Instead he went to the hills above San Salvador to make a last retreat. There he made his confession and told the elderly confessor that he felt his end to be imminent. The prospect weighed heavily on him, filling him with fear; but he would not run away. In this Gethsemane of his spirit, he professed himself ready to drink the cup of suffering to the dregs.

It must have been now that he telephoned a Mexican newspaper reporter and gave him a valedictory message. Jose Calderon Salazar, Guatemala correspondent of the Mexican *Excelsior*, later reported the following words spoken to him by Archbishop Romero:

I have often been threatened with death. Nevertheless, as a Christian, I do not believe in death without resurrection. If they kill me, I shall rise again in the Salvadorean people. I say this in all humility, without boasting.

As a pastor, I am obliged by divine decree to give my life for those I love – for all Salvadoreans, even for those who may be about to kill me. If the threats come to be fulfilled, from this moment I offer my blood to God for the redemption and resurrection of El Salvador.

Martyrdom is a grace of God that I do not believe I deserve. But if God accepts the sacrifice of my life, let my blood be a seed of freedom and the sign that hope will soon be reality. Let my death, if it is accepted by God, be for the liberation of my people, and as a witness of hope in the future.

You may say, if they succeed in killing me, that I pardon and bless those who do the deed. Would that they might be convinced that they are wasting their time! A bishop will die, but the Church of God, which is the people, will never perish. (Reproduced in *Orientacion*, 13.4.80)

*   *   *

The governing junta was falling apart at the seams. Many of its members resigned. At five p.m. on 9 March, Romero said Mass for Mario Zamora, a Christian Democrat politician murdered by a death squad the previous week. Many Christian Democrat leaders attended the funeral Mass. Next morning a workman in the basilica discovered a suitcase filled with seventy-two sticks of dynamite, enough to destroy the whole basilica. It had been primed to explode during the Mass but had somehow failed to detonate. 'I wish to put on record,' commented the Archbishop, 'that far from feeling fear, I am more confident than ever that God takes care of us.'

On 16 March, in a sermon lasting for an hour and three quarters, punctuated throughout by impassioned applause, Romero preached on reconciliation.

> We live in groups, polarised (he said sadly). Perhaps even within the same group, people don't love each other; for there can be no love where people take sides to the point of hating others. We need to burst these bonds of hatred, we need to feel that there is a Father who loves us all and longs for us all. We need to pray the Our Father and tell him, 'Forgive us as we forgive.'

The people hung breathlessly on every word, as he went on to warn all sectors of society:

> Nothing violent can be lasting. There is still the possibility of a reasonable solution. Above all there is the Word of God, which cries today for reconciliation. God wills it – let us be reconciled, and we shall make of El Salvador a land of brothers and sisters, all children of one Father who awaits us all with outstretched arms.

On the previous day, security forces had killed a whole family in the village of La Laguna, as well as eleven other *campesinos*; elsewhere four *campesinos* including two children; and in another village, three. Fear was mounting. On Monday bombs went off in San Salvador and throughout the entire country. The military besieged the national university and bursts of machine gun fire made their staccato din all day. In Colima, eighteen persons died. At the end of the day the nationwide toll of dead was sixty.

All week the terror raged. By the following Sunday, the YSAX transmitter was repaired and Romero's last homily went out to the nation. It was almost as though he knew he was speaking to them for the last time, for he tried to sum up all that he had attempted to teach them:

I have tried during these Sundays of Lent to keep uncovering in the divine revelation contained in the Gospel readings, God's programme of salvation for nations and individuals. Today when our people stand at the crossroads of history, we can say with confidence: the way that better reflects God's plan will win the day. This is the Church's mission. In the light of God's word it is our duty to point to the realities, and to see how God's plan is furthered by us or rejected by us. Let no one take it ill that in the light of God's word read in our Mass we seek to shed light on social, political and economic realities. If we did not, it would not be Christianity for us. It is thus that Christ willed to become incarnate, so that the light that he brings from the Father may become the life of men and of nations.

In a final challenge which must surely have sealed his fate even if it had not already been settled, Romero appealed to the men of the army and the national guard.

Brothers (he pleaded), you are part of our own people. You are killing your own brothers and sisters. No soldier is obliged to obey an order that is contrary to the law of God. Nobody has to fulfil an immoral law . . . In the name of God, and in the name of this suffering people, whose cries rise to heaven each day more despairingly, I beg you, I plead with you, I order you in the name of God: *cease the repression.*

When he had finished, the applause, which had interrupted him five times in the course of this homily, went on for a full half-minute. But in the eyes of the authorities what he had just said was treason. A spokesman for the armed forces described the Archbishop's words as 'criminal'. It was expedient now that 'one man should die for the people'. The forces of law and order could not afford to fail.

Only the last act remained to be played, and the curtain had already risen on it. On Monday morning he went to confession; he was to say the six p.m. evening Mass in the chapel of the cancer hospital where he lived. 'I want to feel clean in the presence of the Lord,' he told his confessor.

The Mass was for the mother of a friend, and unwisely its time and location had been announced in the press. 'Though I walk in the valley of the shadow of death, yet will I fear no evil, for Thou art with me,' he read aloud from the Twenty-third Psalm; and the Gospel reading took up this theme of death and resurrection: 'The hour has come for the Son of Man to be glorified . . . Unless the grain of wheat falls to the ground and dies, it remains only a grain. But if it dies, it bears much fruit . . .'

As he always did, the Archbishop based his homily on the readings:

You have just heard the Gospel of Christ that one must not love oneself to the point of refusing to become involved in the risks of life that history demands of us; and that those who fend off danger will lose their lives. But whoever, out of love for Christ, gives himself to the service of others, will live, like the grain of wheat that dies, but only seems to die. If it did not die it would remain alone. Only in undoing itself does it produce the harvest.

When he had finished speaking a shot rang out. Romero died instantly, shot through a main artery. And in the uproar that was let loose, the assailant or assailants made their escape – and have never been brought to justice.

The news spread like a bush fire and the Salvadoreans were stricken. Thousands waited to see the body as it lay in the basilica, and when on the Wednesday it was moved to the cathedral, the crowds filed weeping past the glass-topped coffin, touching it, pressing against it. With difficulty, and at enormous risk to themselves, *campesinos* poured into the

city, queueing in the blazing sun for their turn to take a last
look at the man they had known as Monseñor.

To the anguished question, Why did he have to die? the
people replied as one: 'because he loved the poor'. In the
cathedral, Fr. Cesar Jerez, provincial of the Jesuits in Central
America, made the same comment. And *The Times* of London in an editorial on the day following Romero's death
backed this view. Romero 'was killed because he had become
a symbol of the need for human rights and social justice.' In
the last weeks of his life he had become a real threat to the
junta, as he appealed to President Carter for an arms embar-
go, and to the military to stop the terror. Worse, perhaps, he
had begun to shake international confidence in the regime's
credibility.

Naturally the junta professed themselves shaken by the
murder, and proclaimed three days of official mourning for
'this most vile of crimes'. As messages of sympathy and of
condemnation of the violence began to flood into the
archdiocesan offices, even the bishops were united in horror.
They excommunicated the murderers and praised their dead
colleague as one who 'remained faithful to his motto of
speaking the truth in an effort to build true peace and justice'.
They spoke of the context of 'violence that reaches the limits
of madness' and praised Romero's tireless campaign against
'institutionalised injustice and abuses against human rights
and the inalienable dignity of man'. This had gained him the
esteem of friends and strangers alike, they admitted, though it
had also 'aroused the animosity of those who felt uncomfortable from the force of his evangelical word and witness. For
being faithful to the Word, he fell, like the great prophets.'
Yet none of them, apart from Rivera Damas, attended Oscar
Romero's funeral, though there were bishops in plenty from
other parts of the world.

And as the thousands gathered on the Sunday morning in
the cathedral square, a sinister epilogue was being prepared.
Members of the popular organisations were getting ready to
march to the square, where a sea of humanity already heaved
and swayed: about two hundred and fifty thousand people,
among them *campesinos* who had come by bus, by lorry, or on

foot. There were no crush barriers, no police to keep order, only a handful of boy scouts.

Mass had already begun on the steps of the cathedral when suddenly the air was filled with the thunder of an explosion. Shots rang out, and the thousands panicked and stampeded, fleeing into the surrounding streets and into the cathedral, screaming, praying, shouting. Most, probably all, of the forty who died that morning, died of heart failure or asphyxiation, or were trampled under foot.

The Archbishop's body was hastily lowered into its tomb. That afternoon an official broadcast placed the blame for the disaster on the popular organisations, but hardly anyone believed that version of events. There were too many witnesses who could give it the lie. Few people doubted that the bomb which caused the panic had been flung from the National Palace on the far side of the cathedral square. Even before Mass had begun, the Nicaraguan Foreign Minister, Fr. Miguel d'Escoto, had been handed a note which told him there were snipers positioned on the palace roof.

That evening, twenty-four of the foreign mourners met at the archdiocesan offices. They issued a statement, signed by eight bishops and sixteen others, in which they rejected outright the government version of the day's events. In their statement they paid glorious tribute to the murdered Archbishop:

> For defending the life of his people and striving for a society of justice and peace, he was murdered, like Christ, at the moment of offertory. From the very beginning of his ministry he had to witness the blood of martyrdom, the suffering of his people. That blood and that pain strengthened him in his determination to be the faithful and understanding shepherd who never abandoned his flock, who lent them his voice and who gave his life for them.

*   *   *

> I come to sing you a sad tale,
> not even the bullets can silence me;
> Monseñor Romero has fallen,

and his body, stretched on the floor,
arouses the people who begin to shout:

We've had enough, we've had enough,
we've had enough of death and falsehood.
We've had enough, we've had enough,
is the cry of El Salvador.

Three years he spent
fearlessly preaching justice and love,
defender of the poor and humble
who suffer at the hand of the exploiter,
voice of the men without voice,
voice of the people of El Salvador.
(Adapted from the popular song, *Basta Ya.*)

It was not only Dr. Lara-Braud who drew the parallels between Romero's life and that of Jesus: the obscure early life culminating in a three-year ministry of prophetic intensity; the love for the oppressed which led him to lay his life on the line; the appeal to all men to unharden their hearts, to change (repent) while there was still time. Oscar Romero had faithfully lived as Jesus in El Salvador might have lived; and he paid the price that his master paid for living the logic of that life. Like Jesus, he had driven the men of power to fear for their own positions and privileges and 'it was expedient that one man should die for the people.'

The poor of El Salvador have long since canonised Monseñor. For them and for those who care for them, Monseñor is the man who told the truth about their misery and who encouraged those who wanted to bring hope to the suffering. Committees, human rights organisations, small churches bear his name; his photograph is treasured, the demand for his homilies phenomenal. Pilgrims visit his tomb and leave messages, cards and flowers. If to be alive is to live in the hearts of the people, then Oscar Romero is indeed living still.

He had to be silenced because the evil he uncovered was too deep rooted, because the good to which he pointed could not be achieved without radical and painful personal conversion. Many who believed him to be right dared not follow where he led because they dared not tread the road to Calvary. In their hearts they must have known that he spoke the truth, that he more than anyone recognised the tortured reality of life in El Salvador for what it was. 'This is the kingdom of Hell,' he had once said. The twin idols of absolute wealth and national security demanded human sacrifice for their survival, and the hundreds of thousands of Salvadoreans who die slowly from hunger or brutally by machine gun or machete, are the unfortunate victims. 'What happens in El Salvador today,' says Fr. John Sobrino, 'can only be described as a new crucifixion; and the Christian is faced with one crucial question: Were you there when they crucified the Lord?'

Oscar Romero had a real faith. He believed in the God who makes an absolute demand of his children: that they should strive to become more human, by ridding themselves of what is less than human in their make-up. He was on his guard against anything that might dehumanise people – in whatever political system. He was not, as his accusers would have it, a dupe of the left; he understood the dangers from that quarter very well. What he wanted was to see man living his life as God willed him to live it: a new man in a new society built on peace, justice and love. He would have no truck with those who preached hatred or looked for revenge. Dialogue, hope, reconciliation: these were the key words in his thinking. 'In dialogue,' he said, '*all* have the right to be heard.' Five days before he was murdered, he was still clinging to the hope that reason would prevail over madness. 'If we are reasonable,' he urged, 'if we make use of our superior capacity for reason, we can resolve the problem peacefully. But if we persist in the polarisation of our society, the spiral of violence will grow and will result in worse misery.'

Reason, as we know, did not prevail. In the first two years after Romero's death thirty-five thousand Salvadoreans died, 15 per cent of the population were driven into exile and more than two thousand 'disappeared'. And there is now no powerful voice to speak for the voiceless. The Church which gave such a clear lead under Monseñor now speaks with many voices and less confidence. But the poor – the *empobreci-*

dos – remain, 'the microphones of God' Romero called them. He foretold that if he died he would rise again in the Salvadorean people. Perhaps that was presumptuous of him. For the moment they are still undergoing crucifixion and the time for resurrection has not yet come. But they treasure the memory of the man who gave them hope, who restored their human dignity and who loved them. For them he will remain one of the most illustrious men in the history of their tragic country – and the most deeply loved of them all.

*   *   *

When Pope John Paul II visited El Salvador in March 1983, he prayed at the tomb of Oscar Romero, praising him as a model bishop and echoing Romero's call for peace and respect for human rights in El Salvador. This apparently routine and innocuous gesture on the part of Pope John Paul was understood on both sides of the divide in El Salvador as some sort of affirmation and endorsement of what Romero had stood for. The authorities were predictably dismayed. Indeed, posters showing Pope John Paul in friendly conversation with Archbishop Romero had already been impounded by the security forces before the visit.

On the eve of his departure from Central America, the Pope had (belatedly) appointed the popular Bishop Rivera as Romero's successor to the see of San Salvador, thereby giving a posthumous seal of approval to the martyred Archbishop. To the great joy of the Salvadorean people, Archbishop Rivera promptly announced that he intended to petition for the beatification of Oscar Romero, their beloved Monseñor.

6.
Maria Skobtsova
1891–1945

I regard Mother Maria as the most outstanding woman of the Russian Emigration. Her life and destiny reflect, so to speak, the destiny of a whole era. In her personality were blended all the qualities beloved in Russian female saints: oneness with the universe, the longing to alleviate human suffering, the spirit of self-sacrifice; and utter fearlessness.

Nikolai Berdyaev

I searched for thinkers and for prophets
who wait by the ladder to heaven,
see signs of the mysterious end,
sing songs beyond our comprehension.

And I found people who were restless, orphaned, poor,
drunk, despairing, useless,
lost whichever way they went,
homeless, naked, lacking bread.

There are no prophecies. But life
performs in a prophetic manner:
the end approaches, days grow shorter;
You took a servant's form – Hosanna.

Mother Maria (from *Stikhi*, trans. by Sergei Hackel)

1

Maria was no more her name than Maximilian had been Father Kolbe's. Her real name was Elizaveta Yurievna Pilenko and she was known to her family as Lisa. In the Baltic town of Riga where she was born in 1891, Lisa's father, Yury, was the Czar's Public Prosecutor. But being a gentle man, liberal in his politics, he did not find the work congenial; and on the death of his father, General Pilenko, he returned with his family to manage the huge estates which he had inherited in Anapa, far to the south, on the north-eastern coast of the Black Sea. Here the family lived in a long, low house set in the midst of vineyards and a fertile sweep of land which stretched as far as the sea. Lisa and her brother Mitia (Dmitri) were lively and energetic children who appreciated each other's companionship and enjoyed this idyllic setting to the full. The vineyards were so fruitful that Yury's fame spread, and he was invited not only to become Director of the famous Nikitski Botanical Gardens near Yalta, but also to take charge of the nearby school of viticulture.

Lisa was thirteen when they moved to Yalta. The year was 1905, a year full of portent for Russia and the world: the year of a General Strike, of anti-Jewish pogroms, of the mutiny of the Potemkin sailors; of revolution and bloody suppression. Yalta seethed with revolutionary ferment. The students at her father's college were a revelation to the young Lisa, with their wild-eyed talk of social upheaval. They held political meetings in the college, which Yury Pilenko did nothing to discourage; a fact which did not go unnoticed by the local authorities. Restrain the students, or get out, they told him in effect. As the students continued their seditious meetings, they and he became prime targets for the police, who one night swooped on the college estate, razing houses to the ground and savagely beating their inhabitants. It was the first of many incidents: on several occasions, students were knocked senseless in the streets and left where they fell.

Lisa was summoned to help clean their wounds, to fetch hot water and bandages. Too young to understand what it was all about, she was nevertheless fiercely partisan: the students were her own family. One day, in her father's absence, she accidentally discovered that the police were about to raid the college. Rushing to a telephone, she gave a breathless warning. When the police arrived, the college fires were burning suspiciously brightly, but no seditious literature was found on the premises. It was Lisa's first act of political resistance. It would not be the last.

On Yuri Pilenko the strain was telling. When a member of his own staff denounced him to the police, he wearily decided to return to the less embattled atmosphere of Anapa. But it was already too late. When he died the following year, Lisa could not contain her despair. Her father's death at a relatively young age was so unfair, so unnecessary; and in her youthful fury she cried aloud that 'there is no God, and there is in the world only sorrow, wickedness and injustice.'

It was the saddest, most negative time of Lisa's life. Her world fell to pieces. Her mother, Sophia, moved the family to an apartment in St. Petersburg, where they would be able to continue their studies. Lisa had always been a brilliant student, but here, in the dank fogs of this northern city, the misery of her father's death still oppressing her, she had neither appetite nor will for study. Starved of the southern sun, she went for long, solitary walks, finding nothing but emptiness as she trudged the dirty snow of St. Petersburg. 'My soul yearned for heroic action,' she recalled later. 'I longed to give my life for all the injustice in the world.'

The urge to self-sacrifice was to outlive the despair. As her energy gradually returned, she was all for laying down her life for her new-found hero, 'the people'.

Attempting to identify with the humblest and poorest, she cut short her hair, dressed simply in a plain skirt and blouse, and begged her mother's permission to give evening classes to groups of illiterate workers. She was gravitating towards the flourishing revolutionary groups in the city, though the first time she attended a meeting of the Social Democrats, whose left wing was Lenin's Bolshevik (or majority) group, she was disappointed. They were not laying down their lives, she noted, 'merely discussing surplus value, capital and the agrarian problem'. When she began to attend the Bestuzhev Courses in philosophy she was attracted to the Social Revolutionaries, though she did not as yet become a member of the party.

Throwing herself with enthusiasm into the political maelstrom of university life, eighteen-year-old Lisa met and impetuously married Dmitri Kuzmin-Karavaiev, the student president and a slightly jaded member of Lenin's Bolsheviks. Later she would admit to marrying him more out of pity than love, hoping perhaps to provide him with some kind of stability.

Marriage did not alter her way of life. She had the satisfaction of becoming the first woman student to enrol in St. Petersburg's Ecclesiastical Academy. Religion fascinated her as much as politics, though she claimed to have lost all belief. In the circle to which Dmitri introduced her, there was plenty of opportunity to test out her ideas. For she now moved into the rarefied world of the Russian intelligentsia, the new Russian Renaissance whose writers, philosophers and poets of genius held forth about the coming Revolution, too idealistic to understand that it would by its very nature devour them. Here Lisa met Nikolai Berdyaev and Alexei Tolstoy who would remain her lifelong friends; here too she met the poet, Alexander Blok, older than herself, married, with whom she established a rare, spiritual friendship. It was her strong maternal instinct that appealed to Blok; and he told her once that even when he could not see her, the knowledge that she was near gave him a sense of security.

The friends met late every evening in The Tower, an apartment whose cupola-shaped roof overlooked the Duma, the seat of government in the Tauride Palace. Night after night Lisa and her husband sat in a dense pall of cigarette smoke, endlessly discussing the existence of God and the necessity for violent social change; until, as dawn rose over the cupola, they brewed a last samovar and ate a breakfast of fried eggs before going home to sleep.

Stirring though they were, these discussions tended to make Lisa sad. She realised how far removed from real life they were, how deep the growing chasm between the intelligentsia and the people. The former talked long and loud about dying for the cause, 'and they would completely fail to understand that to die for the Revolution means to feel a real rope round your neck, to leave life behind for good on just such a grey and somnolent morning – physically and in actual fact, to die.' Their talk of religion too was cerebral and lacked the warmth of faith. Theirs was 'the wisdom of old people who had mastered everything and for whom everything had grown cold.'

Ideas, however brilliantly expressed, would never be enough for Lisa. She was a passionate woman, a woman of action, and her innate enthusiasm, referred to by Ilya Ehrenburg in his autobiography, 'for justice, for man and for God' needed more than verbal fireworks for its satisfaction.

Sadly, the marriage between herself and Dmitri was breaking down. By 1912 they were already going their separate ways; and when Lisa's daughter was born the following year, it was widely believed that another man was the father.* By this time Lisa had returned to Anapa, hoping to find happiness in closeness to the earth. Gaiana, the name she gave to her baby daughter, was a Greek word meaning 'the earthly one'. She was looking for faith. Nearness to the earth implied nearness to the people who worked on it, and nearness to the Christ whom they worshipped. Lisa still denied God; but she had a strong compassion for Christ, who had been scourged, had bled, had died for a cause. As she devoted herself to managing the estate and seeing to the grape harvests, she continued her search, praying 'intensely but fruitlessly' on the cold floor, and all 'to force Christ to reveal himself, to come to my aid . . . No, simply to let me know whether or not he exists.'

The European war had broken out. Lisa was gripped by a profound sense of destiny, a growing awareness of the prophetic role she was destined to play. At the same time she had premonitions of disaster, both personal and cosmic. 'The times are drawing to a close,' she wrote in one of the books of poetry she published in the war years. As for herself, 'a dark cross weighs my shoulders down, my way grows straiter with every stride.'

Always her mysticism was tempered by a strong streak of practicality. Regarding some sort of work for society as a necessity, she finally joined the Social Revolutionary Party, which had by now jettisoned its terrorist wing to become the

* They were legally divorced in 1916. In 1920 Dmitri was converted to Roman Catholicism and, emigrating to France, was ordained a Jesuit priest.

true heir to that nineteenth-century Russian populist tradition in which humane idealism was tinged with spirituality.
Lisa, unlike her friends, was never a Marxist, never tempted
by a totalitarian paradise. In the local party, it was her aim to
proclaim the rights of the individual, whatever his beliefs or
politics.

Events began to move fast. After the March Revolution of
1917, the Social Revolutionaries co-operated with Keren-
sky's provisional government. In the summer Lisa attended
her party's third Congress in Moscow as a delegate from the
south. But in the October Revolution, the Bolsheviks seized
power by a coup d'état; and the moderate socialists were
ousted from the government. Henceforward there would be
only one party in Russia.

Tension throughout Russia was high, and terrorism, in the
shape of Trotsky's newly formed Red Guards, took over from
reason. Hundreds were shot daily without trial, hundreds
more simply vanished. Lisa, horrified by these developments,
decided to assassinate Trotsky before he could do more
damage. Discretion not being her strong point, she made the
mistake of confiding in Alexei Tolstoy. He and her other
friends were so alarmed by Lisa's hot-headedness that they
more or less forced her to abandon her plans and leave
Petrograd (as Petersburg had been renamed in 1914). Bowing
reluctantly to their combined opposition, she left for Anapa
at the end of that fateful year.

The journey south almost cost Lisa her life. When Bolshevik sailors took over the train on which she was travelling with
a companion, they began shooting the passengers. Only
Lisa's quick-wittedness saved her. Claiming to be a friend of
Krupskaya, Lenin's wife, she demanded that a telegram be
sent to the latter informing her of her own imminent execution. Taken in by this trick, the sailors allowed Lisa and her
companion to continue their journey without even being
searched. The two women were, in fact, carrying papers and
documents which would most certainly have incriminated
them.

Arriving safely in Anapa, Lisa was elected to the town
council. By February 1918 she had become the first woman

mayor – a position fraught with danger, which few could have
envied her. For hardly had she been elected than news came
through of fighting between the Red forces and White insur-
gents. The Civil War had begun. As mayor, Lisa shared
responsibility with the newly established soviet in the area;
and she managed to create a good rapport with its Bolshevik
chairman, Protapov. Ignoring politics, she set herself to care
for a flood of homeless refugees from the north, housing many
of them on the Pilenko family estate, and opening a medical
centre where they could receive treatment. Her own people
of Anapa she did her best to protect from the ravages of war,
to keep their lives as normal as possible.

But life was far from normal. One day a band of anarchist
sailors landed in Anapa, drowned the harbour-master and
demanded a prohibitive sum in protection money from the
townspeople. They could not pay, but were terrified of the
sailors who were in ugly mood and threatening to shoot the
leading citizens. Lisa would not be browbeaten. Drawing
herself up to her full height (she was nearly six feet tall) she
gave the sailors a flat refusal. With barefaced courage she
prevailed on them to go away without harming anyone –
though they saved face by returning briefly that night and
kidnapping the chief of police and the schoolmaster whom
they took out to sea and drowned.

But when Protapov of the local soviet was murdered by his
own men, Lisa's courage failed her. Once more she left
Anapa for Moscow, only to find that the Social Revolutionaries were fighting a losing battle for survival. Sadly she returned home. The fortunes of war had shifted, and the town
was now in the hands of White Cossack forces. Lisa was
charged with collaborating with the Bolsheviks. She was
arrested, thrown into her own jail and brought to trial in
March 1919. The townspeople held their breath, fearing the
death sentence for her. They need not have worried: Lisa
defended herself with skill and energy, and after the Cossack
president of the tribunal himself intervened on her behalf, the
result was not in doubt. She was given a suspended sentence
of two months in prison. The president's name was Daniil
Skobtsov. Within a few weeks he and Lisa were married.

The White's victory was short-lived. The tide turned again in favour of the Bolsheviks. In the region around Anapa, the Civil War was over by March 1920, and the Skobtsovs, like thousands of their compatriots, decided to leave Russia 'for a while'. Daniil went first, to look for a job and somewhere for his family to settle.

Lisa was heavily pregnant and expected to go into labour at any moment when she, her mother Sophia and daughter Gaiana set sail from Novorossiisk on the northern shores of the Black Sea. The steamer in which they travelled was one of the last to leave, and for this reason it was crammed solid with frantic refugees. Lisa and her family, unable to afford the price of a seat, were packed into the pitch-dark hold of the vessel, in among a cargo of explosives. It was a brutal introduction to the harsh facts of life for a refugee. Hungry, cold, afraid to move, she was scared of giving birth in that fetid place. But Yury, her son, was not born until the family had reached Tiflis, in the then independent (Menshevik) republic of Georgia. He was born in April, in a wretched, dimly lit rented house. A few months later his parents had a joyful reunion in Constantinople, where the majority of the southern refugees had headed. But the city had nothing to offer them, and they had to continue their journey. Daniil looked for work in Yugoslavia, and the family came to join him there. They stayed for a time, and their youngest child, Anastasia (which means Resurrection) was born there. It was a miserable period: the children were all ill, and there was no work to be found. Wearily they packed up once again and set off on the last stage of their odyssey. They reached France, and stayed there. Only Gaiana would ever return to Russia.

2

Life for the Russian refugees in France was wretched, though France was not unwelcoming. Daniil Skobtsov joined the one million expatriate Russians looking for work. Eventually he secured a part-time teaching-job in a charitable institution; but it was badly paid and did little to help feed his family. The

Skobtsovs' poverty was acute, forcing them into a sordid basement room in a Paris suburb, where they slept on mattresses without sheets, and had no furniture. Lisa, haggard with exhaustion, worked up to twelve hours a day as a seamstress on piece-work, making dolls and painting scarves, ruining her short-sighted eyes for a mere pittance. Their lack of money was a constant source of anxiety, for the children, who had all been ill in Yugoslavia, needed to eat to regain their strength. Mercifully, Daniil found a job as a taxi driver, which at least ensured a regular income.

In the bitter winter of 1925–6 the whole family went down with influenza. All except Nastia (Anastasia) recovered. Even by their undernourished standards, four-year-old Nastia's weight loss was excessive, but the various doctors who came to see her could neither diagnose nor check it. Then one day a new young doctor was brought along and he, without hesitation, told the parents that Nastia had tubercular meningitis. She was rushed into the Pasteur Institute in Paris, and Lisa was allowed to stay with her. For two months, as she watched her child drift painfully towards death, Lisa tried to assuage her own pain by sketching a series of portraits of Nastia. Three of these were drawn at different hours on 7 March 1926, the day that Nastia died.

All that day and all night Lisa kept watch by her child's body. As she sat, she became aware of having reached a watershed in her life, and she wrote:

At Nastia's side I feel that my soul has meandered down back alleys all my life. And now I want an authentic, purified road, not out of faith in life, but in order to justify, understand and accept death . . . No amount of thinking will ever result in a greater formulation than the three words, Love one another, so long as it is (love) to the end and without any exceptions. And then the whole of life is illumined, which is otherwise an abomination and a burden.

Her long search for faith was over. She had been a revolutionary less out of intellectual conviction than out of a passionate concern for justice; and her long years as a wandering refugee had sharpened her concern. Now at last she recognised the religious basis of that search for justice, and as the past sank into the grave with Nastia, she began to take a long fresh look at her life. The moment was, she would say later, 'a visitation from the Lord', a glimpse of the divine plan.

Eventually, they say, time heals – would it not be more accurate to say deadens – all. Normality is gradually restored. The soul reverts to its blindness. The gates to eternity are closed once more . . . But . . . the light of eternity may yet suffuse them if the individual does not become afraid, does not run away from his own self, does not renounce his awesome fate . . . his personal Golgotha, his own freely accepted carrying of the Cross . . .

And I am convinced that anyone who has shared this experience of eternity, if only once; who has understood which way he is going, if only once; who has perceived the One who precedes him, if only once: such a person will find it hard to step aside from this path; to him all comforts will seem ephemeral, all treasures worthless, all companions superfluous if, in their midst, he fails to see the one Companion, bearing his cross.

Upon the death of Nastia, the relationship between Lisa and her husband collapsed. Anxiety for the child had papered over the cracks, but they could be hidden no longer. The couple had fierce arguments over the elder girl, Gaiana, whose legal 'father', Lisa's first husband, had arranged for her to go to a Catholic boarding school in Belgium. Bitterness grew and in 1927 Daniil Skobtsov moved out of the damp basement flat in Meudon, taking young Yury with him. (They had agreed that Yury would stay with his father until he was fourteen, and would then choose for himself.)

Suddenly bereft of family, Lisa found a vocation. She and her mother moved to a room in a more central district of Paris, more convenient for the work she had already started, with the Russian Orthodox Student Christian Movement. The Movement concerned itself not only with students but also with the far greater number of Russian émigrés who were working in the factories of suburban Paris or in the mines and steelworks of the industrial north and east. Poverty and despair had driven many of these uprooted human beings to drink or to drugs; others they had driven mad. The émigré trail was littered with human wreckage.

The headquarters of the SCM was in Paris which, as far as these unfortunates were concerned, might as well have been the planet Mars. To overcome this inaccessibility, several full-time itinerant secretaries were appointed in 1930 to take the Movement's work to the provinces. Lisa Skobtsova was one of these. Elisabeth Behr-Sigel has recorded her impressions at the time: 'She was not pretty, but she was intelligent and extraordinarily alive. Her hair was a mess, her clothes appalling, and she would sit for hours on end discussing literature, politics, metaphysics, theology, with a cigarette always in her mouth.'

Lisa's greatest talent was her ability to get through to the outcasts of society – to the drunk, crazy, depressed and even criminal dregs to whom her work now led her. In an article for an émigré newspaper on 'The Russian Geography of France' she defended the human dignity of those whom the world rejected as scum:

Are they degraded? Yes, indeed.
Rotten? Yes, rotting alive.
Drunk, debauched, dishonest, thieving? Yes, and yes again.
Are they people? Utterly and undeniably, miserable and abandoned people; but people who can be reclaimed by a little human kindness – so that no trace remains of debauchery and lying.

Travelling the country, Lisa became more and more immersed in the sufferings of her unhappy compatriots; and, as she always had and always would, she went far beyond her brief. The 'drunk, despairing and useless' became her especial concern. Arriving in some provincial town as an official lecturer, she would find herself turning into a spiritual ad-

viser, as a queue of people waited to speak to her. 'There
would be people wanting to pour out their hearts,' she told a
friend, 'to tell of some terrible grief which had burdened them
for years, of pangs of conscience which gave them no peace.
In slums like these it is no use speaking of faith in God, of
Christ or of the Church. What these people need is not
sermons, but the most basic thing of all, compassion.'

A group of hard-bitten miners in the Pyrenees showed
active hostility to Lisa when they understood that she had
come to give a lecture. It would be more to the point if she
scrubbed the floor for them, they said. Lisa promptly went for
a bucket of water and a scrubbing brush. When she spilled
water all over herself, the men's hostility evaporated. One of
them took off his jacket and put it round her shoulders. The
ice was broken, and when Lisa had finished her scrubbing,
they sat down at table together for supper. During the meal
she discovered that one of the men was determined on
suicide. Not stopping to argue, she took him to friends of hers
in Toulouse who were willing to give him a temporary home.

In Marseilles Lisa did not even attempt to lecture. Instead
she went off to the notorious bars and dives frequented by
vagrants, thieves and drunks. She sat there with them,
cigarette dangling, listening, consoling, weeping with them,
not least because of her own powerlessness to help. On one
occasion, she braved an opium den in the Old City, dragging
out two surprised young Russian junkies by sheer force.

More orthodox Orthodox eyebrows were raised in horror.
How could she consort with such human detritus? To them
she retorted that such people were not frightening at all, that
her only regret was that she could do so little for them. She
expressed this regret in a poem:

> Again I leave, the poorer,
> for some more distant part,
> The world, try as one may,
> will not fit in one heart.

Ever since Nastia's death, she had been overwhelmed by
the desire to become a mother to all the unfortunates of the

world. She was gripped by a powerful sense of mission, of being fashioned by God as 'an instrument for others to flourish'.

> What am I but a call, a sword in someone else's hand?
> A current, quickened by the rapids,
> a publican who draws attention to men's debts?
> Yet You insist on straitening my ways.
> 'Go, share the life of paupers and of tramps.
> And with an everlasting bond
> secure yourself to them, the world to me.'

Lisa came to a momentous decision. Approaching her spiritual adviser, Fr. Sergei Bulgakov, and her bishop, Metropolitan Evlogii, she asked whether she, a married woman, with two husbands still living, could make her profession as a nun. The two men saw no objection in church law. If Daniil Skobtsov would agree, Lisa might proceed.

An ecclesiastical divorce was granted to the Skobtsovs on 7 March 1932, the sixth anniversary of Nastia's death. That same month, at the Institute of Saint Sergius in Paris, Lisa laid aside her secular clothes and donned a second-hand black habit. As he placed a cross in her right hand, Bishop Evlogii reminded her that every follower of Christ must accept his share of it. Then he gave her a new name: Maria. 'I give you this name,' the bishop told her, 'in memory of Saint Maria of Egypt. Like that earlier Maria who lived a life of penitence in the desert, go forth to act and speak in the desert of human hearts.'

It was precisely what Lisa-Maria intended to do. She had become a nun, as the bishop later realised, only in order to give herself unreservedly to that desert of human hearts which lay all around her.

3

In the early 'honeymoon' months, she did her best to be a conventional nun, but it was not in her to be conventional for long. In the summer of 1932, Maria visited Latvia and Estonia on behalf of the SCM. In those briefly independent republics, Orthodox monasteries and convents survived, sheltered from the chill winds of religious persecution blowing across the border in Soviet Russia. Maria received much kindness – and even a new habit, so shocked were the Latvian nuns by her disgraceful old one. But she was unimpressed by the mediocrity and 'bourgeois piety' of these convents, and was disinclined to follow their example. 'No one there is aware that the world is on fire,' she cried, on her return to France. 'They have no interest in the fate of the world.' Maria wanted to give Orthodox monasticism a new look, better adapted to the suffering of the Russian émigrés and to the world catastrophe which she believed to be imminent. A safe and comfortable convent life, insulated from 'the filth and misery of the world' was not for her. She would be one of those 'fools for Christ's sake' who reject all comfort and security in order to be completely at the service of both God and man.

The rebel had been reborn. To the dismay and anger of the 'truly' Orthodox she wrote, in 1938, what she freely admitted was a call to anarchy:

> Open your gates to homeless thieves, let the outside world sweep in to demolish your magnificent liturgical system, abase yourself, empty yourself, make yourself of no account . . . Accept the vow of poverty in all its devastating severity: destroy all comfort, even the monastic kind.
>
> Our times are firmly in tune with Christianity, in that suffering is part of their character . . . They help us genuinely and completely to accept the vow of poverty, to seek no rule, but rather anarchy, the anarchic life of Fools for Christ's sake, seeking no monastic enclosure but rather the complete absence of even the subtlest barrier which might separate the heart from the world and its wounds.

'The world and its wounds' would always be her way to God. The boundary between the two great Gospel commandments – love God and love thy neighbour as thyself – simply did not exist. 'The way to God lies through love of people;

here is no other way,' she wrote. 'At the last Judgment I shall not be asked whether I was successful in my ascetic practices, nor how many bows and prostrations I made during the liturgy. I shall be asked, did I feed the hungry, clothe the naked, visit the sick and the imprisoned. That is *all* I shall be asked.'

There was no shortage of opportunity. More than other European countries, France had treated her refugees with great generosity; but inevitably there were many who fell through the net of the official welfare services. In an era of economic depression and rocketing unemployment statistics, many of these lacked even a roof over their heads. Without a fixed abode, they could not find work; without work, they could not afford a fixed abode. The streets of Paris swarmed with jobless vagrants.

Maria started with out-of-work girls. Optimistically she took the lease on 9 Villa de Saxe, in a prosperous district of Paris, without having a penny to pay for it. On the day that the lease was to be signed, Metropolitan Evlogii came to the rescue, with a gift of five thousand francs and a warning that next time she would not be so lucky.

'I can spend tonight at home,' she exulted, as she moved into a house where there was neither gas nor electricity and whose furniture consisted of a solitary grand piano. Undaunted, she slept on the floor, wrapped in a blanket, while the huge Bottin, Paris's telephone directory, served as a chair.

Within a few weeks, the house had been furnished with gifts, cast-offs and second-hand junk which she had delighted in collecting herself. When the house was ready, six young women moved in, one of them her daughter, Gaiana, now returned from her boarding school and studying at the Sorbonne. To ensure that the girls had enough space, Maria moved out of her own room into a small opening behind the central heating boiler. Here she pushed her narrow iron bed and, seeing a hole in the floor, she stuffed it with an old shoe.

In the dining-room cum lecture hall tramps came in from the streets to be fed, rubbing shoulders with the writers, philosophers and theologians who used the place as a forum. This was Maria's ideal of 'monasticism open to the world'. Try as he would, Metropolitan Evlogii could not convince her that any other kind of monasticism was possible.

Before long the Villa de Saxe was seen to be too small for the vast numbers that congregated there. In September 1934 Maria moved her operation to a large but crumbling and undistinguished three-storey house at 77 rue de Lourmel in the working-class fifteenth district where many Russians lived. Asked how she would afford the rent, Maria shrugged: 'Here at Saxe I have no room to spread. I can feed twenty-five hungry people. There I shall be able to feed a hundred. There are simply times when I can feel the Lord taking me by the scruff of the neck and compelling me to do what he wants. This is one of them.'

Converting the stables into a chapel, Maria covered the walls with the exquisite embroideries she did so well; adorning the south wall with a tapestry Life of David, while a remarkable Last Supper would soon cover the arch over the sanctuary entrance. At the Villa de Saxe she had painted an icon screen, which she now transferred to Lourmel. As well as this, she made and embroidered the rich vestments required by the Orthodox liturgy.

The house itself, run-down and dirty, was open to the world at large, saved from ugliness by the warmth of its embrace, by the shelter it provided from penury and cold. Soon its eighteen rooms were filled with outcasts and misfits of every sort, the very old, the very young, sometimes entire families. Number 77 rue de Lourmel was entirely a hostel for the needy, with a canteen where they could obtain a cheap (or in some cases free) midday meal of soup and a main course with meat. In 1935 alone, 2,300 dinners were served. What made Lourmel special was the total absence of 'soup-kitchen' condescension. Every effort was made to see that while the customer's hunger was appeased, his self-esteem suffered no damage.

A sympathetic Polish baker provided bread daily free of charge, and continued to do so right up to the time of the German Occupation. But not all the food was so easily come by. Long before dawn, Maria could be seen trudging, with a huge sack over her shoulders and down-at-heel men's shoes on her feet, towards the early morning markets at Les Halles. When the day's trading had finished, she would beg the left-over scraps, the meat bones, fish, bruised fruit or damaged vegetables that no one wanted. With this treasure she filled her sack, heaved it onto her shoulders and made her way to the Métro, where she was a familiar figure. On those rare occasions when someone gave her a sack of potatoes or a box of fruit, she would hurry home, collect one or two of her vagrants and return to Les Halles on foot with a wheelbarrow.

At first Gaiana oversaw the cooking. But one day she dropped a bombshell, announcing that she intended to return to the USSR to marry a Soviet student she had met at the Sorbonne. Maria stormed and pleaded, but it was no use: there was no stopping Gaiana. When she had gone, Maria had to take on the cooking herself. For six months she slaved single-handed in the kitchen, bare-headed, bare-footed and red in the face, stirring huge cauldrons of soup for the midday meal. As she was also carpenter, decorator, seamstress, icon painter and scrubber of floors, it was no wonder that each night she retired exhausted to her little room under the back stairs. But even here she had no peace. Her door stayed open, as a constant stream of people came to consult her.

In 1935 an independent group of Orthodox Christians (with the tacit approval of the Church) decided to undertake a more committed programme of social work. This group, known as Orthodox Action, appointed Maria to be its first President, with Fedor Pianov as its General Secretary and business manager. Their main aim was to help the poor, keeping in mind always that 'man is God's image and likeness, the temple of the Holy Spirit, the incorruptible icon of God.' Money was the chief problem and for lack of it the new organisation might have died at birth. Fortunately help was at hand and contributions poured in from the League of Nations High Commission for Refugees and from certain Anglican and ecumenical sources. With the money Maria rented a spacious but dilapidated house outside Paris at Noisy-le-Grand, as a sanatorium for tubercular Russian patients. Eventually, when the émigrés acquired the same rights to health care as the rest of the population, the house became redundant as a sanatorium and became a rest home for the elderly instead. Closed down during the German Occupation, it reopened after the war and is still in existence as a home for the aged sick.

By this time Maria had been joined by Mother Evdokia, who had made her religious profession shortly before leaving Russia. The two got on well together, Evdokia quite admiring Maria's dynamic approach to monasticism. But the lack of the contemplative side of the monastic life distressed her. Maria was inclined to make up her own rules, and frequently failed to attend the weekday services because she was too busy. She had no intention of allowing herself to be a cloistered nun, whereas in her heart this was what Evdokia wanted to be. After some fairly unpleasant arguments, Evdokia and another nun, Blandina, who had joined the Lourmel household, retired to a more orderly religious life in a convent outside Paris.

In 1936 Maria was devastated by the news from Russia that Gaiana had died from typhus. Grief overwhelmed her, sapping her strength, casting her into a deep desolation of spirit, a dark night of the soul in which there seemed no possibility of hope. Her misery was compounded by the arrival of a new chaplain, Father Kiprian Kern, an ultra-traditionalist priest with whom she could have no understanding. It was an impossible situation for them both, their mutual antipathy keeping them in a state of permanent exasperation. By way of countering her misery, Maria flung herself into hard work: spring-cleaning, stripping paint, washing walls and generally trying to cure herself by exhaustion. Not until 1939 did the tension slacken, when Father Kiprian was transferred elsewhere. His relief must have been as great as hers, for the fault could not all have been on his side. Maria's tolerance was reserved solely for the poor and needy.

Many of the desperate Russian émigrés had drifted to the outskirts of Paris where they lived in squalid slums or shanties. But others led a nomadic existence, with not even a slum roof to their heads. Often they slept rough in the markets of Les Halles where Maria would discover them on her way to buy food. Sometimes she found them in sleazy all-night bars where for the price of one glass of cheap wine they could sit till morning, slumped over the sticky table, head in hands. Maria's pity for these wretches was so great that at times she would disappear for days on end to share in their life.

All of them were welcome at Lourmel. Maria had her critics, of course, who accused her of being too trusting, too easily taken for a ride. She did not care. If she was quite often robbed or cheated, it was a risk she had to take. It was not right to refuse to trust. 'It is not enough to give,' she would say. 'We must also have a heart that gives.'

Just before Christmas 1938, Maria set out to survey the mental institutions of France, with a view to discovering how many Russian-speaking patients were living there. She was shocked by what she found. In one large hospital, in the Jura, virtually all the Russians had arrived since 1920, victims of the European war, the Revolution or the Civil War, or of all three. They had arrived in France speaking no word of French, and the situation had set the seal on their agony. Mentally withdrawing from an alien world they could in no way understand, they had ceased to speak at all, turning, for the most part, into gibbering, barely human wrecks.

Amid so much human wreckage, Maria found three patients sane enough to be discharged from their long incarceration. Alerting the Russian community to her discoveries (which resulted in a committee being set up to help Russian mental patients) she patiently combed seventeen more such institutions. In them she found twenty patients who should never have been there at all.

Some she found homes for, others she brought to Lourmel to help in the kitchen or about the house. The house was well-known now – part hostel, part refuge, part monastery, part canteen, part meeting-house for both intellectuals and derelicts. Maria herself had become a local landmark. A tall, robust, earthy woman, with the flat, ruddy face of a Russian peasant, brown eyes twinkling through cheap steel-rimmed spectacles, plain, unkempt, but bursting with life, she was one of the fifteenth district's more picturesque sights. Reactions to her tended to be extreme: people either loved Maria for her warmth and her joie de vivre, or detested her for her boisterousness and refusal to conform. Criticism was often spiteful, but it can't be denied that she provided plenty of ammunition. Her anarchic, left-wing radicalism, her contempt for rules, the company she kept, her shabbiness and the fact that she still smoked, infuriated the pious, and not only the pious. Then there were her two divorces, a source of scandal and wagging tongues. Daniil Skobtsov and Maria had renewed their friendship and, as he was now helping out at Lourmel, the faithful were scandalised at his frequent presence in the house. 'As a nun,' commented one eminent critic recently, 'Mother Maria was a walking offence.'

Yet in some ways she remained typically Orthodox: in her passionate mysticism, her love for the Resurrected Christ, her feeling for the Cross as the focal point of history, her openness to suffering, her asceticism. But her critics saw only the blemishes, and these were considerable. They did not understand that to her the command to feed the hungry and visit the sick and imprisoned, in short, to immerse oneself in the world, required a total commitment beside which all other rules were irrelevant. In what was perhaps her apologia, the profoundly moving essay on the Second Commandment, written just before the outbreak of the Second World War, she makes it clear that the Christian must give his all – his 'last shirt and last crumb of bread' – for his fellow men:

> It is the only life-giving way. Outside this way of love, there is death by fire and ashes, death from the mutiple hatreds which divide humanity, whether of class, nation or race. Against all such totalitarian concepts we must proclaim one unique reality – the image of God in man . . . Each of us is called to give himself for his friends, to follow lovingly in the footsteps of Christ, towards that Golgotha which is appointed for us.

Often before, she had had this premonition of 'death by fire and ashes', of a personal Calvary; and in that year of 1939, the time was at hand. On his way to a new life in America, Trotsky, (whom years ago she had planned to assassinate) came to Lourmel to see her. War was imminent, he warned. If she stayed in France, imprisonment and death would certainly await her. Better to go, as he was going, to the New World. She smiled at him and shook her head. Nothing mattered except to do God's work, she said. Then would she allow him to do her one last favour, in memory of the past? 'Yes,' she beamed at him. 'It's a very long time since our poor coal merchant was paid.' Trotsky went out and paid the coal bill. When she told this story to her co-prisoners in the concentration camp at Ravensbrück, Maria used to say that God would forgive Trotsky his crimes – 'for the sake of the Lourmel coal bill'.

4

Paris fell to the Germans on 14 June, 1940; one week later France surrendered. Maria, who had long since prophesied, 'We are entering eschatological times . . . the end is already near,' responded with characteristic practicality. 'There will be hunger this winter,' she said briskly. 'We must save those who might (otherwise) perish.'

The canteen at Lourmel was taken over by the local authorities, but the daily routine of the house was largely unchanged. The results of Maria's foraging expeditions to the markets now served to enrich the thin, watery soups and stews delivered daily by the *mairie*. The main difficulty, in those early days of Occupation, was that there were more hungry people and less food to go round.

For the Russians in Paris, the early calm ended abruptly on 22 June, 1941, when Germany invaded the USSR. In the days that followed the invasion, one thousand émigrés were arrested in Paris, among them Mother Maria's friend and colleague, Fedor Pianov. All were taken to the detention camp at Compiègne, 100 km north-east of Paris. Worrying about their families left unprovided for, the prisoners discussed means of getting help for them. A few weeks later, some of the detainees were released, among them Igor Krivoshein, son of a former Czarist Minister of Agriculture. Krivoshein returned to Paris to solicit aid for the prisoners and their families and was advised by a friend to approach Mother Maria. A committee was set up at Lourmel to organise the preparation and despatch of food parcels and to raise funds for the prisoners' dependants.

Meanwhile all Russians in Paris were ordered to register at a Directorate for Emigré Affairs which had a Russian Nazi, Zherebkov, at its head. Mother Maria and her newly appointed chaplain, Father Dmitri Klepinin, a man after her own heart, ignored the order, although failure to register meant the risk of being arrested as enemy aliens. Maria despised the Zherebkovites and all who collaborated with the Germans. Hitler's Germany, she believed, was poisoning the whole of Europe, while Hitler himself was 'a madman, a paranoiac who ought to be confined to a madhouse, who needs a straitjacket and a cork-lined room to prevent his bestial howls from disturbing the outside world.'

Such incautious talk, regardless of who might be listening, was dangerous, but only to be expected from Maria. She did not care who knew about her scorn for the 'master race'. When officials put up posters in Lourmel urging Frenchmen to volunteer for work in German factories, she tore them down. Her lack of discretion reflected both her integrity and her courage, but was uncomfortable to live with. Some of her colleagues resented the way she endangered them.

She cheerfully compounded the danger by installing a powerful radio set on which she tuned in each night to the BBC. A huge map of the USSR covered the whole of one wall in the conference room. Here, every morning, standing on a table, she would plot the course of the German advance, using coloured pins as markers. At this time, the pins moved steadily and inexorably eastwards, but she refused to give up hope. 'I hope Russia will win in the end,' she insisted to the doubters. 'The day will come when we hear on the radio that Russian planes have destroyed Berlin. And then,' she added with spine-chilling accuracy, 'Russia's hour of history will have come. Russia will extend her borders from the Arctic to the Indian Ocean. A great future awaits her. But, oh, what oceans of blood.'

It was not, however, for the Russians, but for the Jews that the Germans had reserved their most terrible venom. At first it seemed to be no more than a simple matter of registration. A decree of 27 September, 1940, defined the term Jew for the French people: 'those who belong or have belonged to the Jewish religion or who possess more than two Jewish grand-parents.' A later decree (April 1941) appeared to emphasise the religious affiliation: 'in case of doubt all persons are considered Jewish who belong or have belonged to the Jewish religious community.'

It seemed likely, therefore, that possession of a certificate of Christian baptism might be a protection against whatever it was the Germans had in mind for the Jews. Few could yet foresee that this would be wholesale deportation and mass-acre; but the menace was undeniable. Hundreds of Jews sought 'mercy baptism' and Father Dmitri was repeatedly asked to provide baptismal certificates for non-Christian Jews. With Maria's whole-hearted agreement, he decided to perjure himself (arguing that Christ would have done likewise in this situation), entering the names of these Jewish sup-pliants in the Lourmel parish register. His card index noted the arrival of no less than eighty new parishioners.

From 7 June, 1942, all Jews over the age of six were ordered to wear the Yellow Star. (They even had to surrender a precious clothing coupon for the privilege.) Shock waves rolled through Paris; there and elsewhere demonstrations took place against this humiliating affront to Jewish dignity. Non-Jews took to wearing the Star, or at least a yellow handkerchief, in sympathy. Jews and non-Jews alike wore the Star with pride in the streets. In a poem written on the day the decree came out, Maria openly showed her sympathies:

> Two triangles, a star,
> King David's – an ancestral blazon.
> No insult this: mark of chosen nation,
> No misfortune: high vocation.

The circulation of this poem in Paris pleased the Jews and almost certainly contributed to her arrest some months later. It would not have occurred to Maria that she should keep silent. 'If we were true Christians, we should all wear the Star,' she argued.

From this time forward, with increasing urgency, Maria and her friends concealed Jews at Lourmel, Noisy, or one of the other houses run by Orthodox Action. They became an integral part of the French Resistance network of refuges and escape routes – not only for Jews but for others whom the Resistance were trying to save, including several escaped Russian prisoners of war. Maria would have liked to be involved even more deeply with the Resistance, but that was not practicable. She had to be content with daily risking her life, securing false papers and documents, feeding and hiding the refugees who were to be smuggled to safety in some remote country area or to what was still at that time unoccupied France.

The Star decree was only the first drum roll in a symphony of unspeakable horror. In July a new decree forbade wearers of the Yellow Star to walk in parks or along main streets; to go to the cinema or the theatre; to eat in cafes or restaurants; to use telephone kiosks, swimming baths or camping sites; to read books in libraries, visit museums or use any but the last carriages on the Paris Métro. Shopping was restricted to the hour between three and four in the afternoon, and a curfew was imposed at eight p.m. Thoroughly alarmed now, many Jews jettisoned the Star. The rush was on for hiding places, for forged papers and for escape routes. For by now it was just possible to guess that this humiliation of the Jews would end in murder.

On the night of 15 July, 1942, the agony of the Paris Jews began in earnest. Nearly thirteen thousand of them were arrested. (Warrants had been issued for thirty thousand, but there had been an unforeseen delay and many Jews had had warning of what was afoot. They had gone into hiding with neighbours.) Patients were dragged from hospital beds, and mental asylums were scoured for the Jewish deranged. Childless individuals were taken direct to Drancy whence they would be packed into trains for Auschwitz. The remaining seven and a half thousand, of whom over four thousand were children, were driven like cattle into the Vélodrome d'Hiver, a little-used sports stadium quite near to the rue de Lourmel. There they were kept for five days without food, under a pitiless summer sun, with one solitary water-tap, ten stinking latrines, and two doctors for all that vast crowd. Into this indescribable hell came Mother Maria on the second day. For three days she stayed, moving among the helpless children, bringing food, trying to calm their fears. The story is told that she prevailed on a group of French dustmen to smuggle out four young children in dustbins. She was ready to continue, but on the fifth day, Nazi overseers drove out all who had no place there, and proceeded to their infamous work. Screaming children were prised away from their distraught parents, and sent on ahead to Drancy and the death camps to the east.

More than ever now Lourmel became a haven for frantic Jews. There were refugees everywhere, in the extension wing, in the shed, on the canteen floor, even in the chapel. A whole family sheltered in Father Dmitri's room, another in that of Yury, Mother Maria's twenty-year-old son, who was now a student at the Sorbonne with intentions of becoming an Orthodox priest later. 'We have an acute accommodation crisis,' remarked Maria with graphic understatement. 'It is amazing that the Germans have not pounced on us.' If the Germans did come looking for Jews, she told Berdyaev, she would show them the icon of the Mother of God. 'The Mother of God might be all right,' he pointed out, 'but live Jews would be more of a problem.'

Indeed the Germans were only biding their time. On the morning of 8 February, while Maria was in the country looking for food, the SS burst in the house in the rue de Lourmel. Not finding Maria, they searched the house and seized her son, Yury. When they discovered in his pocket a letter from a Jewish woman to Father Dmitri, appealing for a baptismal certificate, they took the boy away as a hostage.

Maria hastened back to Lourmel as soon as she heard the news, having learned that her return would secure her son's release. But Yury remained a prisoner. Meanwhile Father Dmitri had been summoned to Gestapo headquarters at the rue des Saussaies, where he was interrogated for four long hours. Though he made no attempt to deny the charges against him, the SS were prepared to let him go in exchange for an assurance that he would help no more Jews. In reply, Dmitri held up his pectoral cross and pointed to the figure of Christ. 'Do you know this Jew?' he asked quietly, and received a blow to the face for answer. 'Your priest did himself in,' Hoffman, the investigating SS officer, told Mother Maria next day. 'He insists that if he were free, he would do the same again.'

It was Maria's turn to be interrogated. 'You brought your daughter up badly,' Hoffman shouted to eighty-year-old Sophia. 'All she can do is help Yids.' Fedor Pianov, who had also returned to Paris in the vain hope of saving Yury, protested at this. At Lourmel, he said, help was given to anyone in need, no matter who they were. Sophia chimed in. 'My daughter is a true Christian,' she told Hoffman. 'For her there is neither Jew nor Greek, only individual people in distress. If you were in trouble she'd help you too.' 'Yes, I suppose I would,' Maria wryly agreed, as she bade her mother goodbye and left Lourmel, head held high. Next day Hoffman returned for a final search before closing down the house. 'You will never see your daughter again,' he told Sophia. Maria had indeed left Lourmel for good.

With thirty-four other women she was sent to the old fort at Romainville, in another part of which Father Dmitri, Yury and Fedor Pianov were being held. From time to time they caught a glimpse of each other. Soon, however, the three men were removed to the immense and filthy camp at Compiègne. Pianov later told how the SS made fun of Father Dmitri: 'About four hundred of us were assembled in the yard. Father Dmitri, his cassock torn, was made into a laughing-stock. One of the SS men began to prod and whip him, calling him dirty Jew. Yury Skobtsov who stood beside him was in tears. But Father Dmitri consoled him, saying that Christ had withstood worse mockery than this.'

Maria too came to Compiègne, but for one night only. It was here that she and Yury met for the last time, before being herded their separate ways into Germany. On that evening, Yury managed to slip across the barrier dividing the men's from the women's barracks. His mother, according to the evidence of other prisoners, was transfigured with happiness at the sight of him, becoming almost beautiful in her joy. From dusk until dawn they whispered together, strengthening each other's resolve. When Yury had gone, Maria stood for a long time motionless, staring into the distance, while tears coursed down her broad cheeks.

'I am utterly at peace and even a little proud of sharing my mother's fate,' Yury wrote to his father and grandmother just before he was deported to Germany. 'I assure you that I shall bear whatever is in store with dignity. I am no longer afraid . . .'

Yury, Father Dmitri and Fedor Pianov were sent to Buchenwald. Only Pianov survived.

5

On the following day over two hundred women left Compiègne. Their transport (number 19,000) was the first to take this particular route. In sealed cattle trucks, without water or sanitation, the women's journey eastward into Germany took three days. When they arrived at Fürstenberg station, they were exhausted but still recognisably women, most of them young, many of them chic Parisiennes, wearing hats, carrying luggage.

Two hours later, the luggage lay in confiscated heaps and the women themselves, grotesque scarecrows in striped cotton twill, heads shaven and with ill-fitting boots on their feet, faced the SS guards and their own hopeless future – in Ravensbrück concentration camp. Herded into barracks where they would sleep two or three to a bunk in long tiers three deep; overworked, starved, humiliated and despairing; a prey to lice and all manner of vermin: in this place the majority of them would die. Of ten thousand Frenchwomen there, only two thousand would return; and at the final count it was estimated that seventy-two thousand women and children, of all European nationalities, died in Ravensbrück. And the greater number of these would never know why they had been brought there.

Here, Maria accomplished her Christian mission in a way she could not have foreseen. Or had she perhaps envisaged this fate when she wrote shortly before her arrest: 'I am Thy message, Lord. Throw me, like a blazing torch into the night, so that all may see and understand what it means to be Thy disciple.'

To the SS she had no name. She was merely prisoner 19263 assigned to Block 27 in the south-west corner of the camp. The long years of self-denial, the austerity, the lack of privacy that had always been her lot, stood her now in good stead. Knowing why she had been arrested helped her to accept her fate. Her robust constitution, wide-ranging interests and habit of prayer saved her from being utterly disorientated by the conditions prevailing in Ravensbrück. Others were not so fortunate. There, in the camp, human misery and suffering were taken to breaking point. At three each morning, the women had to stand out in the open in all weathers, until everyone had been counted, a procedure (known as the Appel) that regularly took five or more hours. Maria took it calmly; many could not.

Maria would not succumb to despair, and struggled to save her companions. 'Whatever you do,' she begged them, 'continue to think. Don't allow the flame of your spirit to die. In the conflict with doubt, cast your thought wider and deeper. Do not let your thought be debased, let it transcend the conditions and limitations of this earth.' To illustrate her meaning, she pointed to the camp's three crematoria whose chimneys continuously belched out smoke, a constant reminder of their nearness to death. 'It is only here, immediately above the chimneys, that the smoke is oppressive,' explained Maria. 'When it rises higher, it turns into light clouds before being dispersed into limitless space. In the same way our souls, once they have torn themselves away from this sinful earth, move by means of an effortless unearthly flight into eternity, where there is life full of joy.'

It was essential to the Nazi philosophy to degrade and brutalise the human spirit before destroying the body. Maria fought back. On Easter Day 1944 she decorated the windows of her barracks with astonishingly beautiful paper cut-outs, using paper stolen from the Germans. The other prisoners turned to her for comfort. Her French was somewhat fractured, (she had never really mastered the pronunciation) but, as they gathered round her bunk, ten or twelve at a time, she would talk to them of history, of politics, of Byzantine art, of literature, of the Russian Church, of the great characters of the Russian Revolution. The women listened transfixed to the stories of this rich and amazing life. Maria had the gift of bringing her subjects alive, the ability to make these tormented girls forget, if only for a short while, the degradation of their present existence. Particularly in the dark days in early 1945, when famine stalked the camp and women forgot everything – their dreams of home and family included – except the craving for food; when they were reduced to slavering fantasies about imaginary menus, writing down lengthy descriptions of dishes – in such a wilderness of the spirit, such abandonment of the soul did Maria fight to save their humanity.

She laid aside her own food for them. When, as occasionally happened, someone working on the outside brought her a potato or a carrot as a gift, she would save this treasure for her companions. But most of all she helped them by talking them out of their obsession with food, drawing their minds away onto a less destructive plane, talking to them of the beautiful things that man had made with his art. Many of her companions, remembers Genevieve de Gaulle, who was with her in Ravensbrück, 'sensed the presence of God in her'. In all of them 'she rekindled . . . the flame of thought which still barely flickered beneath the heavy burden of horror.'

Often she spoke of her religious beliefs, and from a prayer book which one girl had managed to preserve from the SS searches, she would read aloud from the Gospels or Epistles, following her readings with a brief meditation.

'She took us all under her wing,' said another survivor. 'We were cut off from our families; yet somehow she provided us with a family.' Maria was mother to them all, but particularly to the young Soviet women soldiers in Block 31 whom she adopted as her own, hugging them like children when they were afraid. By rights these girls were prisoners of war, but the Germans had chosen to treat them as partisans and had sent them to this concentration camp. Maria admired and loved them. She acted as interpreter for them, and it was like the rue de Lourmel all over again as they crowded round her bunk, listening to her talk of the old Russia she had known, begging her to tell them about the West, about which they knew nothing at all.

Maria translated their Russian soldiers' songs into French and had the whole camp singing them beneath their breath. Once, as she was talking to one of 'her' Russian girls just before roll-call, she failed to notice the approach of a female SS guard. The woman screamed an obscenity at her and struck her across the face with a leather strap. Maria went on talking to her companion, as though the SS woman did not exist.

Every minute of every day death hovered over the camp. Maria had long ago ceased to fear it. It was not that she did not love life, but that she loved eternity more: death was merely a birth into eternity, suffering was the necessary birth pangs. The night might be dark indeed, but she never doubted the dawn. Composing a message for her confessor, Father Bulgakov, she asked a fellow-prisoner to memorise it and deliver it if that were ever possible. 'My state at present,' it went, 'is such that I completely accept suffering in the knowledge that this is how things ought to be for me; and if I am to die, I see in this a blessing from on high.'

As the months dragged past, the endless standing around in sub-zero temperatures during the daily Appel took its toll on Maria. Her legs became swollen and raw so that she could scarcely stand. Nevertheless she forced herself, in that pre-dawn hour before the dreaded roll-call, to walk with a group of her friends, leaning heavily on one of them, telling stories, dreaming dreams, describing plans for the future: for books she would write, relief work she would do, bridges she would build between her beloved Russia and the West.

She was sure that the Russians would be the first on the scene to liberate them. Rosane Lascroux was equally sure that it would be the Americans and British. They took a bet on it, Maria promising a gift if Rosane should be right. When news of the Allied landings in Normandy in 1944 reached them, she kept her word, telling Rosane that she would embroider a cloth to commemorate the landings. Hidden in her mattress, Rosane had a triangular piece of white cotton which the SS had originally ordered the women to wear on their heads, but which they had later withdrawn. She was glad now that she had kept hers hidden. One of the girls, whose job it was to look after the SS shirts, found some dye; two others stole some lengths of cable from the Siemens factory where they worked; another stole a needle. All of these crimes, if discovered, would have been punishable by death.

Maria stripped the protective fabric from the cable and separated it into single threads. Standing upright on the Appel ground, supported from behind by another prisoner, Maria worked to create a thing of beauty amid such ugliness. She worked without a pattern and with scarcely a glance at the tiny corner of cloth which protruded from her striped uniform, and to which she diligently plied her needle, pushing the whole thing out of sight whenever the SS appeared. Rosane Lascroux had studied English, and she scrawled an Anglo-Saxon-type inscription in the dust, a word at a time, for Maria to copy. The finished masterpiece for which so many had risked their lives, became the greatest treasure of the women of Block 27. It depicted the arrival of the men from the north in their boats; and their victory over the evil usurpers of the land. 'Then they came, the Norsemen – the lofty fortress they besieged, and within their arms befell the rich booty. Fiercely they fought, the brave invaders, for the filthy devils were doomed to death. Meanwhile rejoiced the peaceful folk.' The Anglo-Saxon may be less than exact, but the spiritual power of this small piece of cloth is beyond measure.*

In the last months of 1944 and the beginning of 1945, the always pitifully inadequate food ration was cut by half. Sanitary conditions reached danger point as, in a Block meant for eight hundred, more than two and a half thousand women

* The cloth is still in the possession of Rosane Lascroux, and is, she claims understandably, her greatest treasure. On her death it will pass to the Russian Orthodox Church.

slept three to a bunk, ravaged by typhus and dysentery, eaten alive by lice. These walking skeletons represented a threat to the SS as the war drew to a close, and as the Red Army drew near. Anxious to eliminate all traces of their inhuman crimes, the SS began systematically to destroy not only records and installations but the more unfit prisoners as well. Himmler had already sent out an order that all women prisoners who were ill or unable to walk should be summarily disposed of.

When the SS began to issue pink cards, promising easier conditions for the old, the ill and the exhausted, Maria, along with thousands of others, fell for the deception. The pink card, they were told, assured its bearer of a place in a nearby Youth Camp, where there would be more food, exemption from hard labour, a bed for every individual, and no roll-calls. It sounded like paradise. Though experience should have taught them better, in a place where already groups of the sick had been poisoned by injection, on the grounds of curing their insomnia, hope sprang eternal, and the prisoners were willing to grasp at any straw. After two years in Ravensbrück, Maria was among those who accepted the pink card. Several of her friends tried to dissuade her, but she rebuked them for undue pessimism. She was, she told them, 'delighted' to have the card.

All through January 1945, doomed and desperate women, many of them 'guinea pigs' who had been subjected to medical experiments, were rounded up and removed to the Youth Camp – in reality an extermination centre with the capacity to feed the newly enlarged crematoria twenty-four hours a day.

What had the women really expected? Did they really fall for the SS promises? Not only were roll-calls not abolished, in this final circle of hell, they sometimes were made to last the whole day through. The bread ration was cut from a nominal 150 grammes a day to 60 grammes, eked out with half a ladleful of turnip soup. In temperatures well below freezing, with the snow thick on the ground, blankets, coats and jackets were forcibly removed. Then even shoes and stockings were taken away. Each day an average of around fifty prisoners died from 'natural causes' such as these.

When Soviet artillery could be heard in the distance, more desperate measures were applied to reduce the incriminating human evidence. Medical supplies were withdrawn from the 'hospital' and plans to poison the sick patients were put in hand – though after 22 January, it became easier to gas them.

The first gassings took place in a couple of hermetically-sealed vans, using Cyclon B pellets which poisoned the victims en route. But from 2 March Ravensbrück acquired its own gas chambers, and with them the capacity to exterminate one hundred and fifty victims a day.

By this time Mother Maria's condition had become critical. Jacqueline Péry, who occupied a bunk above hers recalls:

> She always now remained lying down between roll-calls. Already she scarcely belonged to the land of the living. Her face was striking to observe, not because of her ravaged features – we were accustomed to such sights – but because of its intense expression of terrible inner suffering. Already it bore the hall-marks of death. Nevertheless Mother Maria uttered no complaint. She kept her eyes closed and seemed to be in a state of continual prayer. This, I think, was her Garden of Gethsemane.

Before this, she had tried to work on yet another embroidery, but she had lacked the strength. It was an icon depicting the Mother of God with a crucified Christ-child in her arms. 'If I manage to complete it,' she had said, 'it will help me to leave this place alive. If I don't manage, that means that I shall die.'

For five weeks she survived the Youth Camp. Then, inexplicably, she was one of a batch of prisoners transferred back to the main camp. The women in Block 27 could scarcely recognise Maria. One of them, Inna Webster, 'froze with horror when I saw the change in her appearance. All that was left of her was skin and bone, her eyes were festering, and she exuded that nightmarish sweet smell of those infected with dysentery.'

All through March roll-calls and selections filled the prisoners' lives. Mother Maria rose from her bunk at the last possible moment and stood for hours supported against

another prisoner. Even for the dying, attendance was obliga-
tory; and many women died on the Appel ground. On the
Wednesday of Holy Week, a macabre weeding-out of the
unfit took place. Summoned to the Appel ground, the women
were ordered to run, five at a time, in front of an SS officer
who carefully observed their legs, as though at a cattle market. A gesture to the left with his whip meant death. Then the
condemned prisoner's number was taken, the women were
stripped down to their shifts, and a tarpaulin-covered van
took the day's total of the damned to the Youth Camp or
directly to the gas chambers.

It was normal now to expect random swoops on the barracks at any hour. The more enfeebled and ill prisoners,
particularly those who bore the tell-tale scars of medical
experiments, had to be hidden away from the marauding SS
intent on feeding the crematoria fires. Twice Maria was
concealed between the roof and ceiling of her hut; at other
times she was pushed hastily beneath the bottom bunks. The
terror generated by the constant alarm and uncertainty drove
many of the women out of their minds; but Maria, who spoke
little now, retained her calmness and tranquility. 'She offered
herself consciously to the holocaust,' Jacqueline Péry witnessed later, 'helping each one of us to accept the cross. Right
to the end she radiated the peace of God and communicated
that peace to us all.'

On Good Friday a delegation from the International Red
Cross was turned away from the camp gates on the grounds
that the Commandant was too busy to see them. He was
indeed. That afternoon the whole camp was ordered on
parade. Once again the wretched women were commanded to
run, in fives, before Deputy Commandant Schwarzhüber. A
survivor has testified to Schwarzhüber's mood of manic cheerfulness: 'He was literally beaming, brimming over with
bonhomie and good cheer, and when my rank passed in front
of him "in fives", he leaned benevolently forward toward us
and said in German, "Just march quite calmly . . .", and
then, with a look of depraved complicity, "Your heart is
beating fast, isn't it?"'

Several hundred were condemned that afternoon, dismissed to the left with a wave of Schwarzhüber's hand. An unprecedented panic broke out, as the doomed women went crazy with fear, struggling hopelessly to escape. Nine of them broke loose and managed to escape into the barracks, but they were dragged out again. Cynically the SS held out pieces of bread to tempt the famished prisoners onto the trucks, then withdrew them when their victims crawled on board.

Maria, still trying to convince her companions that they might yet survive, was among the women who were driven off that afternoon to the Youth Camp. Of her actual end there is no doubt – she is on the list of those gassed on the eve of Easter, 31 March. But there are two versions of what actually happened on Good Friday – and, given the panic and confusion of those hours, it is not surprising. In the first version, Maria's legs failed the test of Schwarzhüber's scrutiny and she was therefore among those condemned to die. The other version claims that she took the place of another woman in the ranks of the doomed. There are two eye-witnesses, both Communists, with no vested interest in fabricating such a story, to the fact that 'she went voluntarily to martyrdom, in order to help her companions to die.'

We shall never know for certain. Perhaps it was at the final selection, made later that day when the vans arrived at the Youth Camp, that Maria volunteered to die for another. One can say only that such a heroic gesture sounds entirely possible for one who had so consistently sought 'to quench the world's sorrow with (her) self.'

On the way to the Youth Camp, they took away her spectacles, in spite of her agonised protests that without them she was virtually blind. She was not among those who were consigned immediately to the gas chambers. Somehow she survived the night. When they finally dragged her away to death, she could neither stand nor see.

It was the following day, Easter Sunday, that the Red Cross gained admittance to Ravensbrück camp, and negotiated the immediate release of three hundred Frenchwomen. They were just too late to save Maria.

7.
The Unknown Martyrs of the Twentieth Century

Bonhoeffer, King, Kolbe, Luwum, Romero, Skobtsova – all six were victims of fascism or of right-wing reactionary forces. The imbalance is so striking that this last chapter must make some attempt to redress it. For how may one speak of twentieth-century martyrs and not refer to the millions who have perished under regimes of the left?

This is not to say that all the 'unsung martyrs' of the world are to be found at this end of the spectrum; they are found elsewhere in terrifying numbers. In fact a peculiar horror of the persecution of Christians today is that much of it is carried out by governments which claim to accept Christ and to be the upholders of Christian morality and values. Karol Wojtyla, later to be Pope John Paul II, referred to these regimes in an address to his fellow-Cardinals in 1977.

Even where Christ is accepted there is at the same time opposition to the full truth of his Person, his mission and his Gospel. There is a desire to 'reshape' him, to adapt him to suit mankind in this era of progress and make him fit in with the programme of modern civilisation – which is a programme of consumerism and not of transcendental ends. There is opposition to him from these standpoints, and the truth proclaimed and recorded in his name is not tolerated. This opposition to Christ which goes hand in hand with paying him lip-service – and it is to be found also among those who call themselves his disciples – is particularly symptomatic of our own times.

Oscar Romero was far from being the only victim of that kind of persecution, the indirect opposition to Christ which calls itself Christian. But the opposition to Christ carried out under the various Communist governments of the world is more overt, and massive: 'an undisguised rejection of the Gospel,' to quote Wojtyla again, 'a flat denial of the truth about God man and the world as proclaimed by the Gospel.'

To the victim it can make very little difference whether the torturer or executioner is of the political right or left. The pain of dying is the same; the fear, the sense of isolation do not vary; the hour of choice involves the identical confrontation of the claims of God and Caesar, of the true universal God and the false man-made idol.

For better or for worse ours is an age of political and ideological extremes. Both extremes may shriek their hatred of each other but they are brothers under the skin, their blueprints for a new world including the suppression of all those who do not agree with them, and the raising up of the new idol, the faceless, all-powerful state. Hence, for both of them, the paraphernalia of the police state and the depersonalisation of the human beings who live in it are inevitable.

On the face of it the left, with its accent on the universal brotherhood of man, has the higher idealism. But in choosing to impose those ideals by force, it has caused untold and unnecessary suffering; and the totalitarian left has claimed as many, if not more victims than its blood-brother of the right. The ordeal of believers in the Soviet Union since 1917, and in Ethiopia since 1974, makes the goings-on in the Roman circuses seem like the unsophisticated antics of children. Under one-party regimes which intend to control the whole of a man's life in its spiritual as well as its physical dimension, the essential dignity and freedom of the human personality go by the board. Systems which claim to exalt man deprive him of the very freedoms on which his humanity depends. Since the heart of the Christian message is that every human being has the dignity belonging to a child of God, it follows that there is no room for Christians in any totalitarian state. By its very nature the Christian challenge is seen as subversive.

*   *   *

Official policy in the USSR has long been to remove all vestige of religious belief from the hearts of its subjects. For writing the verse: 'You can pray freely, but just so God alone can hear,' Tanya Khodkevich received a ten-year prison sentence. Yet she had uttered no less than the truth. For although Christians, or at least those who are officially registered, may worship in a church, they may not live out their Christian belief nor speak of it to their children. Religious indoctrination of the young is a serious crime; many children have been taken away from their Christian parents to be placed in special boarding schools.

Is it surprising that many – possibly the majority, human nature being what it is – have bowed to the intolerable pressure and forsaken or compromised their beliefs? Yet there has been no lack of brave men and women who have defied the injunctions, professing themselves believers, and willing to pay the price of their audacity. And their number continues to grow. A combination of harsh repression, flagging economy and disillusionment with a hollow ideology, has led to a spiritual rebirth not only in the Soviet Union but throughout a large part of its satellite empire of Eastern Europe. There is a craving for truth in societies which are collapsing from hypocrisy and 'double-speak'; and the search reveals itself as a search for religious faith.

When, in 1927, Metropolitan Sergei (later Patriarch of Moscow) opted for discretion rather than valour and declared his allegiance to the Soviet regime, a number of believers broke away from the official Orthodox Church. In the two years that followed most of the rebel bishops were rounded up by the KGB or had gone 'underground'. By the mid-thirties, most of these had been unearthed and executed with unspeakable brutality.

Today, no regime wants to make martyrs. In an age which proclaims freedom of conscience, everyone professes religious freedom, and persecution has become more subtle. The martyr is made to seem a fool, inconsistent, even a liar, an 'enemy of the people'. He is manipulated by the regime so that his witness may be destroyed. He is a disgraced and discredited clown.

Father Dmitri Dudko, who became a believer while serving in the Soviet Army as a conscript during the Second World War, once looked like a threat to the regime. He was arrested shortly after the war for publishing a poem lamenting the destruction of the holy places in Russia. At the time he was not a priest. After eight and a half years in a labour camp he became one. 'If you want to believe,' he said, 'you have to stand there next to Christ as he is nailed to the Cross. In Russia today that's the only way you can believe.'

He preached fearlessly in spite of numerous warnings from the police. Even when he was moved to a country district, people, especially young people, followed him to listen to his sermons. All through 1979 he was harassed by the KGB, and was moved to yet another country parish, this time demoted to 'second priest'. Yet still the people came. On 15 January, 1980, he was arrested in church. Before he was taken away he blessed the people there, asking them to pray for him and for each other. Five months later he appeared on television admitting to 'systematic fabrication and dissemination abroad of anti-Soviet material'. It was such an unlikely confession that his friends had no hesitation in attributing it to the application of psychotropic drugs. Next day Father Dmitri was allowed home, and since that time he has stated emphatically that his beliefs are as they always were: 'I am the same as I was,' he wrote in a secret (*samizdat*) article. 'Pay no attention to my statement to the press or to my speech on television. They are not mine. My books and sermons are mine.' His writings are all on the theme of repentance and forgiveness, and the voice of Father Dmitri continues to express the conscience of the Russian Orthodox Church.

What Christians are doing is refusing to live a lie. They are standing up for the human values which Soviet society so conspicuously lacks. Vladimir Shelkov (an Adventist) was a heroic figure who spent twenty-three years of his life in prisons and work-camps. His fourth prison sentence – five years in a strict-regime camp – was imposed in 1979 when he was eighty-three years old, and he died there within a year. While offering loyalty to the legitimate demands of the state (as most Christians do) Shelkov always defended the right of believers to follow their consciences when those demands were in conflict with the law of Christ. Begging his fellow Adventists not to give way under police interrogation, he told them: 'Be ready to suffer, do not betray your brethren, and keep silent like Christ before Pilate.'

In the eyes of the Christians, it is indeed Christ who is on trial. 'Today here, as in Pilate's day, Christ our saviour is being judged,' said Georgi Vins at his trial in 1975 when he was sentenced to five years' forced labour and five further years in Siberia. (His father, also a Baptist preacher, had died in prison in 1945, claiming always that his only crime was 'faithfulness to the Lord'.)

Vins, the leader of the non-registered Reform Baptists of the USSR, who broke away from the 'official' body in 1961 – now lives in New York, for (in total ignorance of what was taking place) he was flown out by the Soviets after an exchange agreement with President Carter. He now edits a newsletter which gives information about his co-religionists in Russia. On 28 April, 1982, the following item appeared:

A letter from a Baptist prisoner Pyotr Rumachik to his family indicates that he is in grave danger and does not expect to live out his sentence in a Soviet labour camp. Rumachik, fifty-two, Vice President of the Council of Evangelical Baptist Churches in the Soviet Union, is serving a five-year sentence in labour camp for his faith in God. For over a year he has been deprived of meetings with his family and they have been unaware of his state of health and living conditions. His correspondence to the outside is either held back or does not get through at all. Rumachik, however, succeeded in secretly getting a letter to his family. In it he writes: 'And what will next year bring? Only God knows; it seems likely, though, that I will be having a meeting with Him . . . Despite everything my spirits have not fallen. I don't feel too bad at all – something like Nikolai Khmara felt.' (Khmara was burned with hot irons by prison officials in Slavgorod, Siberia, after his trial in January 1964. The KGB and prison officials were attempting to force him to deny God. He died in prison.)

Anti-religious pressure is constantly applied and discrimination against believers (in the matter of jobs, education, etc.) is systematic. In the late 1960s Maria Vasilyevna was a teacher in a state school, much loved by all her pupils who called her affectionately 'our Miss Maria'. The director of the school, a party member, suspected her of being a Christian and devised a cunning trick to make her reveal the fact. The whole school was summoned to walk over an icon of the Mother of God placed like a bridge over a ditch in the school courtyard. When Maria Vasilyevna came up with her class, she stopped and said in a clear voice exactly what the director wanted to hear. 'What you ask would be for me personally a crime,' she said. 'I am a believing Orthodox Christian, and I shall not walk over the holy icon of the Mother of God and the God-child.' She was taken away and never seen again. Rumour had it that she was shot.

For a soldier to refuse the military oath of allegiance to the Soviet state has always been a serious crime. Two brothers from Sharlyk refused with the words: 'We have not refused to serve in that army which goes with Christ, with God. But to serve in an army which is against God and Christ, that we cannot and will not do. We are Christians.' It was winter. Wearing summer clothing they were made to set out on a 150 km journey to Orenburg on foot. Both of them froze to death on the way.

Today's conscripts who refuse to take the oath, many of them Baptists or Jehovah's Witnesses, often meet a violent and mysterious end; like twenty-year-old Vanya Druk, a quiet boy and a teetotaller, who was stabbed to death in what the authorities called a 'drunken brawl'. And since the 1970s a new and sinister way of dealing with nonconformists of whatever kind has been to consign them to a psychiatric hospital. To the dogmatic Soviet mind religious belief is symptomatic of mental illness. In 1977 a 35-year-old truck driver, Michael Vasilyevich Avdeyev, an Orthodox Christian of peasant family, was admitted to hospital with nephritis. In the ward he began to pray out loud, protesting that he was going to die. Having thus proved himself insane, he was transferred to the hospital's psychiatric wing and certified as 'socially dangerous'. Here he continued to pray and ask forgiveness of those around him, saying as before, 'I'm dying,

I'm dying.' A boy who was in the same ward related afterwards that a doctor came along and said to Avdeyev: 'Well, you're obviously ill, so I shall give you an injection to make you better.' He did so, and the patient immediately died.

In the course of this century, many small independent countries were forcibly swallowed by the giant Soviet Union; 'dumped down the sewer pipes', as Solzhenitsyn so graphically put it. The countries on the Eastern shores of the Baltic – Estonia, Latvia and Lithuania lost their independence in 1940, after Russia and Germany had carved up Eastern Europe between them. In those countries the full fury of persecution was unleashed. About 150,000 people, including most of the Lutheran, Catholic and Orthodox bishops and many clergymen, were deported to labour camps in Siberia or Central Asia. Others were simply shot. Between the end of the war and Stalin's death in 1953 half a million more were deported. Though the churches are still in existence, they are hobbled, the strongest and most active being the Roman Catholic Church in Lithuania, which commands the overwhelming support of ordinary Lithuanians and is a seemingly irremovable thorn in the side of the Soviets.

Lithuanians, like their neighbours, the Poles, are deeply nationalistic and deeply religious, and, as in Poland, the Catholic Church in Lithuania is identified with the deepest aspirations of the nation towards freedom. In 1980 the Catholic Committee for the Defence of Believers' Rights (founded in November 1978) wrote to the Prosecutor of the Supreme Soviet, listing numbers of priests and nuns assaulted, beaten or inflicted with third degree burns. On the night of 11 October, 1980, for example, Fr. Leonas Sapoka, parish priest of Luoke, was asleep in his flat when a group of men broke in, tortured him for several hours and left him lying dead on the floor.

It seems to us (the letter ran) that among all these offences: the robbing of churches, arson, desecration of the Blessed Sacrament, torture and murder of priests, there is some kind of internal, organic unity. And thus it is natural that the faithful characterise these offences as a conscious and deliberate campaign against the rise of the authority and influence of the Church in Lithuania. Mr. Prosecutor, please take speedy measures to punish the Soviet mafia and to bring the offenders to trial, since these offences directed against the Church and the priests are not only very damaging to the Church but they especially compromise the Soviet government which protects only the atheists and those who work to destroy the Church.

This petition and others like it have been signed by tens of thousands of Lithuanian Catholics, and many priests, in full acceptance of the possible consequences. Father Leonas Mazeika (aged sixty-three) was one of 118 priests from a single diocese who signed a similar petition to their Supreme Soviet, expressing support for the Catholic Committee's appeal for greater religious freedom, in accordance with the provisions of the Helsinki Treaty. He was murdered. Neither in his case nor in that of Sapoka has a single suspect been questioned by the police.

Among Lithuanians one man is a legend: Mindaugas Tamonis, described as 'one of the moral giants' of the country. In 1974 this 33-year-old engineer, married with two children, had a good job, was well thought of in his field and was expected to go far. But in that year Tamonis refused to repair a monument to the Red Army at Kryzkalnis until a monument had first been erected to the Lithuanians who had died in the Stalinist terror. That refusal brought to an end both his career and his life. Dismissed summarily from his job, he was declared mentally ill and incarcerated in a psychiatric hospital, after answering a 564-point questionnaire on his religious beliefs. After three months of electric shock treatment he was released, a chronic invalid quite incapable of work. This did not prevent his writing to the Central Committee of the Communist Party calling for a more humane attitude within the Party, an end to falsehoods and hypocrisy and also to discrimination against believers. In the letter he described himself as 'a convinced twentieth-century Christian.'

The wrath of the Central Committee soon descended on his head. Tamonis was returned to the psychiatric hospital where he was injected with Moditen-B, a depressant drug which is a medicine for the mentally sick but lethal to the healthy. Though they then released him, he was forced to have more injections. On 5 November, 1975, he was found dead on a railway line.

The *Chronicle of the Lithuanian Catholic Church* No. 20, a *samizdat* publication which focuses attention on religious liberty, national issues and human rights, published an obituary which accused the KGB of Tamonis's death. Moditen-B, they declared, 'kills secretly and silently, until a human being is left with nothing but a body . . . He was our conscience . . . ,' they went on, 'one of the first of our generation to find the living, warm Christian God.'

The *Chronicle* itself, in whose production and distribution many of the Catholic clergy are involved, seems so far immune to the attacks of the KGB, though many of those connected with it have been given harsh sentences in strict-regime camps. It has opened the eyes of many people, proving itself 'the conscience of our nation, the voice of our struggling Church, and a cry for help which has resounded through the world.'

It was the Vatican newspaper, *Osservatore Romano*, which first reported (25 September, 1975) the execution by hanging of Father Michael Lutsky of the Western Ukraine. The report noted the prevalence of religious persecution throughout the Ukraine. Soviet police, it claimed, had had Father Lutsky under close surveillance and had warned him three times that celebrating Mass and distributing the Eucharist were illegal in the Soviet Union. Father Lutsky was aroused at dawn on 30 January, 1975, by a group of men who begged him to 'visit a sick Christian'. It was a trap. They led him to a nearby wood and hanged him from a tree. A suicide note in the dead priest's pocket fooled nobody.

Czechoslovakia carries a heavy load of persecution. In the early Stalinist days the churches were all but destroyed and there has been discrimination against believers ever since. In fact the situation for Catholic priests, Protestant pastors and the average Christian is as difficult in Czechoslovakia as in the USSR: the Church is effectively gagged.

Yet reports continue to reach the West of Slovak priests who continue the struggle. In 1979 a refugee brought first-hand information about the trial of Father Milan Gono, a secretly ordained Slovak. On his arrest in 1979 Father Gono was charged with 'theft of socialist property', though a detailed search of his and his parents' apartments revealed no trace of stolen goods. During the search, however, the police stole everything Father Gono possessed: his typewriter, books, writing paper and money.

Three months after his arrest he was charged, obscurely, with sexual misconduct. Then the real reason for his arrest became apparent: his secret priesthood had somehow been discovered. At his trial, an elderly nun and another secret priest were forced to give evidence of Father Gono's pastoral activities. The Chairwoman professed herself shocked at the idea of 'secret' ordination – in a country whose constitution guaranteed freedom of religion. Whereupon the courtroom was convulsed with uncontrollable mirth, until the Chairwoman threatened to clear the court if it did not stop.

Father Gono declared that he would never renounce his priesthood, and was given two years' forced labour. But an appeal was lodged and a new trial date set for 26 July, 1979. On 21 July he fell from some scaffolding and was killed, or so the official report claimed. His body was handed over to his parents on condition that they did not bury him as a priest. It showed extensive injuries and facial wounds which had been stitched. Several weeks later the parents learned (through the warder who had been in charge of their son) that he had died under interrogation, refusing to divulge the names of other secretly ordained Slovak priests.

One of these could well have been Premysl Coufal, a monk who worked at the agricultural institute in Bratislava. When the secret police discovered his priesthood, they tried to browbeat him into informing on others. On 8 January they arrested and interrogated him. When they let him go, he avoided all his friends, for fear of incriminating them in any way. But his freedom did not last long. At the end of January the police presented him with an ultimatum: collaborate, or else . . . He was given until 23 February to decide. When Coufal did not turn up for work on 24 February his colleagues reported his absence. They found his flat locked, though there was no sign of a key. When the police broke in they found Coufal dead in the bathroom, with a faint smell of gas in the air. There was no explosion when a match was struck, so the gas tap could not have been on for long. In spite of this anomaly, the official verdict of suicide by gas poisoning was brought in. But – and perhaps the seeming concession was intended as an awful warning – his friends were allowed to see the corpse. Father Coufal's wrists had been cut, his nose broken and his skull smashed in.

Nowhere has the persecution of Christians been more virulent than in Albania, that tiny country of 11,000 square miles and two million people, which has truly earned its title, 'land of martyrs'. Albania is the only state in the world whose constitution does not pay even lip service to religious toleration. In 1967 it was officially claimed as 'the first atheist state in the world' and its rulers followed up the claim with an all-out onslaught on religious belief and practice unequalled for ferocity anywhere in the modern world.

At the last religious census, taken in 1937, 70 per cent of Albanians were revealed to be Muslim, 20 per cent Orthodox and 10 per cent Roman Catholic. The Communist government was quite impartial, attacking them all with equal savagery. Mosques were destroyed and muftis imprisoned and executed alongside Catholic and Orthodox bishops and priests.

The original constitution did in fact guarantee 'freedom of conscience and religion', regarding religion as a private matter with no public significance. But the Chinese-style 'ideological and cultural revolution' of 1966 changed all that, and religion became a prime target for organised defamation, humiliation and destruction. All buildings for public worship were closed, and those who wilfully continued to practise their religion were either imprisoned or executed. Priests who had not been sent to labour camps had to take a secular job. Today they are an ageing and depleted band, secretly cele-

brating Mass and listening to religious broadcasts from Italy
and Greece. Speaking of Albania in 1972, Pope Paul VI said
with sadness: 'With the shepherds stricken and the flock
dispersed, we cannot see what human hope remains there for
the Church. But we must go on hoping, even if it is hoping
against hope.'

Reports trickle out infrequently. One of these told of
seventy-year-old Stephen Kurti, one of a long line of Alba-
nian Catholic priests killed since the Communist take-over. In
1945 Father Kurti was arrested on a trumped-up charge of
spying for the Vatican and given a death sentence which was
later commuted to life imprisonment. After eighteen years in
prison he was released and returned to pastoral work. But
then came the cultural revolution. When the government
declared all religious practice to be illegal he took a job as a
clerk in a co-operative. But the arrival of soldiers to demolish
his church was more than he could stand, and he fought them
off with his bare hands. For such antisocial behaviour he was
sentenced to sixteen further years in prison.

In prison he agreed to a mother's urgent request to baptize
her new-born child. But news of this reached the authorities.
Father Kurti was handed over to a firing squad and his few
belongings were sold publicly in the town square at Milot
where his trial had taken place, in a former church. It was
announced that the priest had been executed 'for subversive
activities designed to overthrow the State'.

Bishop Ernest Coba, the Apostolic Administrator of
Shköder, was a man much loved for his tireless work among
the poor and sick. Because of his eloquent preaching he was
singled out as 'an agitator', and for many years was hounded
and humiliated in public. Wearing a clown's motley, with a
placard hung around his neck proclaiming 'I have sinned
against the people', the bishop was made to sweep the streets
and clean out the public lavatories. In 1974 they finally
deported him to a labour camp where he continued to minister in secret to the other prisoners. On Easter Sunday, 1979,
the bishop was caught in the act of saying Mass and was
mercilessly beaten. Next day he was found dead.

It is hard not to share Pope Paul's belief that in these

countries – and also in countries like Ethiopia where the Churches are being systematically destroyed and their leaders murdered – the situation is all but hopeless. Yet at the same time it is clear that as long as there are men and women like Georgi Vins, Maria Vasilyevna, Dmitri Dudko and Bishop Coba, the flame of faith will refuse to be extinguished.

Virtually all the leading activists in the Orthodox, Baptist and other churches in the USSR are now in prison or labour camps, and except in Lithuania the open dissent of the post-Helsinki seventies has been somewhat cowed. And yet throughout Eastern Europe (except, significantly, in industrialised East Germany and Yugoslavia, where conditions for believers are relatively easier and where a Western-style consumerism prevails) most of the religious denominations have seen a substantial increase in their membership. There can be no doubt of a growing interest in Christianity, most markedly among the young people whose spirits have been starved by an arid materialism and a diet of propaganda, and who are seeking a trustworthy moral authority. Moreover, in these countries where the ruling ideology forbids people to gather except at officially controlled and mandatory public demonstrations, there is a hunger for a type of society which is based on something other than mutual fear and suspicion.

In the past sixty-five years many more Christians have given their lives in witness to Christ than in the three hundred years which followed the Crucifixion. Not even the gladiators and wild beasts of Decian and Diocletian have matched in ferocity the tidal waves of hatred unleashed in our own century. What is the mysterious secret of those who are prepared to endure the unendurable for the sake of what they believe to be eternal truth? Why is it that, surrounded by the majority who give way to despair or compromise, or who die in the prison camps with hatred in their hearts and curses on their lips, there are always to be found those rare beings who are prepared to love to the limits and beyond? These are the men and women who, at the furthermost edges of endurance, prove that humankind, though fallible and weak, is tinged with the divine; that there is in all of us something greater than ourselves. 'The spirit cannot die,' wrote the Czech poet,

Franz Marc, 'in no circumstances, under no torment, despite whatever calumnies, in no bleak places.'

Andrei Sinyavsky who spent 1966–71 in a forced labour camp, is one of the most prophetic and significant writers of our troubled century. While in the labour camp he wrote: 'The good thing about this place is that a man feels that he is nothing but a naked soul.' In that nakedness of soul Sinyavsky discovered life stripped down to its essential elements. What was important could be clearly seen, and all else was dross. 'We came into this world,' he explained, 'in order to understand certain things; very few things, but exceptionally important ones.' In discovering God, he found freedom, and came to understand that the real prisoners were those who believed that power and material possessions represented the highest point of man's achievement.

'The deeper the sorrow, the nearer is God,' quoted Sinyavsky, from a story which Georgi Vins tells:

> One day in a town in the far East (of Russia) a column of prisoners was being marched from a transit prison to a goods station for embarkation. After the column ran weeping women, seeing off their fathers, husbands, sons . . . A young Orthodox priest was marching in the column beside my father. His wife was hurrying alongside after the column. As she took leave of him, she cried: 'Vasya! Don't lose heart! The darker the night, the brighter the stars!' The priest's heartening reply rang out above the column of prisoners: 'The deeper the sorrow, the nearer is God!'

Perhaps few have the strength to reach such insights in the Gulag Archipelago. To read Solzhenitsyn overwhelms one with despair and desolation. But the fact that even a few human beings keep the flame of humanity alight gives hope that the battle will never be lost.

People like the martyrs, sung or unsung, show us that a human life is capable of rising above apparent banality, and suggest a meaning for the daily treadmill of boredom, disappointment and failure which is the nearest most of us get (or want to get) to martyrdom.

How do we reach that inner freedom which alone can offer the peace we seek? The martyrs by their example assert that it is by refusing to put our own interests first, by being willing to count the world well lost for the sake of Christ's call to 'love one another'. It is the hardest task in the world, for it is a call not only to suffer but to forgive those who do us harm. A Russian bishop once said that only the martyr has the right to stand before the judgment seat of God and say 'According to Your word and Your example I have forgiven. Will You forgive them also?' Though we cannot control the external circumstances which crush us, the inner response is still ours to make. It is the last and incomparably the greatest of the human freedoms.

In Germany, the Nazis came for the Communists,
And I didn't speak up because I was not a Communist.
Then they came for the Jews
And I didn't speak up because I was not a Jew.

Then they came for the Trade Unionists
And I didn't speak up because I was not a Trade Unionist.
Then they came for the Catholics
And I was a Protestant so I didn't speak up

Then they came for me. . . .
   By that time there was no one left to speak up for anyone

Pastor Martin Niemöller

Concise Dictionary of Religious Quotations,
Editor William Neil
Mowbrays, Oxford

Bibliography

1. Dietrich Bonhoeffer

Bielenberg, Christabel. *The Past is Myself*. Chatto & Windus.
Bonhoeffer: An Illustrated Introduction. Fount Books, Collins.
Bonhoeffer, Dietrich. *Christology*. Fount Books, Collins.
The Cost of Discipleship. SCM.
Ethics. SCM.
Letters and Papers from Prison. ed. Eberhard Bethge. SCM.
Life Together. SCM.
No Rusty Swords: Letters, Lectures and Notes from the Collected Works of Dietrich Bonhoeffer. Vol. I 1928–36. Fontana Library, Collins.
The Way to Freedom: Letters, Lectures and Notes from the Collected Works of Dietrich Bonhoeffer. Vol. II 1935–39. Fontana Library, Collins.
Bosanquet, Mary. *The Life and Death of Dietrich Bonhoeffer*. Hodder & Stoughton.
Cox, Harvey. *The Secular City*. SCM.
Dying We Live: Letters written by prisoners in Germany on the verge of execution. Fontana Library, Collins.
I Knew Dietrich Bonhoeffer: Reminiscences of His Friends. Collins.
Johnson, Paul B. *A History of Christianity*. Pelican Books.
Muggeridge, Malcolm. *A Third Testament*. Collins and BBC.
Shirer, William. *Berlin Diary (1934–41)*. Pan Books.
The Rise and Fall of the Third Reich. Pan Books.
Taylor, A. J. P. *The Course of German History*. Methuen University Paperbacks.

2. Martin Luther King Jr.

Ansbro, John J. *Martin Luther King Jr.: The Making of a Mind*. Orbis Books.

King, Coretta Scott. *My Life with Martin Luther King Jr* Hodder & Stoughton.

Oates, Stephen B. *Let the Trumpet Sound: The Life of Martin Luther King Jr*. Search Press.

3. Maximilian Kolbe

Dewar, Diana. *Saint of Auschwitz*. Darton, Longman & Todd.

Frankl, Victor E. *Man's Search for Meaning: An Introduction to Logotherapy*. Washington Square Press.

Gans, Charles and Whale, John. 'The spreading stain on the robe of the Auschwitz saint.' *Sunday Times* 27.3.83.

Garlinski, Jozef. *Fighting Auschwitz*. Julian Friedmann.

d'Harcourt, Pierre. *The Real Enemy*. Longman.

'Maximilian Kolbe, A Saint for our Times.' *Messenger* September 1982. (Articles by Piero Lazzarin, Bernard Przewozny-Porter and Gianfranco Grieco.)

Maximilian Kolbe, Hero of Auschwitz. Crusade of Mary Immaculate Press.

Moorman, John R. H. *Saint Francis of Assisi*. SPCK.

Simon, Ulrich, E. *A Theology of Auschwitz*. Gollancz.

Winowska, Maria. *The Death Camp Proved Him Real*. Prow Books.

I owe an especial debt to Jan Jozef Szczepański for his brilliant and sensitive article 'Święty' which appeared in *Twórzość*, April 1974, and was reproduced in the special Polish edition of *Osservatore Romano* which commemorated the canonisation of Father Maximilian in October 1982. Any mistakes in translation must be attributed to me.

4. *Janani Luwum*

Brown, Bishop Leslie (formerly Archbishop of Uganda). Transcript of a talk in the series 'Reflections', broadcast on BBC World Service, 15.4.81.

Faupel, J. F. *African Holocaust*. Geoffrey Chapman.

Ford, Margaret. *Janani, the Making of a Martyr*. Marshall, Morgan & Scott.

Grahame, Iain. *Amin and Uganda: A Personal Memoir*. Granada Books.

Hastings, Adrian. *A History of African Christianity 1950–75*. Cambridge University Press.

'King Freddie'. *Desecration of My Kingdom*. Constable.

Kivengere, Festo. *Hope for Uganda and the World*. African Evangelistic Enterprise.

I Love Idi Amin. Marshall, Morgan & Scott.

Listowel, Judith. *Amin*. IUP.

Miller, Charles. *The Lunatic Express: An Entertainment in Imperialism*. Ballantine Books.

Roscoe, John. *The Baganda: An Account of Their Native Customs and Beliefs*. Frank Cass.

Smith, George Ivan. *Ghosts of Kampala: The Rise and Fall of Idi Amin*. Weidenfeld & Nicolson.

Thoonen, J. P. *Black Martyrs*. Sheed & Ward.

Wilkins, John. 'Uganda's New Martyrs.' *Tablet* 18.2.78.

Wright, Michael. *Buganda in the Heroic Age*. Oxford University Press.

5. *Oscar Romero*

Brockman, SJ, James R. *Oscar Romero, Bishop and Martyr*. Sheed & Ward.

Camara, Helder. *Church and Colonialism*. Sheed & Ward.

Erdozain, Plácido. *Archbishop Romero, Martyr of Salvador*. Lutterworth Press.

Gheerbrant, Alain. *The Rebel Church in Latin America*. Pelican L. A. Library.

Keogh, Dermot. *Romero, El Salvador's Martyr*. Dominican Publications.

La Vos de los Sin Voz: La Palabra Viva de Monseñor Romero. Colección La Iglesia en American Latina.

A Martyr's Message of Hope: Six Homilies by Archbishop Oscar Romero. Celebration Books.

Paredes, Ivan D. *Evolucion de la Iglesia Salvadoreña 24 de marzo 80/28 de marzo 82*. Estudios Centro Americanos.

Presencia de Monseñor Romero en la Hora Actual. eca piensa así 2. Universidad Centroamericana, Jose Simeon Cañas – El Salvador.

Sobrino SJ, John. *Romero, Martyr for Liberation: The Last Two Homilies with a Theological Analysis*. Catholic Institute for International Relations.

6. *Maria Skobtsova*

Boegner, Philippe. *Ici On A Aimé les Juifs*. J. C. Lattès.

de Gaulle, Geneviève. 'Voix et Visages' *Bulletin mensuel de l'Adir* jan–fév 1966.

Hackel, Sergei. *Pearl of Great Price: The Life of Mother Maria Skobtsova*. Darton, Longman & Todd.

'What Can We Say To God?: The poetry of Mother Maria Skobtsova' *Sobornost* series 7, no. 5.

Krivoshein, Igor. An article, trans. Rosane Lecroux.

Marrus, Michael R., and Paxton, Robert O. *Vichy et les Juifs*. Calmann-Lévy.

Meine Zelle Heisst: Welt. Transcript of film made by Deutsches Fernsehen TV.

'Mère Marie 1891–1945'. *Contacts: revue francaise de l'Orthodoxie* XVIIᵉ année, no. 51, 1965.

Rougier-Lecoq, Violette. *Témoignages, Ravensbrück: 36 Dessins à la Plume*.

Smith, T. Stratton. *The Rebel Nun*. Souvenir Press.

Zhaba, Sergei. An article, trans. Marie Kastchenko.

7. The Unknown Martyrs of the Twentieth Century

Aeschliman, Michael D. 'Prison-camp Prophet'. *Tablet* 24.11.79.

Beeson, Trevor. 'Albania: Land of Martyrs'. *Christian Century* 26.9.73.
   Discretion and Valour: Religious Conditions in Russia and Eastern Europe. Fount Books, Collins.

Bourdeaux, Michael. *Faith on Trial in Russia*. Hodder Christian Paperbacks.

Chernov, Fr. Antony. 'The Catacomb Church in the Russian Land' trans. Vladimir Moss. Unpublished MS.

'A Chronicle of Current Events no. 62'. *Journal of the Human Rights Movement in the USSR*. Amnesty International Publications.

Dumitriu, Petru. *Incognito*. Sphere Books and Collins.

Bishop Kallistos of Diokleia. 'What is a Martyr?' *Sobornost* 5/1, 1983.

Moss, Vladimir. 'The Catacomb Church: The Last Fifteen Years' February 1983.

Sapiets, Marite. 'Lithuania's Unofficial Press' *Index on Censorship* 4/1980.

Solzhenitsyn, Alexander. *The Gulag Archipelago*. Fontana.

Tomsky, Alex. 'Modus Moriendi of the Catholic Church in Czechoslovakia' *Religion in Communist Lands* 10/1, 1982.

Urban, George. 'A Conversation with Leszek Kolakowski' *Encounter* January 1981.

Vins, Georgi. *Georgi Vins: Three Generations of Suffering*. Hodder Christian Paperbacks.

Walters, Philip. 'Christians in Eastern Europe: A Decade of Aspirations and Frustrations' *Religion in Communist Lands* II/1, 1983
   'Christian Samizdat' *Index on Censorship* 4/1980.

Wojtyla, Karol. *Sign of Contradiction*. St. Paul Publications.

Most of the case histories in this chapter are from the archives of Keston College in Kent, by courtesy of Rev. Michael Bourdeaux.